The Irish 100

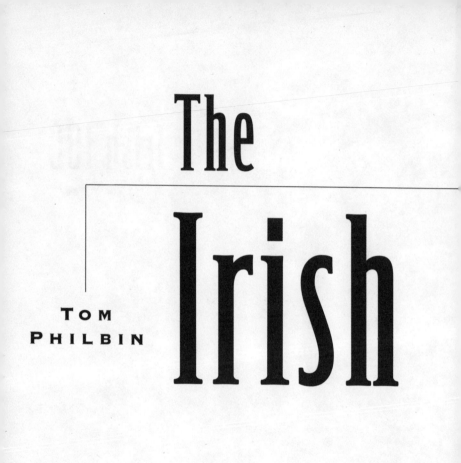

The

Irish

TOM
PHILBIN

ഗ

A RANKING

OF THE MOST

INFLUENTIAL

IRISH OF

ALL TIME

ഗ

100

**Andrews McMeel
Publishing**

Kansas City

www.andrewsmcmeel.com

99 00 01 02 03   RDC   10 9 8 7 6 5 4 3 2 1

Library of Congress Cataloging-in-Publication Data
Philbin, Tom.
    The Irish 100: a ranking of the most influential Irish of all time / Tom Philbin.
    p.   cm.
    ISBN 0-8362-6841-5 (hd: alk. paper)
    1. Ireland—Biography. 2. United States—Biography. 3. Irish Americans—Biography.
    I. Title.
CT863.P48   1999
920'.00929162073—dc21

                                                                            98-22700
                                                                            CIP

Design by Mauna Eichner and Lee Fukui

For Honora

ꙮ

A long time ago, when I was a good boy you used to put a "duckie" (a wedge of butter) in my hot oatmeal. I hope you'd think this book worthy of a duckie, too.

Contents

∞

Author's Note

In researching any book, authors learn that, inevitably, some sources disagree on some facts. I want to note that every attempt was made to put only the truth in this book and that every logical source I could think of was consulted to achieve that end.

Acknowledgments

ʚɞ

Many people think that writing a book is about writing. But good books are mainly about research. The more you do, the better the book. And you can't do it alone.

I was fortuante to get help from a variety of people, many of whom I don't even know the names of—anonymous people in libraries and other institutions in America and Ireland and just ordinary people who would call me to share a "little something" that might be useful for the book.

I thank them all.

I am also grateful for the in-depth research assistance given me by Joan Seaman and my daughter Mary, who is a reference librarian. Thanks very much also to Irish historian Dr. Edward Clark and scholar Elizabeth Toomey for vetting the book and providing very helpful input.

I am also very grateful to the editors at Andrews McMeel for their caring and their high-line professionalism.

Introduction

༄༅

There are a host of startling things about the Irish and Irish Americans:
Around the time of the Great Famine (1845–1850), which was
caused by the failure of the potato crop (and by ill-conceived and callous
policies of the British government), the average Irishman's daily diet consisted of buttermilk, which provided vitamin A and fat, and potatoes,
which fulfilled all the remaining nutritional needs. And how many potatoes, on the average, did he eat per day? About fourteen pounds.

And in the 1600s Oliver Cromwell of England slaughtered some
750,000 Irish people.

Ireland now has half the population (because a lot of people died or
emigrated as a result of the famine) it had in the mid-nineteenth century.

Native Irish were treated as subhuman by the British. They were
discriminated against in America, too—and the discrimination was on a

level that some people claim was even worse than any other immigrant group was subject to.

A vast number (perhaps two-thirds) of the Union soldiers in the Civil War were Irish or of Irish extraction.

Quite a few people whom one might never suspect were Irish have Irish blood in them, people such as Walt Disney, Henry Ford, John Lennon, Paul McCartney, Ulysses S. Grant and a host of other American presidents—and many more. Even people with non-Irish names, such as Father Theodore Hesburgh and Margaret Sanger, are closet Irish.

Compiling a list of the most influential Irish—and I considered for the list the Irish born and Irish Americans—of all time is not easy. It's not that easy to know who should be on the list and who should not—because a lot of people who ultimately didn't make the list could well have, people such as Sandra Day O'Connor, Robert Kennedy, Helen Hayes, Jackie Gleason, Davy Crockett, "Buffalo Bill" Cody, Arthur Guinness, Sam Houston, Neil Armstrong—and many more.

But the question, of course, is who is the most influential. Not the most famous, the most influential. Certainly, for example, Paul McCartney is more famous than Cyrus McCormick, but Cyrus's invention, the reaper, had a lot more impact than Paul's music—and therefore Cyrus has had more influence.

Nor did I find it a walk in the park ranking the people. In compiling the list, I asked myself: What impact did the lives of these individual people have on the lives of their fellowman? I realized that the definition of "impact" can vary: everything from shoring up people's sense of identity and making them feel good (as I think people such as John McCormack and Thomas Moore did) to freeing people who have been enslaved. After a while, it came to me that those who have had an impact on someone's freedom or similarly important "spiritual" values are more important than those who have exerted other types of influence and must go higher on the list (it's hard to enjoy a song or be entertained if you're living in slavery). There are a lot of people who affected the freedom of others, such as Daniel O'Connell, Michael Collins and Eamon de Valera, but there are also people such as Edmund Rice, founder of the Irish Christian Brothers, who had a profound impact on thousands of lives over the years; Rachel Carson, who really started the age of ecology; and Margaret Sanger, who brought birth control to the world.

In calculating influence, I tried to get a better grasp of the full effect people had. For example, Henry Ford made the automobile a practical reality. If you think it through, though, you come to realize that not only did he make transportation better, but he also affected manufacturing, jobs, the way people live, air quality—and more. He had a lasting impact in important ways.

Similarly, James Joyce had a big impact on how a lot of other writers write. And there is what can only be described as a cottage industry of people who analyze Joyce's works. But who is to say what kind of influence he also had in breaking down the mores of his day—and yours? I'd say it was significant.

Oscar Wilde is on the list not for his literary output, though that is no mean achievement, but for the effect his trial—and tribulations—had on other gay people through the years. What happened to him must have beamed home a clear message to thousands of gays who followed: If you're in the closet, stay there.

Sometimes influence is more spiritual than actual. Perhaps the clearest example of this is Cuchulain, the legendary Irish warrior. In times when the Irish felt they were nothing—and there were plenty such times—it must have been good to think that, inside, you were potentially a great warrior, like Cuchulain. Indeed, according to some historians, rebels in the great Easter Rising of 1916, specifically, were inspired by the deeds of Cuchulain.

I have not prepared this book like a legal brief: I do not argue or even state in every case why a person is on the list. I think, though, that if you think about a person's impact, in most cases you will see the method to my particular madness, why I made the choices I did. I think in most cases people will at least agree that most of the people belong on the list, though their ranking may be sometimes in dispute.

In most cases, I have given what one critic who vetted this book called "the Irish connection" of Irish Americans; that is, where in their family tree the Irishness comes from—but not in all cases. Sometimes it's not known, and I had to have something approaching solid evidence before considering someone for the list. Edward R. Murrow, for example, said he had Scotch-Irish ancestors who, he believed, jumped off a boat in 1670—but he's not on the list.

There are some truly wondrous human beings on this list, towering figures who, I must say, being of Irish extraction myself (all of my grandparents were from Ireland, and they married Irish Americans), make me proud. Who could not be proud to share his heritage with a Rachel Carson, who taught us how to think of our environment differently; or a Daniel O'Connell, who freed Catholics in Ireland from bondage; a Catherine McAuley, founder of the Sisters of Mercy; five great Nobel laureates in literature; that little GI from Texas, Audie Murphy, who was the most decorated American soldier of World War II; or General Ulysses S. Grant, who, when informed by his doctor that he was terminally ill with throat cancer, started to write his memoirs in a race against death so that his family would be financially cared for. I am proud. More than a little.

The vast majority of the people on the list have had positive influences, but not all. I would not consider Oscar Wilde's good, nor would I consider Michael Collins's life purely positive in its effect, nor would I consider publisher Joseph Medill—who I think was in serious need of institutionalization—totally positive.

But they all share one thing: They are the most influential Irish of all time (in my view).

Erin go bragh.

Tom Philbin

The Irish 100

St. Patrick

(CA. 386 A.D.—461)

Patrick's influence was simple and profound, and he is indisputably the most influential Irish person of all time for two reasons, either of which would put him at the top of the list: Though there were a few scattered Christian settlements in Ireland before Patrick came, he brought Christianity to Ireland in a deep, pervasive way.

Also, he created the conditions for Ireland to become "the isle of saints and scholars" and allowed civilization to be saved. At the time Patrick lived, Europe was overrun by barbarians, and the writings that recorded Western culture, the manuscripts of Greek and Latin writers, both Christian and pagan, were in danger of being lost forever. However, the monks in Ireland copied them, and those same monks then went to Europe and with missionary zeal strove to reintroduce this culture during the Dark Ages—and succeeded.

The irony is that Patrick, or Patricius as he was called in Latin, the greatest Irish saint of all, was not born Irish. Born in Britain, he was the son of a deacon and the grandson of a priest. He lived in an area of Europe that was occupied by Romans and was known as a Romanized Celt. He had had a calling to the priesthood but had no intention of visiting Ireland, which was across the sea, far away for that time. However, the Irish were seafaring warriors who often raided the Continent to kidnap children, turning them into slaves.

One day, when Patrick (his name then was Succat) was sixteen years old, an Irish raiding party led by Niall of the Nine Hostages kidnapped him and took him across the water to Ireland. Forced to become a shepherd, he spent seemingly endless days walking nude or half nude and half starved, tending to the animals.

For six years he endured the pain, physical deprivations, and aching emptiness inside, as he reports in his autobiographical *Confessio* (which scholars say is historically viable). But always he plotted to escape, knowing that if he were caught, he could be executed.

Then one day he saw his chance: A group of Irish wolfhounds was being shipped to the Continent. With the help of some sympathetic sailors, Patrick stowed away on the ship, hid among the dogs, and successfully escaped.

He was reunited with his family in Britain, went on to be a priest, and years later, his kidnapping was just a bad memory.

But one night he had a dream, in which a voice called him back to Ireland to "walk once more amongst us."

It was a call from God.

Patrick answered the call and headed back across the sea to Ireland, the place he both hated and feared.

He was not attacked, and he became one of the first traveling missionaries, going from place to place—probably in the north—spreading the word of Christ. He succeeded in changing the Irish living there because he understood them. On the surface they were warlike, pagan, bloodthirsty, and profane, but he knew that deep inside they wanted what everyone wants: peace, faith, hope, love, and charity. He gave them these things without trying to change them, and many accepted Christianity and started to preach his way themselves.

In an interview with *Irish America* magazine, scholar and author Thomas Cahill, who wrote the best-selling book *How the Irish Saved Civilization,* says, "We think [of Patrick] as sort of this stern-looking bishop with a miter on his head, and he's nothing like that at all.... He was extraordinary in two ways: The greatness of his heart and the insight that he had into the psychology of an alien race." And he was very human: "He had a temper," Cahill says, "that could flare dangerously when he perceived an injustice—not against himself but against another, particularly someone defenseless. But he had the cheerfulness and good humor that humble people often have. He enjoyed this world and its variety of human beings—and he didn't take himself too seriously. He was, in spirit, an Irishman."

A number of fictions exist about St. Patrick, most of which are contained in the biographies written about him during the first two hundred years after he died. Perhaps the greatest legend about him concerns the snakes in Ireland. It is said that Patrick banished "the demons of paganism." Of course, Ireland has no snakes now, and there is evidence that it never did, this observation having been reported by the Graeco-Roman writer Solinus two hundred years before St. Patrick was born.

His feast day is March 17, the day of his death. Parades marking it are held all over the world.

Michael Collins

(1890–1922)

Perhaps the most surprising thing about many of the great revolutionary figures who populate Irish history is that they were so young—and many of them never grew old. Such a figure was Michael Collins, who was born on October 16, 1890, and was assassinated on August 22, 1922, at thirty-two years of age.

Most Irish revolutionaries also failed, despite heroic efforts, to achieve anything. This was not the case with Collins. He did not die in vain. Indeed, he achieved a lot of good—and bad—and a good case can be made for his being number two on a list of the most influential Irish of all time on the basis of one event: In a treaty he helped negotiate in 1921 and then signed, the twenty-six southern counties of Ireland were freed from oversight by England while the northern six counties—Ulster—stayed under English control. That partition led to decades of strife and bloodshed in Northern Ireland, where Catholics and Protestants, as well as the British army and the IRA, clashed.

Collins was born in Clonakilty, County Cork. His father was a farmer, and Michael was educated at Clonakilty National School, where he showed a particular aptitude for finance, a skill that would later serve him well. When he was sixteen, he went to London, where he became a clerk and then joined a firm of stockbrokers. But his true calling was not math or stocks; it was revolution and driving the English out of Ireland. While in London he joined the Irish Republican Brotherhood, the precursor of the Irish Republican Army.

Collins was a minor player in the Easter Rising of 1916, something that did not, on the face of it, amount to much. He and a few hundred others encamped in the general post office on Sackville Street in Dublin and opened fire on the British soldiers, while Eamon de Valera occupied the Boland Street Bakery. The rebels were put down in five days, and many prisoners were taken, including Collins, who was sent to serve time in a prison.

The failure of the rebellion was fine with most of the Irish citizenry, as some 90 percent of the population had opposed it in the first place. At one point, when the bedraggled prisoners were led to prison, they passed through a gauntlet of people that jeered at them, with women being particularly vituperative.

That might have been the end of it. The British would simply wait for the next feeble rising some years hence. Except they made a mistake.

They started hanging the prisoners, fifteen in ten days, and gradually the tide of public opinion turned against them—and toward the rebels. It was a climate in which more rebellion could occur, but this time it would be a different kind of warfare; Michael Collins would ensure that.

While in prison, Collins was planning to fight anew, and when he and his colleagues were freed, they tried a different method of attack: They fought the British guerrilla style. Collins was superb at it. (A number of historians consider him the father of guerrilla warfare.) Instead of confronting the British directly, he fought from the shadows, using spies, some of whom infiltrated British police operations. He engaged in subterfuge and conducted surprise lightning strikes that the British had great difficulty coping with.

In fighting this war, Collins had a heart made of stone. He did whatever had to be done. For example, he once learned that England was sending a crack team of spies, called the Cairo Group, to track him down and kill him. Collins's spy network obtained a group photograph that clearly identified all of the British spies. A day later, Collins's death squad shot all of the British agents dead at the same time.

He was very organized, and his background in finance helped him gather contributions from people sympathetic to the cause and keep track of the funds. He sometimes handled large sums of money, particularly contributions from America, but there was never a hint that any of it was stolen or squandered.

Collins rose within Sinn Féin, the political party of the IRB, and the Volunteers groups, and also became a member of the Supreme Council of the IRB, a very powerful position. Sinn Féin had been victorious in the election of 1918, and following the creation of Dáil Éireann (the Irish Parliament) Collins became minister of finance and minister of home affairs.

For five years Collins and the IRB provoked the British, whose reaction was to overreact, even shooting into a crowd of people at a hurling match, an incident that was vividly (but not terribly accurately) depicted in the movie *Michael Collins*.

Finally, the British called for a truce, and Eamon de Valera was poised to negotiate a treaty. He quickly saw, however, that he could not negotiate something that would please everyone in the Irish camp, including the purists in the IRB. So he got Michael Collins to do it—a move a number of historians look on as Machiavellian: Collins couldn't do it either, but he was able to help negotiate a treaty (on December 6, 1921) that was to give dominion to the twenty-six southern counties (Ireland got its independence in 1949). When the British negotiator signed, he told Collins he was "signing his death warrant," but he seemed to be speaking figuratively. Collins was reported to have a sad little smile on his face when he responded that he "might be signing my actual death warrant." Collins looked on the treaty as a stepping stone to the future. As his pen scratched across the paper, he did, in effect, lay down his life for the Ireland he envisioned.

De Valera was opposed to the treaty, and a vote was held in Ireland and Collins's side prevailed. But ultimately the vote triggered a civil war between pro- and antitreaty forces in which more than four thousand Irish were killed, far more than were killed by the British in the fight for independence.

Collins was murdered by the opposition—men he had fought side by side with in the Easter Rising of 1916—on a rural crossroads in Béal Na Bláth in the west Cork countryside. Many Irish felt he had capitulated to the British and betrayed them by getting them into an untenable arrangement. In September 1997 more than one thousand people and an honor guard gathered there to remember him, all standing silent as bagpipes keened, the Irish flag snapped in the wind, and the strain of a lone bugler mournfully played "The Last Post."

Collins once said, "Individuals are imperfect, liable to error and weakness. The strength of the nation will be the strength of the spirit of the whole people." But it is individuals—such as Michael Collins—who are needed to lead the way.

Charles Stewart Parnell

Charles Stewart Parnell was a powerful speaker, one reason he was so effective in creating what is widely regarded to be, as John Ranelagh writes in *Ireland: An Illustrated History,* "the most powerful political movement in Irish history."

Dr. Walter McDonald, professor of theology at St. Patrick's College in Maynooth, Ireland, recalled once hearing Parnell, a handsome, dark-eyed man, speak: "He was very nervous; not, however, as if he were afraid of the audience or doubtful of his own powers, but as if he were one seething mass of energy, seeking to burst into volcanic eruption, but kept under firm control. He spoke a good deal with clenched right hand, and one could see the nails digging into the flesh, while up along his back the tightly fitted frock coat showed the muscles playing as an instrument."

Parnell was born in Avondale, County Wicklow, on June 27, 1846. His mother was a daughter of Admiral Charles Stewart of the U.S. Navy, and his father was a Protestant landowner of nationalist sympathies.

When he was very young, Parnell was weaned on the idea that England did not belong in Ireland.

Parnell's most important involvement in politics was as a member of the Home Rule Party, whose tenets stated that the Irish Parliament would conduct its own affairs while the British Crown would be responsible for international problems.

When Home Rule's leader, Isaac Butt, died, Parnell took over. In addition to being a convincing speaker, he was an adroit parliamentarian, using filibusters and other stratagems to achieve Home Rule victories.

But what was to be Parnell's crowning glory occurred in 1879, when he was invited by Michael Davitt, founder of the Land League, to become its president. The group had a single goal: to banish the system of landlordism, which had long abused Irish tenant farmers.

Using parliamentary ploys, agitation, the boycotting of farms, and any other tactics they could, Parnell and his cohorts plowed away. (Incidentally, the word "boycott" came from Captain Charles Boycott of Lough Mask House, County Mayo, who was its first victim; see Number 10, Michael Davitt.)

There was some resistance by the British, but their leaders had come to realize that the time of landlordism was past, and the Land Act of 1881, which gave tenants proprietorship of the land, was implemented. Parnell had succeeded—in three years—in destroying a system that had existed for centuries.

Like all great Irish leaders, Parnell saw the destruction of landlordism as a stepping-stone to freeing Ireland from British rule completely. He continued to fight, in particular for more home rule, and for-mulated a bill, the Home Rule Bill of 1886, which, though ultimately defeated, was acknowledged by the likes of Prime Minister William Gladstone to be just.

Parnell was riding high, but he had enemies. The *Times* of London reported that Parnell had said—and there was a letter in Parnell's hand-writing to prove it—that he had advocated the murder in 1882 of two important British officials. Public opinion swung against Parnell, but he fought back and vindicated himself by proving the letter was a forgery. Public opinion swung back to him, and he became known as "The Uncrowned King of Ireland."

There was no telling where Parnell might have taken Ireland. But then it was revealed that he'd had a ten-year affair with a married woman, Kitty O'Shea (who had borne him three children), and atti-tudes toward the Home Rule political movement became ensnarled with attitudes toward Parnell's morality. Gladstone asked him to step down. But Parnell made a fatal mistake: He chose to fight, and this split the Home Rule Party in two camps.

Parnell continued to fight, but in the midst of the turmoil, on October 6, 1891, perhaps because of the stress, he abruptly died. His legacy to his party was ten years of internal dissension—and ineffective-ness in bringing about any further significant change.

The loss of Parnell was profound—how profound, one can never know. But it brings to mind one of the most rueful phrases there is: "If only . . ."

4 Daniel O'Connell

Daniel O'Connell had been a witness to violence. He had seen it up close during the French Revolution as well as at the public hanging of Robert Emmet in 1803 after a failed rising. But he had also experienced it in his own life. At one point O'Connell had criticized "the beggarly corporation of Dublin," and one of its members, a man named D'Esterre, was affronted. He challenged O'Connell to a duel. The duel took place, and O'Connell killed D'Esterre. The event traumatized O'Connell, and he vowed never to use violence again. "Not for all the universe contains would I consent to the effusion of a single drop of human blood, except my own."

And he didn't. Like Martin Luther King Jr., he accomplished much with a blend of political astuteness and clever stratagems.

O'Connell came to prominence in the 1820s. The Act of Union, joining England and Ireland, had been created at the turn of the century, but the lot of the Catholics had remained essentially the same as before:

13

If you were Catholic, you were barred from many things, such as political office.

O'Connell was a larger-than-life figure, a big man with big appetites, a cutting wit, and a sometimes profane way of speaking. But he was also a master politician and a mesmerizing public speaker. Moreover, he was a man of the people, particularly rural people, who were the most victimized.

O'Connell, who had been a very successful barrister before getting involved in politics, had one goal: Catholic emancipation. His stratagem was to form the Catholic Association in 1823. For the first time, someone galvanized rural Catholics into a political force. The association required that dues be paid—a shilling a year. Although many Catholics could not afford even that, some two hundred thousand could.

The Catholic Association had a loud voice, and its members kept up a variety of other pressures, with O'Connell leading the way with electrifying speeches and great courage. Eventually, England came to see that emancipation was a better option than rebellion.

It granted Ireland emancipation, and from then on O'Connell became known as "The Liberator." Joy ran rampant in the country, and something else: a new pride and dignity.

But O'Connell didn't stop there. Using the same pressure tactics, he tried to take down the Act of Union. But whereas the British did not fear emancipation greatly, they feared repeal, as it would result in Ireland's independence. Their fears were stoked by the Young Irelanders, a militant group that advocated the use of arms. (O'Connell was at odds with this group because of its willingness to use violence.)

The British clamped down on O'Connell, trying him on trumped-up charges of sedition and sentencing him to a year in jail, of which he served three months. But he had failed to repeal the Act of Union.

O'Connell lived by his principles. He was vocal in his opposition to American slavery; he even said that the Americans were wrong to have mounted an armed insurrection in America. He was hardly a saint, though, and was probably a womanizer; indeed, it is said that when he was seventy he embarrassed his sons by making a pass at a young Protestant lass.

But he more than deserves his place on a list of influential Irish. His contemporary, John Mitchel, wrote of him in 1849, "Pray . . . that the good God who knew how to create so wondrous a creature may have mercy on his soul."

Henry Boylan eloquently summed up what O'Connell had done in *Dictionary of Irish Biography:* "His great achievement, Catholic Emancipation, is overshadowed by his failure to win repeal. But he showed the people of Ireland, long used to defeat, that victory could be achieved, and that the power to achieve it was theirs, given the right leadership. It was a lesson that sank deep into the Irish consciousness."

Eamon de Valera

There are different opinions about the impact of Eamon de Valera on Ireland, some quite negative. For example, author Frank McCourt characterized him as a "drag" on Ireland's progress in the twentieth century. However, one thing about de Valera is indisputable: He dedicated his life to freedom for and betterment of his countrymen, which included his risking his life and spending time in prison. Though there might have been individual acts of other Irish that were greater than anything de Valera ever did, his impact on the country was massive, and he richly deserves the sobriquet "Father of Modern Ireland."

De Valera came, as it were, a long way from Brooklyn, New York, where he was born on October 14, 1882. His given name was Edward, but he changed to the Irish equivalent, Eamon. If he had stresses throughout his adult life, he had stresses when he was young, too.

Eamon's Irish-born mother, Catherine, was not yet married when she emigrated—or fled—from Ireland in the 1870s. At the time, Ireland was experiencing a partial failure of the potato crop, and anyone who had heard about or experienced the Great Famine was not about to endure the same thing again. Arriving in New York, she became a domestic servant, or "Brigid," as such servants were called, to a French family named Giraud. The well-off Girauds employed for their children a music instructor named Vivion de Valera, who was Spanish, and it wasn't long before he and Catherine were involved, then married.

The marriage was haunted by Vivion's illness. He was advised by his doctors to go to Denver, which he did, but the change didn't help. In 1864 he died.

This story has not been confirmed; in fact, Vivion de Valera may have deserted Catherine and Edward. One writer who checked for the marital records of Catherine and Vivion could find none. All his life, Eamon heard the charge that he was illegitimate.

Following his father's death, Catherine treated him more like a problem than a loved one. She deposited him in the home of a friend, Catherine Doyle. From that time on, all he remembered of his mother were the occasional visits of a woman dressed in black.

When he was two years old, his mother sent him to live in Ireland with his grandmother, and it was there that he was later influenced by a Land League priest named Eugene Sheehy, from whom, he said, he learned patriotism.

Ultimately, Catherine was remarried, to an Englishman named Charles Wheelwright, and settled in Rochester, New York. Her relationship with Eamon was not unfriendly, but he lived in Ireland and she in the United States.

De Valera excelled in school, being particularly skilled in mathematics, and after a while he won a variety of scholarships and awards. In 1903 he was made a professor of mathematics at Rockwell College, County of Tipperary.

In 1908 he joined the Ard-Charaobh of the Gaelic League, the beginning of what biographer Henry Boylan said was "a life-long devotion to the Irish." It was there that he met an instructor four years his senior, Sinéad Flanagan, whom he would ultimately marry.

In the early 1900s a strong feeling of nationalism had developed in Ireland, and when de Valera attended a public meeting in Dublin in 1913, he was fired up by it. He became a captain in a volunteer force, and plans were made for a rising.

When the rising—the famous Easter Rising—began on April 24, 1916, de Valera commanded one of the forces covering the southeastern approaches to the city. When the rising was put down he was arrested, court-martialed, and sentenced to death. (It has been said that he was saved from execution because of his American birth, but there is no proof of this. His mother also came back and appealed for his life.) Perhaps the reason he was not executed was that a general revulsion of killings by both British and Irish citizens had developed.

Following his release in 1917, de Valera began a lifelong career in Irish politics. For his first position, he was appointed president of Sinn Féin (pronounced Shin Fane), Arthur Griffith having stepped aside.

For the next fifty years, until his retirement in June 1973, de Valera was intimately involved in Irish politics, his career going from the heights—as leader of the country—to the depths, when he took part in the civil war triggered by the Treaty of 1921, "the war of the brothers," and was forced to witness and take part in the deaths of men whom he had fought beside against the British.

De Valera was a master politician, and one of his greatest feats was keeping Ireland neutral during World War II, when both the Allies and the Axis were pressuring Ireland to join them.

One action that has been roundly criticized is the economic war he precipitated between Ireland and England, which involved each country's barring the importation of the other's products. It caused great hardship. But he was also a man who was three times premier and founder of Fianna Fáil (the political party whose name means "armed men of Ireland") and president of Ireland from 1959 to 1973.

The list of honors bestowed on de Valera is long, and when he was buried at Glasnevin Cemetery after a state funeral, the greatness of the man could still not diminish a sad and central fact: The ending of partition—for which he had fought so hard for so many years, the central goal of his life—had eluded him.

John Devoy

(1 8 4 2 – 1 9 2 8)

In 1861, when he was nineteen, John Devoy decided to get military training in preparation for fighting England. He picked an unusual method, a kind
of on-the-job training: He joined the French Foreign Legion. He served a year, and when he returned
to Ireland he was ready to fight. That story is just one in
a life that reads more like a movie script than a real life.

When Devoy returned, he became active in the revolutionary Fenian
group that was secretly organizing Irish soldiers within the British army.
But in 1866 he was caught, brought to trial, and sentenced to fifteen years
in prison.

He served five years and then was released on condition that he live
outside the United Kingdom. The way things worked out, it would have
been better for the British if they had allowed him to stay.

Devoy emigrated to America and worked as a journalist in both
Chicago and New York. Eventually settling in New York, he joined Clan
na Gael, an Irish American organization whose goals included galvaniz-

ing American opinion against the British and collecting and sending donations to a variety of groups in Ireland. The group also tried to shape American public opinion in Ireland's favor.

When fellow revolutionary Michael Davitt came to America, Devoy and Clan na Gael formed a "new departure" philosophy, by which constitutional and revolutionary nationalists formed a common front on the issues of land reform and self-government, the two most pressing issues in Ireland.

In 1879 Devoy took a big risk: Contrary to the terms of his release from prison, he returned to Ireland to aid the Irish cause.

Devoy's boldest foray of all was his secret trip on the whaler *Catalpa* to Australia to execute a successful escape plot for six Fenians who had been languishing for years in an Australian jail. (See Number 92, John Boyle O'Reilly, for details.) The event gave Clan na Gael tremendous credibility as an organization.

While in New York he founded two newspapers, the *Irish Nation* and *Gaelic American,* and he helped support the *United Irishmen,* which was superbly edited by Arthur Griffith. Support was also given to the Irish volunteers and to St. Enda's College in Dublin, which had been founded by Patrick Pearse, a martyr in the Easter Rising. The school was devoted to increasing the use of the Irish language.

When World War I broke out, Devoy and his comrades tried very hard to keep America neutral; in other words, to discourage it from supporting England.

But undoubtedly, Devoy's greatest role was as the symbol of Ireland in America. He had a small office in a hotel room in New York City and was visited there by thousands of people who wished to talk, to plan, to contribute. In sum, Devoy was the single most important Irishman in America. And England hated that because there was no way to stop him.

In 1919, Clan na Gael was paid a visit by Eamon de Valera, and it did not turn out well. A power struggle ensued between de Valera and Devoy over control, and de Valera and Devoy split.

Devoy had one last hurrah. In 1924 he returned to Ireland to attend the newly revived Tailteann Games and received a hero's welcome. When he returned to America, he wrote *Recollections of an Irish Rebel*, which was published in 1929, the year after his death.

The end of Devoy's life was sad. He died in Atlantic City, New Jersey, on September 28, 1928, almost impoverished and alone—he had never married. But as someone said at his passing, "He didn't die unknown. The Irish knew it, and the British knew it real well."

Patrick Pearse

Perhaps no one looks like a revolutionary, but Patrick Henry Pearse looked even less so, and some historians would argue that he didn't have the heart for it either. Before the Easter Rising of 1916 in Ireland, Pearse was a schoolteacher, as well as a writer and poet of some note—and a spellbinding public speaker.

He was also a man with a great reverence for Irish culture and language. Until the 1830s the vast majority of people in Ireland spoke and read Gaelic, but in 1831 the use of the language was outlawed by the British. Then, when the Great Famine came along in the 1840s, Irish was used mostly by the peasantry and became a symbol of inferiority. The language gradually faded, pushed along by practices in school that included punishing young students for lapsing into Irish.

But Pearse cherished and used Gaelic, reveled in Irish culture, and sought to inspire his students the same way. The great warrior Cuchulain was one of his favorites, and he taught his students that Cuchulain was not a savage warrior but a "small, dark, sad Boy, comeliest of the boys of Eire."

At the end of the year, Pearse would send the boys home with stories of the great Irish hero ringing in their ears and hearts, feeling the way he felt about Cuchulain himself. These stories were alive in him when he started to plan the Easter Rising with others of the IRB. And as they fired on the British those days in Dublin, Cuchulain was not far from the thoughts of many of them.

For a long time, Pearse had thought that the way to achieve Irish independence was through peaceful means, but there came a time when he, like so many other Irish revolutionaries, concluded that only a revolt that involved bloodletting would set Ireland free. So he dedicated himself to that task.

On August 1, 1915, the body of one of the Fenians, Jeremiah O'Donovan Rossa, who decades earlier had plotted against the British but had gone to America to work on the *Irish People* newspaper, was returned to Dublin. He had finally come home, and Pearse delivered a powerful oration at the graveside that was to become famous and was the measure of his resolve:

> The fools, the fools, the fools!—they have left us our Fenian dead, and while Ireland holds these graves, Ireland un-free shall never be at peace!

Pearse was one of a handful of men who actually planned the details of the revolt, and though at one point the British sensed that something was brewing, most officials scoffed that anything would come of it. Still, they debated back and forth whether to arrest Pearse and his cohorts, and finally on Easter Monday morning, lead by Lord Winmere, they decided to do just that.

They were too late. The attack had begun.

The revolutionaries held out for five days, but on April 29 at a quarter to four in the afternoon Pearse, who had become commander in chief of the IRB, was forced to surrender. He and other ringleaders were arrested.

Their efforts seemed to have done nothing, but the British turned public opinion against themselves with the executions of the rising's ringleaders.

Patrick Henry Pearse was the first to be executed, and it was clear that the judge who passed sentence did not relish the idea. Later, he would remark that it was terribly difficult sentencing a man of such courage to death.

Though others were killed, Pearse's death had a greater impact because he was a leader, a poet, a speaker, and someone who had perpetuated the love of things Irish. When he was killed, a part of Ireland died with him. His death affected his countrymen greatly.

Just before he died, Pearse wrote a final letter to his mother, a stunning, moving document informed by everything he was—including a desire to make his mother feel good on the most terrible day any mother can have. What he wrote to his mother—who was not allowed to see him—was on a single sheet of paper and is today on display in the National Museum of Ireland:

Dear Mary, that didst thy first-born son
Go forth to die amidst the scorn of men
For whom he died
Receive my first-born son into thy arms
And keep him by thee till I come to thee.
Dear Mary, I have shared thy sorrow and
soon shall share thy joy.

St. Brigid

Brigid, known as "Mary of the Gael," is the most venerated of all female Irish saints, thought to be on a level with St. Patrick and Colmcille. She is also the patron saint of students and dairy workers. Her feast day is celebrated on February 1.

Various accounts of her life have been written, but the central influence of her life is that she was a major force in the spread of Christianity in Ireland.

She started her ministry in Ireland about twenty years after St. Patrick's death and continued the work of Patrick all over Ireland, as well as in her famous monastery in County Kildare.

There are many stories in medieval hagiography of the miracles attributed to her. Perhaps the most famous is that of St. Brigid's Cross. According to legend, the saint converted a peasant on his deathbed by explaining the Redemption to him, using as a visual aid a cross made from rushes.

Brigid's involvement with the spread of Christianity alone would put her near the top of any list of influential Irish, but the impact she had on people who would pray to her in times of trouble and the reverence shown for her (indicated by how many Irish women are named after her) are almost equally significant.

Robert Emmet

(1778-1803)

Robert Emmet had a very brief life—he was only twenty-five years old when he was hung, then beheaded and drawn and quartered by the British. But the impact of his death has resonated since it occurred in 1803. Any revolutionary—and that's what Emmet was—who followed was sure to have thought about him or perhaps been inspired by him—particularly by the final, electrifying speech he gave while looking into the face of his own mortality.

Emmet was the son of a physician and student at Trinity College, Dublin, and was a member of the Historical Society. Early on he distinguished himself as an outstanding orator—and rebel: When the lord chancellor of England visited the school to gauge support for the rebellious United Irishmen group, Emmet, one of its leaders, was summoned before the prestigious visitor. Emmet became so incensed that he removed his name from the college's books, thus ending any prospects of a professional career.

A few years earlier, in 1798, Emmet had witnessed the failure of Theobald Wolfe Tone's rising, but that debacle did not dim Emmet's goal, which was freedom from England, achieved by violent revolution.

In April 1799 he went to Europe and met his brother, Thomas. Together they asked a number of governments for help. They met with Talleyrand and Napoleon, and despite the diminutive French leader's dislike of the English, Emmet and other leaders questioned his sincerity when he expressed concern for Ireland.

Ultimately, they decided not to seek French help, and Robert returned to Ireland and set about the task of organizing and arming his countrymen. They established arms depots, drew up battle plans, and hoped that help would come from other countries. Robert got promises of help from people all over Ireland, including the North, and working from his base in Dublin, he prepared his plan.

But there was a problem he did not see: One of his inner circle, a man named Bernard Duggan, was a British spy. As preparations for the rising were made, Duggan reported everything to the British undersecretary, Alexander Marston, who readied a trap.

On July 16, an explosion occurred at one of the depots where Emmet had hid his explosives. Worried that he would be discovered, Emmet moved the plans up and set a place named Costigan's Mills for the assembly of the army. Only about a hundred men showed up, but they set out to attack Dublin Castle. On the way he encountered Arthur Wolfe, the lord chief justice, and his nephew, and the band killed them. Emmet fled to the Dublin mountains. However, he was drawn to visit a woman he loved, Sarah Curran, at Harold's Cross and was arrested by Major Henry Sirr, a man radically opposed to Ireland's independence.

Emmet was tried for treason. He gave a stirring speech that included the battle cry that can still be heard:

> Let no man write my epitaph. . . . When my country takes her place among the nations of the earth then, and not till then, let my epitaph be written.

On September 20, 1803, Robert was publicly executed on a Dublin street. His brother, Thomas, escaped to America, where he became a lawyer, eventually becoming New York State attorney general in 1812.

The poet Thomas Moore wrote many ballads about Emmet, including "O Breathe Not His Name" and "She Is Far from the Land."

10

Theobald Wolfe Tone

Since 1169, when they had been invaded by the Normans, the Irish had been subject to four other invasions, but until the mid-1600s none of the invaders ever quite succeeded in subduing them. On the contrary, the Irish "conquered" the invaders by absorbing them into the Irish way of life.

But in the mid-1600s, following the Reformation in England, Oliver Cromwell came to Ireland, and oppression wore a new, dead-eyed, horrific face. Indeed, Father Andrew Greeley says in his book *The Irish-Americans: The Rise to Money and Power* that Cromwell "won his place in history as the first modern practitioner of genocide. During his decade-long invasion of Ireland, the population of Ireland was cut in half, from eight million to four million—and in the two centuries that followed, Ireland went though an era of rebellion, atrocity, repression, misery, famine, punitive legislation, sullen resentment." In particular, in the 1700s Irish Catholics and to some degree Protestants were subject to the Penal Laws, which regarded the Irish as ignoble savages, subhuman creatures not deserving of the kindnesses ordinary people receive. More than one historian has compared their treatment to that accorded slaves in the Old South. They could not vote, practice their religion (under penalty of death), or go to school (if caught, they were executed); they were half starved, and paid unconscionably high taxes.

At the end of the 1700s, however, the English became aware of that typically Irish characteristic: never saying die. Many sensed that Irish revolution was in the air, even though many of the Penal Laws had been repealed or simply not enforced. To quell the unrest, England passed more liberal legislation; this placated people to some degree, but not completely.

Theobald Wolfe Tone was one person who was not buying in.

Tone, son of a Protestant Dublin tradesman, had been a mercenary in France during the revolution there and was in complete sympathy with the Catholics. He referred to the Penal Laws as "that execrable and infamous code, framed with the art and malice of demons, to plunder and degrade and brutalize the Catholics."

He vowed to do something to help his fellow Irishmen. In 1792 he formed the Society of United Irishmen and issued a pamphlet that articulated the goals of the society:

To subvert the tyranny of our execrable government, to break the connection with England, the never failing source of all our political

evils and to assert the independence of my country . . . and to sub-
stitute the common name of Irishmen in place of the denominations
of Protestant, Catholic and Dissenter.

These were fighting words. But Tone was a true revolutionary, and
his eyes were always on freedom. He would settle for nothing less.

When he published the pamphlet, he was still working within the
political system. He organized a group of delegates in the Irish Parliament and in 1793 was able to push through the Catholic Relief Act,
which gave Catholics some new rights, including the rights to vote and
enter the professions. But Catholics were still not allowed to run for
office. Tone, guided by the French Revolution's precepts of liberty, equality, and fraternity, concluded that nothing but violence would work.

Then fate played into his hands.

Louis XVI had been executed by the revolutionaries, and the French
declared war on the Netherlands and its ally England. Tone knew that
England would now be more than a little preoccupied with France. The
time seemed ripe for armed revolution.

He traveled to France and arranged for aid to help make an insurrection work. Then he returned to Ireland and readied for battle.

On a cold winter day in 1796 fifteen thousand French soldiers
boarded forty-three French ships and headed for Bantry Bay, Ireland. The
fight for Irish independence was to begin.

But unlike World War II's D-Day, which was blessed with good
weather, this invasion was bedeviled by stormy weather. The ships could

not anchor in the choppy seas, and they were forced to return to France. The battle was off.

Tone planned and plotted again, but in 1798 the British swept across to Ireland, arrested the United Irishmen's leaders, and flogged them with cat-o'-nine-tails. The actions threw gasoline on the fire. A spontaneous rebellion started with farmers and intellectuals attacking the British, mainly in Counties Mayo, Wicklow, and Wexford. The British responded with a force of sixty-five thousand soldiers and quickly quelled the rebellion, slaughtering men, women, and children.

The last bitter battle was at the appropriately named Vinegar Hill, where the rebels were defeated and their leaders hanged. The British set about torturing those who had survived to discourage further rebellion.

Tone, meanwhile, had been in France when the spontaneous revolution erupted. In August he returned to Ireland, this time with only a thousand soldiers. His attack was quickly quashed.

On October 12 he returned again, with three thousand French soldiers, and they engaged in a naval battle with the British fleet. His small force was defeated, and he was captured. He was returned to Dublin, tried by court-martial, found guilty, and sentenced to be hanged. He asked to be a shot like a soldier rather than hanged, but when this request was denied, he performed his final act of defiance, cutting his own throat with a penknife.

The memory of Tone and his fight would linger long in the Irish soul, and he would be with them permanently in spirit and serve as inspiration for future Irish.

Michael Davitt

(1846–1906)

In 1880 Captain Charles Boycott, a landlord in Lough Mask who had a reputation for grossly unfair rents and tenant abuse, abruptly found himself given the "silent treatment" by the people in the county where he lived. No one was willing to perform any of the basic services he required on his land. He had been ostracized, or—as the world would later characterize what had happened to him—"boycotted." The action was engineered by Michael Davitt and was part of a larger strategy to effect overall change in the way the landlord system worked in Ireland.

Davitt's motivation for change went back a long way. In 1850, as a result of the Great Famine, his family had been evicted from their small farm in Straide, County Mayo. Davitt was only four when this occurred, but he remembered a bit of it. What he didn't grasp, his father, an activist against unfair landlord practices, enlightened him about later, inculcating his son with his own beliefs.

As a man, Michael Davitt was easily recognizable—he had only one arm, his right one lost at the age of eleven in a cotton mill while he was working on the farm. Early in his career, he was involved with the Fenians, a militant and militaristic group, and in 1868 he also became the secretary of the Irish Republican Brotherhood.

In 1870 he was arrested for his activities and sentenced to fifteen years in prison. He served almost half of this—seven years—at Dartmoor prison; then he was released because of pressure bought to bear by Charles Stewart Parnell and Sir Isaac Butt.

Then Davitt and his comrade John Devoy formulated a new approach toward land reform that they called the New Departure. There followed the formation of Davitt's Land League, which basically worked by ostracizing greedy landlords.

Both Davitt and Devoy thought that the land development would be followed quickly by Ireland's independence from England, but then Parnell fell and the split in the Home Rule Party Parnell headed set them back "for generations," according to one historian.

Davitt became member of Parliament of a variety of counties, visited America, and published six books. He died on May 30, 1906, and was buried at Swiade, in land that was free—land that had, however, not been free when he was born there some sixty years earlier.

Arthur Griffith

(1 8 7 1 — 1 9 2 2)

Arthur Griffith did not fit the heroic mold. He was a small, bespectacled man, and his life, at least in terms of military action, hardly compares to the lives of some of the superstars of Irish revolution. But on December 6, 1921, he was in London sitting next to Michael Collins, and he was the first person to sign the treaty of 1921. Like Collins, he took a big risk. But he did a good deal more than that.

The fall of Charles Stewart Parnell in 1890 had been a blow to the Irish, who all thought independence was on the horizon. The country was looking for new approaches to gaining independence, and Arthur Griffith had some ideas.

Griffith was born in Dublin and, while still a young man, became a member of the Gaelic League. He also joined the Irish Republican Brotherhood. But in 1896 he seemed to give up Irish politics, probably feeling that nothing could be done, at least at the time. He went to Africa to work in the gold mines.

Two years later he was back, returning at the request of his friend Willie Rooney to edit a newspaper called the *United Irishmen.* In 1904 he wrote and published a series of articles that detailed his new approach to ridding Ireland of English domination. The articles, which were turned into a pamphlet that carried the unlikely title "The Resurrection of Hungary," were based on his studies of how the Hungarians had acted under Minister of Justice Ferenc Deák after 1848. Griffith wrote that following their example could aid Ireland in forming its own national assembly to set their own laws, as well as tribunals to supersede English courts.

Griffith called the new policy "Sinn Féin" ("we ourselves" in English). A new newspaper was started to supplant the *United Irishmen,* which was embroiled in a lawsuit, and Griffith dubbed this *Sinn Féin.* It was to become the permanent name of the political arm of the Irish Republican Army.

In 1912 the Home Rule Bill was passed, but it did not significantly alter Irish rights. As a result, new movements were sought, and the philosophy espoused by Sinn Féin was adopted by many.

Meanwhile, the Ulster Volunteers were formed to fight home rule, and in 1913 the Irish Volunteers were formed to counter them. Griffith lent his support to the latter group, taking part in a secret importation of arms to Howth in July 1914.

He went much further than that. When World War I started, some political leaders in Ireland exhorted Irish youth to join the British and fight for "small nations." But Griffith suggested the opposite course in his newspaper, and ultimately the British suppressed the publication.

Griffith did not fight in the Easter Rising of 1916, which did not endear him to the dominant, militant wing of the Irish Volunteers. Nevertheless, the British saw him as a threat, constantly reminding the Irish people in his writings of his nationalistic goals.

Sinn Féin benefited from the rising of 1916. When the tide of public opinion turned against the British, Sinn Féin came into its own because the group was openly hostile toward the British. At a Sinn Féin convention of 1917, the strength of the movement was clearly indicated by the turnout: Thousands attended.

Griffith had been head of the movement, but he stepped down in favor of Eamon de Valera.

In 1918, the Irish held their own general election, and Sinn Féin was overwhelmingly victorious. The movement declared the Dáil Éireanne the legitimate parliament of Ireland and formed a republic independent of England with de Valera as president and Griffith as vice president. This was beyond anything Griffith had imagined.

Joseph P. Kennedy

(1888–1969)

Joseph P. Kennedy could have been the protagonist of one of Harold Robbins's novels. He had the necessary character traits, and his life story reads perfectly as a novel's plot. At one time the wealthiest man in America, Kennedy was a man consumed by ambition: He ached to be president of the United States. When his own political dreams were dashed, he drove his sons to recapture them and suffered the soul-searing trauma of losing three of them and one of his daughters. (It was the kind of life loss about which someone once said poignantly and accurately: "There is a name for it when you lose a spouse, but there is no name for when you lose a child.") At the end of his life the image is fittingly Robbinsesque: an old man sitting in a wheelchair, his health and his dreams gone, perhaps looking forward to death more than anyone could possibly realize.

Kennedy was born in Boston, into the helter-skelter politics of that time, the son of a liquor dealer who was also a ward boss. Joe was tough and bright; he attended Harvard, where he did well but always felt, he told friends, that because he was Irish Catholic he was never really accepted by the Boston Brahmins who dominated the school.

He did even better after he graduated. At twenty-five he took over a modest bank, the youngest bank president on record, and built it into a highly successful enterprise.

It is said that he longed to have as his wife Rose Fitzgerald, the daughter of "Honey Fitz," the mayor of Boston, and perhaps the most sought-after young woman in the city. "It was," said an observer, "a matter not of love at first sight but a way to fulfill ambition."

They were married and took up residence in Brookline. That is, Rose did so. Kennedy was often in New York, pursuing his interests in the stock market, which at the time was a wild, unregulated place. He was said to have worked ferociously to make money there and that nothing—and no one—would stand in his way. He said of his methods then: "I have to make this money fast, before they make laws against what I'm doing."

In the 1920s Kennedy went west and started to invest in low-budget films, which practically manufactured money; he made $5 million very quickly. His only mistake was a big-budget picture he tried to make with Gloria Swanson, with whom he was having an affair. She was but the crown jewel in a long line of Hollywood affairs—or consumables.

By 1928 Kennedy was back in the stock market, but by early 1929 he sensed that something was wrong and started to sell. In October, when the market crashed, Joe Kennedy got away unscathed—and millions richer.

At a time when other businessmen were Republicans and backing Republicans, Kennedy was a Democrat and put his backing and resources behind Franklin Delano Roosevelt and his New Deal. Later, Roosevelt awarded him various governmental posts and in 1937 appointed him U.S. ambassador to Great Britain. Thus he was poised to make a run for the presidency after Roosevelt left office.

Meanwhile, Hitler was on the move, and it was then that Kennedy made his politically fatal mistake: He stated that the United States should stay neutral in World War II. It was not a popular position, and there were charges that he was anti-Semitic. Pressure built, and in 1940 he was forced to resign the ambassadorship. His political career was over.

At home, his family had enlarged considerably: By 1932 he had nine children, four boys and five girls, one of whom, Rosemary, was mentally retarded. His relationship with Rose can hardly be described as romantic. She had to have known about at least some of his affairs, and in this case "some" was more than enough to drive a wedge between them.

He instilled in his children his own competitive drive and told them that when they lost, crying wasn't allowed.

Historians say that Kennedy continued to dream of the presidency— but this time through his sons. Kennedy earmarked his eldest son, Joe Jr., for the presidency, and he indeed would have had all the pedigree needed. He was handsome, smart, and a fighter pilot war hero.

But Joe Jr. volunteered for a very dangerous bombing mission. His plane was loaded with extra bombs, and on the way to the destination the plane blew up.

However, Kennedy was not finished. He had someone else waiting in the wings, and one day John F. Kennedy would indeed run for and capture the presidency.

Joe Kennedy's influence was massive, not only because of his own individual impact but because of the deeds of his progeny. Indeed, it is likely that his influence will be felt for decades.

In 1961 he suffered a stroke, which left him debilitated, and he died on November 18, 1969.

14

Rachel Carson

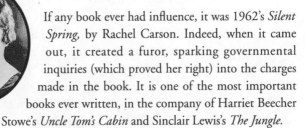

If any book ever had influence, it was 1962's *Silent Spring,* by Rachel Carson. Indeed, when it came out, it created a furor, sparking governmental inquiries (which proved her right) into the charges made in the book. It is one of the most important books ever written, in the company of Harriet Beecher Stowe's *Uncle Tom's Cabin* and Sinclair Lewis's *The Jungle.*

Carson shared with the writers of those other seminal books passion—a passion to reveal and to warn people how the careless use of pesticides was destroying the land and the creatures that depended on it. But the book did much more than that.

Carson meticulously researched this book: She was a marine biologist and knew how to investigate nature, understanding how interdependent things in nature could be. As she had written in her earlier book *Edge of the Sea,* "Each living thing is bound to its world by many threads, weaving the intricate design of the fabric of life."

Carson got her love for the land and her respect for all living creatures from her mother, Irish American–born Maria McLean, who was a schoolteacher and musician. (Her father, Robert's, mother and father were immigrants from Ireland.) Her mother also encouraged her to explore literature and pointed Rachel onto the path to becoming a writer. Indeed, Carson was greatly encouraged when she sold a story to a children's magazine, *St. Nicholas,* and received $10 for it.

When Carson entered Pennsylvania College for Women (later Chatham College), she intended to major in English, but then she took a biology class by Mary Scott Skinker that electrified her. She found it all so fascinating that she gave up her literary goals and became a scientist.

In 1929 she received a fellowship at the Woods Hole Marine Biological Laboratory in Massachusetts and found the study of the sea enthralling. She followed this with a fellowship at Johns Hopkins University. She then received an M.A. in zoology from the University of Maryland and began teaching there.

In 1935 her father died abruptly, and Carson, searching for ways to support herself and her mother in the Depression, linked up with the U.S. Bureau of Fisheries in Washington on a part-time basis, writing radio broadcasts about life in the ocean. In 1936 she became the first full-time female employee of the bureau, continuing her writing and scientific investigations.

She was asked to write a fisheries booklet. However, when she turned the manuscript in, the bureau turned it down as inappropriate. Nevertheless, her boss was so impressed that he suggested she submit it to *The Atlantic.*

This she did. The article was published as "Undersea," and the editors asked her to submit more material. When the magazine hit the stands, the article was so highly praised that Carson was encouraged to expand it into a book. She did, calling it *Under the Sea-Wind.* It became a best-seller.

Through the war years and after, Carson continued to write government publications. She then took some time off to write a book, with the help of a Eugene F. Saxton fellowship. She called it *The Sea Around Us,* and it also vaulted onto the best-seller lists and stayed there an astonishing eighty-six weeks.

People were fascinated by the scientific explanations and insights, but many people thought it was so beautifully written that it was poetry. Carson didn't deny it. She said, "No one could write truthfully about the sea and leave out the poetry." With the money from the book, she became a full-time writer and wrote a series of books that detailed life in the sea.

But Carson had noticed, more than most anyone else, storm clouds on the horizon. The threat was simple: people. They were indiscriminate about their use of the land and chemicals, killing off all kind of creatures and disrupting the fabric of life she was writing about. She researched the book thoroughly, and the result was *Silent Spring.* She was attacked viciously by business and chemical companies, but government inquiries at the time proved that she was right.

While on the surface the book was about pesticides, it was really a call to humans that we must be careful with our environment; if we kill it, we will die too. In a way, Carson triggered the ecological concerns that are commonplace now.

She developed cancer and heart disease when she was only fifty-seven years old and died. In 1980 President Jimmy Carter presented her with a posthumous Presidential Medal of Freedom and said of her, "Always concerned, always eloquent, she created a tide of environmental consciousness that has not ebbed."

Margaret Sanger

(1879–1966)

The event that changed Margaret Higgins Sanger's life happened one sweltering day in the summer of 1912. Sanger, a nurse, accompanied by a doctor, went to the run-down Lower East Side New York City apartment of one Sadie Sacks. Sacks, a very poor woman who could barely care for the children she already had, had become pregnant—again—and, like many women in her plight, had tried to give herself an abortion. But she was dying.

Margaret, daughter of a poor immigrant Irish father, Michael, and an Irish American mother, Anne, had long been opposed to women giving birth to an army of children, which was a way of life—and death—at a time when no effective birth control methods were available. Her own mother had given birth to eleven children and had died by the age of forty. Though her mother had been tubercular, Margaret had long thought that having all those children had contributed to her death.

The doctor saved Sacks, but as they were about to leave, the woman pleaded with him to provide some way to stop a pregnancy other than condoms or coitus interruptus. If he didn't, next time she tried an abortion she could die.

The doctor's advice was simple: "Have Jake sleep on the roof."

Sacks turned to Sanger, who told her she would return and talk to her. But she never did return. And eventually she learned that Sadie Sacks had again tried to give herself an abortion—and had died.

Suffused with guilt and sorrow, Sanger vowed that she would teach women about what she dubbed "birth control." She vowed to find ways that were simple, cheap, and effective. This was a woman's—a person's— right.

For the next two years she researched birth control methods in the United States and Europe and in 1914 published many of her findings— though the 1873 Comstock Law prohibited sending detailed how-to information through the mails—in a publication she called *The Woman Rebel*. This publication articulated the message that women had rights when it came to their bodies and that it was okay to enjoy sex and not become pregnant.

That same year Sanger followed this publication with a bombshell dryly titled *Family Limitation*. It gave state-of-the-art methods, complete with explicit drawings on how to effect birth control. She lugged the manuscript to twenty publishers before one agreed to print it, and when it was distributed, it was in great demand.

Her speeches and other work eventually came under the scrutiny of beady-eyed Anthony Comstock, who enforced the law with his name on it. When he learned what she had done, he set the legal machinery to put her in jail into action by charging her with nine counts of sending birth control information through the mail.

The night before the trial—facing forty-five years of incarceration—Sanger fled to Europe. There, her education in birth control, feminism, and socialism was expanded upon. When she returned home, the indictment was quashed. People listened to what she was saying. And Anthony Comstock had died.

In October 1916 Sanger opened the first birth control clinic in the country, in New York City. It was mostly a source of information on venereal disease and birth control methods, and it also tracked patients' medical records.

A few years later, she and a sister, Ethel Byrne, launched *Birth Control Review,* which was distributed to health professionals and was designed to keep them apprised of issues and methodologies available for birth control. In 1921 she assembled the first national conference on birth control, which drew doctors and other professionals from all over the country.

Sanger had married William Sanger in 1902 and borne three children. She divorced Sanger in 1920 and in 1922 married Noah Slee, a wealthy businessman who helped finance many of her projects.

On January 3, 1936, she and her adherents won a big victory in the case *The United States* v. *One Package.* Here it was decreed that a doctor could legally receive a package—which happened to contain a contraceptive device—that had come from Japan. The way was cleared for wide distribution of the devices. Sanger spread the word worldwide and in 1952 established the International Planned Parenthood Federation.

Sanger exerted tremendous influence not only on America but throughout the world, from the marble halls of San Francisco to the humble mud huts of Africa. Her work has meant longer life for many women and a great reduction in childbirth deaths. Because of Sanger's work, many children enter the world being wanted rather than as the result of a biological imperative. Her work has meant more freedom for women everywhere.

Sanger's was a life spent in struggle and conflict: conflict with law enforcement, conflict with the Catholic Church, conflict with others' religious beliefs—and more. And she went to jail eight times.

And, of course, her life was one filled with triumph.

The woman who did all this was by no means a saint, though her diminutive, wholesome good looks made her look like one. She had a sometimes prickly personality surrounding what was really an indomitable heart. You either hated her or loved her. Without question, the latter was more common.

16

William Holmes McGuffey

(1800–1873)

In the 1830s, William Holmes McGuffey contracted with a publisher to develop a series of books that would teach people how to read. He did, and at one point there were more than 150 million copies in print. Besides showing Americans how to read, the McGuffey Eclectic *Readers,* as they came to be known, taught America how to behave.

William Holmes (his mother's maiden name) McGuffey had a Scotch-Irish heritage. He was born on a farm in Washington County, Pennsylvania, close to the Ohio border, on September 23, 1800. In 1803, the same year Ohio entered the Union, McGuffey's father, Alexander, moved his family across the border into a windowless log cabin near Youngstown, Ohio.

McGuffey learned how to read, write, and do arithmetic thanks to his mother and so-called subscription schools, usually conducted by ministers. His father, a scout and frontiersman, appreciated the value of education and tried to make it easier for William to read at night by constructing an adjustable lamp stand for him.

By the time he was fourteen, McGuffey, who had launched a teaching career by instructing his sisters and brothers, opened his own school, charging forty-eight children $2 each. He went on to further education himself at a variety of schools, ultimately entering Washington College in Pennsylvania in 1820.

In his senior year he left the college and accepted a teaching position in Paris, Kentucky. Then, on a visit to Lexington he had a chance meeting with a man named Robert Hamilton Bishop, who was to become the first president of Miami University in Ohio. Hamilton offered him a job teaching classical languages (McGuffey could speak seven foreign languages, including Hebrew and Greek).

His first year on the faculty was particularly good: Through his brother Charles, a retailer in Oxford, Ohio, he met Harriet Spining of Dayton, Ohio. They were married in 1827, and by 1833 McGuffey had constructed a brick house, the handsomest in the area, across the street from the college.

McGuffey wrote four readers, but there were six in all. One was a primer that, as William E. Smith of Miami University once wrote, "introduced children to the code of ethics which ran through the four readers." The second and third readers contained stories that people "would never forget," such as "The Dying Boy" and "George's Feast." In the fourth the stories were meant to be read aloud. The fifth reader, by McGuffey's brother, Alexander Hamilton McGuffey, contained instructions in rhetoric. It was called "Rhetorical Guide," and the sixth contained selections from the fourth and fifth.

Through the stories McGuffey threaded the virtues of individual morality, thrift, sobriety, and hard work—the Protestant ethic.

It was estimated by one analyst, Harvey C. Minnish, that "each Reader was used by ten pupils before it was worn out or laid aside." And of its influence, Minnish said, "Except for the Bible, no other book or set of books has influenced the American mind so much."

Unfortunately for McGuffey, individual virtue was not in the forefront of the mind of his publisher (Truman and Smith in Cincinnati). McGuffey got a royalty of 10 percent, up to a limit of $1,000 worth of books sold. Meanwhile, the publisher, for whom the books had made millions many times over, sent McGuffey a barrel of smoked hams each year and an annuity until he died in 1873.

Not that McGuffey suffered that much; he was a born teacher and stayed that way (except for stints as president of Cincinnati College and Ohio University) until he died.

Catherine McAuley

(1 7 7 8 – 1 8 4 1)

Catherine McAuley's parents died when she was young, and she lived with relatives. But in 1803, she was invited to live in and work at the Coolock House estate of Catherine and William Callaghan in Dublin to take care of Mrs. Callaghan, who was in frail health. It was an event that was to affect the lives of millions of people for decades to come.

Catherine's father had been a very compassionate man. It was not uncommon for him to invite the poor children in the neighborhood into his house, where he would teach them the tenets of the Catholic faith. Catherine did the same. At Coolock House, she began catechetical instruction with the household servants and with the poor children of the village, and she taught needlework.

Meanwhile, her responsibilities at the house increased. Catherine Callaghan became sicker, and McAuley took over the management of the house more and more. She also took over what could be called the spiritual management of her charge. She spent hours and hours reading the

Bible to Mrs. Callaghan, who found it a great comfort. Before she died, inspired by McAuley's compassion and grace, Catherine Callaghan converted to Catholicism.

Death seemed to haunt Catherine McAuley. It wasn't long after Catherine Callaghan's death that Anne Conway Byrne, Catherine's cousin, died, leaving four small children. With characteristic compassion, Catherine brought them to Coolock House to care for them.

Around 1822 William Callaghan's health started to fail, and he began looking for a way to dispose of his estate. Catherine had been with him for twenty years, and he decided to give a portion of it to her and the rest to Robert Powell, his niece's husband. Then he overheard Robert comment that after William died, he and his wife would control the estate, putting Catherine into a subservient position. William revised his will and made Catherine the sole heir.

He died on November 22, 1822. As soon as the will was read, the Powells began to contest it. But it had been written tightly, and Catherine ended up with Callaghan's entire fortune as well as Coolock House, worth about $1 million by today's standards.

McAuley had long dreamed of teaching poor children, and the money gave her the opportunity to do so. She planned to use the estate as a residence and school as well as a place of worship. Gradually, her vision expanded to include a variety of services for adults and children. She also decided she needed a formal social service center. She leased property in Dublin's Baggot Street, a rich neighborhood, worked out a plan, and the building began.

The choice of an affluent area was intentional: McAuley hoped that seeing the straits that the people who entered the building were in would prompt the rich to offer their help. Many of them did. In the three years it took to construct the building, Catherine continued to help young women and others, and traveled to France to learn the latest education methods. On September 24, 1827, the Feast of Our Lady of Mercy, the house on Baggot Street was opened. Catherine and her coworkers decided to call it the House of Our Blessed Lady of Mercy.

A core group of twelve women lived in the house and worked with the young people. Over time, they started to dress the same and act the same and to call one another "sister." At the same time, the Archbishop of Dublin encouraged Catherine to form a religious congregation. Assured that it would not be cloistered, she consented. She and a group of women took vows and formed the Sisters of Mercy in 1831. Gradually, she started new houses in other areas of Ireland, and eventually the Sisters of Mercy would be in virtually every country, the largest order of nuns in the world.

Catherine McAuley died on November 11, 1841. The positive influence she had on others in her life, as well as the influence of the order she founded, is incalculable. At her core, she was a person who felt huge compassion for others and followed her impulses. And she was a woman of simple but profound faith. "Each day," she said once, "is a step we make towards eternity, and we shall continue thus to step from day to day until we take the last step, which will bring us into the presence of God."

18

Niall of the Nine Hostages

(FOURTH—FIFTH CENTURIES)

One of the great kings of Ireland, in legend and in fact, was Niall of the Nine Hostages. Not only was he influential in his own time, but he was also the founder of one of the longest dynasties in Irish history. He had fourteen sons, and their progeny were to reign as ard-reighs (kings) for six hundred years. Yet he performed one act that had profound consequences.

Niall was the son of Eopcahid Muigh-medon, who in the fourth century became king. His mother was named Carthann. But Niall's father had two wives, and his other wife, Mong-Fionn, was a Machiavellian personality whose goal was to banish Niall and his mother.

While she succeeded in subjugating his mother to the slavelike existence of a person who carried water to the court, Niall was spirited away when a very young boy by the great poet Torna, who reared and educated him. As soon as he was old enough, Niall returned and rescued his mother, restoring her to her rightful place.

There are many legends about Niall, at least one of which detailed how his father decided that of all his sons, Niall was most qualified to be king.

The father had designed a kind of Rorschach test for his sons. They were at a smith's forge when suddenly it caught on fire. The king told his sons to descend on the forge as fast as possible and save what they could. Son Brian saved a chariot; son Ailill rescued a shield and sword; Fiacrha, the old forge trough; the hapless Fergus, only a bundle of firewood. Niall saved the anvil, anvil block, sledges, and bellows—the core items in the smith's business—and his father immediately knew that it was Niall who should succeed him.

But Mong-Fionn had other plans. She succeeded in getting her brother Crimthann selected, the plan being that he would act as king until her son Brian was of age. However, Crimthann had ideas of his own. He turned out to be a strong, good king, reigning for twenty years.

Mong-Fionn never lost sight of her goal, and in one horrendous act she cleared the way for Brian: She served Crimthann a drink with poison in it, first drinking from it herself to prove that it was harmless. Both she and her brother died. But her dream died with her, and Niall succeeded Crimthann as king.

Niall followed up with a series of warring exploits. First he sailed to the north of Scotland and conquered the Picts. He also invaded Britain and warred with the Romans, driving them out of the land they were occupying, and returning to Ireland with hostages and booty. Historians think that he also made incursions into Gaul. On one of these trips, a captive named Succat, taken by Niall's armies, was carried back to Antrim. Under the name Patrick he was to become the greatest figure in the history of Ireland.

Niall's reign and life ended in 404, when he was ambushed by an arrow. His death marked the dawn of Christianity in Ireland.

19

Edmund Rice

(1762–1844)

Perhaps the most intriguing thing about Edmund Ignatius Rice, who founded what today is known as the Irish Christian Brothers, is that at one point in his life he was married and had a child. It is not the kind of detail one usually finds in the biography of a religious personage.

Rice was born at Westcourt, near Callan, County Kilkenny, and grew up at a time when poverty and hardship were particularly in evidence. Rice, who in 1779 had gone to work for his uncle, a wealthy export merchant who lived in Waterford, was a kind and charitable person. For many years he helped the impoverished of Waterford with food, clothing, and shelter. In 1790, his uncle died, leaving him the business, and at the age of twenty-eight, he found himself wealthy.

He continued to expand the business and built a highly successful life in Waterford. In 1785 he married and had a daughter.

Then everything changed. In 1789 Rice's wife died, and instead of continuing with business as usual, Rice decided to devote himself to the service of God.

Rice had always been a devout, charitable person. With encouragement by Pope Pius VI and the local bishop, and starting with a core of a few men, in 1802 Rice started building a school for young, poor boys. The school melded learning with religion, and boys who attended it ultimately received their First Holy Communion. The overall goal, of course, was not just education but salvation.

The early years were not easy. A number of people who had helped him left, and the pupils themselves were, as Brother Patrick E. Jacob writes in a short biography of Rice, "ignorant, wild, and unused to the discipline of school life." Rice used the money he had made in business as well as donations to keep the school going, though at times it was difficult. But the school survived.

Around 1820, Rice and others in the school drew up a "plan of life," as Brother Jacob writes, and submitted it to Rome for approval. On September 5, 1820, the plan was approved by Pope Pius VII. Two years later, on January 20, 1822, the brief from Rome was formally accepted by the brothers. A new religious order was admitted to the Church, and Rice was known thereafter as Brother Edmund Ignatius Rice and was elected superior general.

Over the years, the one school in Waterford grew to many. By the time Brother Ignatius retired in 1838, the Christian Brothers had established twenty-two houses in Ireland and England.

Rice died on August 29, 1844.

William J. Brennan Jr.

(1906–1997)

President Dwight D. Eisenhower once said that during his time as president he had made "two mistakes, and both of them are sitting on the Supreme Court." One was the chief justice, Earl Warren. The other was Associate Justice William J. Brennan Jr.

When Eisenhower appointed Brennan, he was embroiled in the 1956 presidential campaign, and it was a purely political move. He needed a bloc of Catholic voters, and appointing one of their own would surely be appreciated. Brennan seemed to fit the bill perfectly. Born in Newark, New Jersey, he was Irish American, a practicing Catholic with three children, and his legal pedigree was impeccable. He had graduated from Harvard Law School in the top 10 percent of his class, had been an outstanding trial attorney in the fledgling field of labor law for fifteen years, and had worked his way up through the New Jersey judicial system to a spot on its supreme court, where it was rumored that one day he would be appointed chief justice.

Eisenhower, and the people who first suggested Brennan for an appointment to the Supreme Court, viewed Brennan as a moderate. But a close look at his record as a jurist in the Garden State would have disabused anyone of that notion; he was essentially a liberal. In the thirty-four years from 1956 to 1990 that he spent on the court, Brennan's beliefs and his ability to translate them into law had a profound effect on the American way of life. He brought to light issues that had never really been considered before.

In an article by Nat Hentoff that appeared in *The New Yorker* on March 12, 1990, Burt Neuborne, a New York University Law School professor and a frequent commentator on Court TV, was quoted as saying that Brennan was the most important Supreme Court jurist since Chief Justice John Marshall, who had served on the court from 1801 to 1835.

Even the conservative journal *National Review,* emphatically no fan of Brennan's, acknowledged his importance in an article, "The Mind of Justice Brennan: A 25 Year Tribute," by Stephan J. Markman and Alfred S. Regnery, that appeared in the magazine on May 18, 1984. Wrote the authors:

> An examination of the opinions, and his influence on the opinions of his colleagues, suggests there is no individual in this country on or off the Court who has had a more profound and sustained impact on public policy for the last 27 years. . . . That the Brennan agenda has become America's social agenda is all the more remark-

able because it was and still is an agenda almost entirely at variance with that of the citizens of the country and their elected representatives. Justice Brennan, more than virtually anybody else in public life today, has made a difference.

While Brennan was involved in a wide variety of cases that were complex, the principle that informed his decisions was simple: He felt that the role of law in society, and of judges in giving meaning to that role, is to protect the essential human dignity of every individual. The Constitution must be interpreted toward that end, and government must be accountable to it, as well as the Court's procedures and rules. In 1954, before his Supreme Court appointment, he gave a speech before the Irish Charitable Society in Boston, saying, "We cannot and must not doubt our strength to conserve, without the sacrifice of any, all of the guarantees of justice and fair play and simple human dignity which have made our land what it is. . . . Ours is a system of government based on the dignity and inviolability of the individual soul." His belief in the dignity of people, said Chief Justice Earl Warren, "was unbounded . . . and he believed profoundly that without such dignity men cannot be free."

Early on, Brennan became a close ally of Warren (whom Brennan called "Superchief") and used his considerable gifts as a writer, scholar, intellect, and perhaps, above all, conciliator to get major rulings approved by the Court's majority. It is said that he used to ask his new law clerks to identify the most important principle of constitutional law and then, answering his own question, raise a hand with five fingers extended and gleefully proclaim, "You can't do anything around here without five votes."

Brennan was always willing to dilute some of his positions in order to get a majority agreement. For example, in *Plyler* v. *Doe* (1982), which involved a Texas law that denied the children of illegal aliens educational opportunities, Brennan wanted to strike down the law. But after negotiating with Justice Lewis Powell, who was concerned that they would be making a sweeping constitutional statement about education as well as about illegal aliens, Brennan modified his position. Powell then joined him to create a majority decision that resulted in something that was not exactly what Brennan wanted but still made it difficult for the state government to discriminate against aliens.

Brennan was never above having his young law clerks find out what other justices were thinking on a particular case. He would then benignly assault the justice or justices not only with well-reasoned arguments but also with his considerable warmth, charm, and personality to get them to change completely or modify their position. (He has been variously described as being like an Irish uncle or grandfather.) And perhaps his fellow justices were more prone to listen because they knew that he also was capable of changing a position for them. Indeed, close examination of his record reveals that many of his decisions were closer to the center—somewhere between conservative and liberal—than to the purely liberal, as, say, the decisions of William O. Douglas were.

Brennan viewed the Constitution not as a document to be looked at in terms of what the founding fathers had been thinking at the time they wrote it—the way many conservative constitutional scholars do—but, as he said in a 1964 speech, as "a living process responsive to changing human needs." In essence, he sought to interpret constitutional law in light of modern realities.

During his tenure (he retired for health reasons), Brennan's work on the Court increased the rights of people accused of crimes, helped establish affirmative action, gave women the right to abortion, gave individuals the right to sue governments, brought gender discrimination to the fore, increased social welfare, and more. But at the heart of Brennan's rulings was always his concern for the dignity of the individual.

Perhaps no case illustrates that better than *Goldberg* v. *Kelly* (1970), which involved cutting off the welfare benefits of a person without a hearing. Writing for the majority, Brennan said that the Fourteenth Amendment guarantees "due process," and this applies to the termination of welfare benefits; a notice and hearing are required before they are cut off. "Termination of aid pending resolution of a controversy over eligibility may deprive an eligible recipient of the very means by which he lives while he waits."

Conservatives long regarded Brennan as the most dangerous justice, saying that he used the Supreme Court to legislate the worst laws in America. (In 1956 Joseph McCarthy was the only senator not to vote for his elevation to the Court.) History will perhaps ultimately decide who is right.

If Eisenhower and his advisers had investigated Brennan's childhood, they would have seen someone who might one day be problematic for them. In the 1890s Brennan's father, who had emigrated to America with his bride from County Roscommon, Ireland, supported himself as a coal shoveler for a brewery. He became a social activist—because of oppressive experiences not only in Ireland but also in America—and he passed his philosophy on to his son. As Brennan once said, "My father was the most influential person in my life." The apple, as they say, does not fall far from the tree.

Ulysses S. Grant

(1822–1885)

Did Ulysses S. Grant have character? When he was informed by his doctors that he was dying of throat cancer, he knew he would have to do something to earn money before he died so his family would be financially secure. He and his son had been hood-winked by a business partner, and the family coffers had been left empty. So he arranged to write his memoirs, and he wrote as he died, in what was a race against death. One can only imagine what he was going through. But he pressed on, finishing the task three days before he died. He produced a book that has been cited by historians as among the finest military memoirs ever written. It made a lot of money, and U. S. Grant had, as it were, won his final battle.

While Grant was a great writer, more than one biographer has hailed him as the finest soldier of the nineteenth century. That statement would be hard to debate. Yet this greatness was well hidden as he grew. He seemed, really, very ordinary.

Grant was born Hiram Ulysses Grant in Point Pleasant, Ohio, on April 27, 1822, the eldest child of Jesse Root Grant, owner of a prosperous tannery business, and Hannah Simpson Grant. In 1823 Jesse moved his family to Georgetown, Ohio, and it was here that Ulysses—or Hiram, as he was known then—grew up.

It was an unremarkable childhood, and he achieved nothing notable in school. The only special talent he had was an ability to calm nervous horses.

Nor did he show the burning ambition symptomatic of extraordinary people. It was his father who was ambitious, and through a local congressman he wangled Grant an appointment to West Point. Grant didn't want to go but relented out of filial duty.

Grant had a concern as he left for the Point, though: the initials on his trunk. They spelled "H.U.G.," and he knew that this was something that would invite ridicule. So he switched his name from Hiram Ulysses to Ulysses Hiram Grant. If he thought life was going to be easier when he arrived, he was wrong. Somehow the congressman who had secured the appointment had told the school his name was Ulysses S. Grant. When he tried to identify himself differently, they said he wasn't the appointee. Either he was Ulysses S. Grant, or he could head back to Georgetown.

So Grant changed his name again, to Ulysses S. Grant. Years later, another congressman asked him what the "S" stood for. His response: "In answer to your letter of a few days ago asking what 'S' stands for in my name I can only answer *nothing.*"

Grant didn't glitter as a student. He liked to read novels, though he had a particular proficiency at math. And he graduated in the middle of his class in 1843.

After West Point, he was commissioned second lieutenant in the Fourth United States Infantry and fought in the Mexican War (1846–1848) and in all major battles up to the capture of Mexico City. He performed well and was made a first lieutenant.

He had been a good soldier but not a happy one. Years later he would admit that he had thought the war was unjust and felt he should have resigned.

On August 22, 1848, Grant married a woman named Julia Dent. She was a sister of one of his comrades at West Point. Grant's family—he and Julia had five children—was the center of his life. When he was ordered to the Pacific coast in 1852, he couldn't afford to take them with him. Out there all alone, he grew despondent. Finally, there was only one thing to do: resign his commission and return to civilian life.

This he did, but with mixed results. By 1860 he was reduced to working with his in-laws in a leather goods shop in Galena, Illinois.

Then Fort Sumter was fired on. Because Grant had had military experience, Governor Richard Yates asked him to lend a hand. He took a ragtag collection of volunteer soldiers and quickly turned them into a cohesive unit. In time, Yates appointed him a colonel commanding the Twenty-first Volunteers. Thus Grant entered the Civil War.

Grant and his troops started to engage the Confederates in battle, first at Belmont, Missouri, with mixed results. President Lincoln appointed him brigadier general on August 7, 1861.

Six months later, he won two victories, the first by overrunning the Confederate stronghold at Fort Henry in Tennessee, and then Fort Donelson, twelve miles away. Grant's response to a Confederate general's statement that the rebels were ready to surrender and wanted to know what the terms were became famous: "No terms," he said, "except an unconditional and immediate surrender can be accepted." And that's just what the Confederate general did. The victories were the first significant ones for the Union, and Lincoln appointed Grant major general.

Grant's next major battle, at Shiloh, almost brought him down. The Confederate troops surprised Grant and his men, and they suffered terrible loses. The next day Grant rallied, but the newspapers excoriated him for being drunk. (This was not a new charge. People also speculated that he had been fired from the army when he left it earlier, because of drinking.) General Henry Halleck was dispatched from Washington and relieved Grant of his field duties, taking over himself.

Grant denied the charge of drunkenness and in a letter to his wife wrote, "We are all well and me as sober as a deacon no matter what is said to the contrary." He survived the debacle because of Lincoln's loyalty: Lincoln would not fire a general who was fighting a war. Grant resumed command as major general of volunteers.

Grant's greatness as a soldier emerged in the battle for Vicksburg. He was a superb military tactician, knowing how and where to employ his troops, how to mount surprise attacks, where the enemy was vulnerable, and how to attack it.

Vicksburg was well fortified, but before attacking it Grant first cut off all communication among the rebel units. When he attacked, the rebels were in a state of mass confusion. Grant lay siege to the city on May 19, 1863. On July 4 he accepted its surrender.

Shortly thereafter, Lincoln made Grant commander of all Union armies in the west, and he continued his exploits, including charging to the rescue of Union soldiers under siege in Chattanooga, Tennessee.

In March 1864 Lincoln made Grant commander of all Union armies. He immediately established two major commands, one under General George G. Meade, whom Grant traveled with, and the other under General William Tecumseh Sherman. Meade attacked Robert E. Lee's forces in Virginia, while Sherman moved against Atlanta.

For the first time, Grant used the telegraph as a weapon of war, directing the two Union forces like a boxer; jabbing here, throwing haymakers there.

Grant's final campaign started on March 26, 1865, and ended on April 9 on the courthouse steps in Appomattox, Virginia, with Confederate general Robert E. Lee surrendering to Grant. Seventeen days later, the last rebel unit surrendered to Sherman. The war was over. The terms of surrender were generous.

Grant's joy at the war being over was short-lived. On April 14, John Wilkes Booth fired a bullet into the brain of President Abraham Lincoln, killing him.

Grant had faith that Lincoln's successor, Andrew Johnson, had reconstruction policies with which he could reestablish equity in the Union, and Grant went off to engage in army business. But as time went on, he became increasingly concerned with Johnson's work and was particularly concerned that blacks were not being protected. Ultimately, his differences with Johnson came into the open, and he decided to run for president against Johnson.

He won, but a presidency is not run like a military campaign. Grant's two terms in office were not viewed as successful, his second term being plagued by the Whiskey Ring scandal, which involved corruption at high levels in the White House, including some of his appointees.

In retirement, Grant satisfied a lifelong ambition by traveling around the world, including "coming home," as he described it to his wife, to the land of his paternal great-grandfather John Sampson, who had been born near Dungannon in County Tyrone.

John F. Kennedy

(1 9 1 7 – 1 9 6 3)

Many of the details of John Kennedy's life after he became president are familiar to many people. Far less is known about the years leading up to his presidency. And it is these years that perhaps tell more about who he was and what he became than anything else.

As suggested by biographers, Kennedy was guided—even goaded—to seek the presidency by his father, Joseph P. Kennedy. After the death of Joseph Kennedy's oldest boy, Joe Jr., on a bombing mission in World War II, Joe Sr. focused on his next oldest son.

JFK seemed to have the background to be a political candidate. He served as skipper of a PT (patrol torpedo) boat; when the Japanese sank it, he spent thirty-six hours in the water, not only saving himself but also keeping an injured comrade alive.

More than being a war hero, Kennedy was bright, a Harvard graduate like his father, and good-looking with a quick, toothy smile and a lightning wit. He should have had the drive to attain a political goal. Like the other Kennedy children, he was taught by his father to be highly competitive.

But at first he seemed indifferent to politics. In fact, he wanted to be a writer. Nevertheless, Joe Kennedy wanted him to run for office. They zeroed in on a congressional seat in the Massachusetts delegation—a good stepping-stone to greater heights—and Kennedy started to campaign for it.

He had a secret during that campaign, one that he kept for his entire life: He was in poor health. He had badly injured his back during the war and was always in some sort of pain from it. More important, though, he had been diagnosed with Addison's disease, a circulatory malady that is potentially fatal. It was a wonder, biographer Doris Kearns Goodwin said, that no one spotted it because if you just looked at him, you could see that he was emaciated.

But no one did, and his congressional opponent, John Russo, was not prepared for the blitzkrieg-style campaign the Kennedys mounted. JFK and other family members worked night and day, Joe Kennedy behind the scenes. Longtime Massachusetts politician and House Speaker Tip O'Neill later said that the Kennedys had money, and that money could do wonders in a political campaign, particularly when it came to advertising.

There were also allegations that the Kennedys pulled a scam by getting onto the ballot a person who had the same name as Kennedy's opponent. So when the voters stepped into the voting booth, they were faced with the confusing choice of John Russo No. 1 or John Russo No. 2. Kennedy won the election handily, and he was off to Congress.

He proved to be an indifferent congressman, relying on aides to brief him on various issues. But he won reelection, and in 1948 he ran for the Senate. Political pundits of the time thought he did not have much of a chance. He was running against Henry Cabot Lodge, a Boston Brahmin who had compiled a good record and whose name and family were well known in Massachusetts.

But again, no one counted on the determination of the Kennedys, their electioneering skills, and the wheelbarrows of money that Joe Kennedy was willing to spend. JFK was packaged—"like soap flakes," someone said—and his advertising campaign was an onslaught.

As in his congressional campaign, Kennedy worked hard, traveling all over Massachusetts, hand extended, toothy smile flashing, wit working, warm, knowledgeable about the issues. And he made inroads, particularly with women, who were drawn to him. He was, quite simply, an attractive man whom women could easily fantasize about.

Kennedy beat Lodge, and when he did so he seemed to become more interested in politics. He succeeded in winning a second term and was catapulted into national politics.

At the 1956 Democratic National Convention, Kennedy was a key player, selected to introduce Adlai Stevenson, the presidential candidate. And it was at this convention that Kennedy made a fateful decision that could have finished his political career: He decided to go for the vice presidential nomination.

The voting was close. Kennedy was seriously in contention (even leading) until the third ballot, when he was defeated by Senator Estes Kefauver.

It was the luck, as they say, of the Irish. Stevenson, of course, was buried by Eisenhower in a landslide. Historians feel that Kennedy's presence on the ticket would not have enabled Stevenson to win, and the young senator from Massachusetts could thenceforth have been branded a loser. For Kennedy, losing the nomination was a blessing in disguise.

As the 1950s wound down, Joe Kennedy started a new campaign, to capture the ultimate prize, the presidency. His dream was still alive.

He had to overcome a number of hurdles, not the least of which was that he was considered too young to be president (he was thirty-nine in 1956)—and, of course, the fact that he was a Catholic. There had never been a Catholic president.

But Joe Kennedy worked on it. And JFK also got a lot of publicity from the book *Profiles in Courage,* which was published in 1956, became a best-seller, and won a Pulitzer Prize. At the Democratic National Convention in 1960, the nomination for president was a nail-biting cliffhanger, and only the very last vote—from the state of Wyoming—gave Kennedy the 765 votes he needed to win.

Then the campaign started in earnest; money was said to gush from Joe Kennedy like the Colorado River. There were allegations that he used it not only to cajole and persuade, but to bribe. It is known that one publisher, to whom he loaned five hundred thousand dollars, later endorsed Kennedy for president.

But undoubtedly the single greatest asset for Kennedy in the campaign was the fledgling, problem-plagued, but powerful medium of television. He engaged in a series of debates with Richard Nixon, organized by producer Don Hewitt, and the country saw Kennedy up close for the first time—and he looked good. A few years earlier, according to Doris Kearns Goodwin, cortisone had come on the scene and had "rescued him" from the emaciated look—and the risk—of Addison's disease.

It was not that Kennedy beat Nixon in the debates. It was rather that Nixon did not beat Kennedy. Kennedy came across as articulate and charming, and he certainly seemed old enough and experienced enough to be president.

Kennedy won the election by a hair—114,000 votes, the slimmest margin of any presidential election in the twentieth century. It was said that his margin of victory came from two places: Texas, the home state of his running mate, Lyndon Johnson, and the Chicago of Mayor Richard Daley, a friend of Joe Kennedy.

Much has been written about John F. Kennedy of an exposé character, much of it negative. Much that is positive has also been written, and he certainly had an effect on young idealists, who did indeed ask themselves what they could do for their country—and then did something. Maybe Kennedy and the brilliant group of people around him could have done more, but they had only a thousand days.

One achievement he will always be remembered for by the people of Ireland, and by Irish Americans, was his visit in 1962 to the home in County Wexford that his great-grandfather had left so many years before. Kennedy came home not as a groveling, filthy peasant but as president of the United States of America. It was a moment that nothing can diminish, nothing can tarnish.

23

Peter J. McGuire

(1852–1906)

Peter J. McGuire, "The Father of Labor Day" and a driving force of the American labor movement in the 1800s, was the founder of the United Brotherhood of Joiners and Carpenters and the cofounder with Samuel Gompers of the American Federation of Labor. If he were alive to see what has happened to unionism in the United States, he would probably immediately organize a nationwide strike.

McGuire spent his early years in a tenement in New York City, enduring a life that he characterized as a "living grave." The experience was seared into his consciousness; partly as a result, he spent his entire life trying to make life better for other ordinary people. The way he saw to accomplish that was by providing good jobs. He wanted to see a day, as he said in 1891, "when the toiler's income shall not be limited to the barren point of mere existence . . . [and when] there shall be no army of hungry, idle men, vainly seeking work, whose little children bend above the lathe and loom; when those who toil are known as the noblest in the world."

He was born in America on July 6, 1852. His mother, Catherine Hand O'Riley, had emigrated from Ireland during the Great Famine, in which six of her eight children had died. In New York City she met John J. McGuire, himself an immigrant. They married and started a family in a tenement that was typical of the time: six families crowded into a building designed for one family's use. Peter was the first of five children they would have.

In 1863 Peter's father joined the Union army, and Peter was forced into the role of breadwinner—at age eleven. He took a variety of jobs—cleaning shoes, selling newspapers, cleaning stores—until he landed a permanent position as an errand boy for the Lord & Taylor department store.

Out of necessity, his formal education ended early, but he lived in a racially mixed neighborhood, where he was able to absorb practices from a variety of cultures. Playing marbles on the corner, he learned how to speak German, and his early experience was to serve him well later, when he organized diverse ethnic entities into a union.

At one point, he attended courses at Cooper Union in New York City, a meeting place of radicals and reformers. It also was a place where he sharpened his debating and speech-making skills, learned economics, labor law, and much more, and was to meet Samuel Gompers, another great labor leader.

When he was twenty, he made his first foray into labor protest, marching along with one hundred thousand workers who were striking in support of an eight-hour workday. It was only a one-day affair, but later he would say that seeing so many people moving along was an important lesson to him on the value of a mass labor movement.

He had gotten a job as a piano maker when he was seventeen, and when he was twenty-one he exhorted his coworkers to strike because of an arbitrary wage reduction. The movement failed. He left and found another job at a wood-finishing shop. At that time, American industry was booming, and by 1873 everyone expected that the fortunes of the average person would boom too. But the boom went bust. McGuire lost his job and joined the ranks of an army of unemployed in what was, in its harshness, exceeded only by the Depression of the 1930s.

McGuire was not the type of person to go into a corner and cry. He did his crying, as it were, from soapboxes he stood on, rallying people to exhort the city to suspend rents and supply public relief.

The newspapers of the time were in the pocket of the moneyed; *The New York Times* wrote that "agitators [like McGuire] will find no support among the great masses of the laboring classes" and demonstrated its racism by blaming the foment on a "foreign class" of workers.

McGuire was gaining a reputation as a fomenter and public speaker, and people whose bellies were filled with fear for both now and the future were listening and reading the handbills that the young man and his friends distributed. Then something happened that reduced him to tears: The New York City police convinced Peter's father to characterize Peter as engaging in "radical and atheistic behavior," according to writer

Mark Erlich. Erlich quoted Samuel Gompers in his biography: "McGuire was tender-hearted, and the treatment hurt, but he stood by the cause."

Then, on January 13, 1874, what was to be the watershed event of McGuire's life occurred. Continuing the efforts to increase workers' rights and benefits, ten thousand workers gathered in Tompkins Square Park in downtown New York City to express their support for labor. Without warning, the police, on foot and brandishing batons, swept down to break up the rally. All day the chaos and harassment continued, and to a large degree the meeting was broken up, with many in the crowd bloodied and arrested. But as with any unfair treatment, there was a reaction. On that day Peter McGuire—and a number of other dedicated young men—decided to devote their lives to the labor movement.

Shortly thereafter, McGuire formed the Workingman's Party, and he traveled around the country and spoke to groups of workers, enrolling new members, even traveling on freight trains when he couldn't afford standard travel. "During one six-week stretch," Erlich said, McGuire was said to have "made 107 speeches, usually to audiences of several thousand." His speeches focused on jobs, the economy, wretched working conditions, and low pay. The only way to guarantee security and a good job, he told his audiences, was to organize.

In the 1870s he moved to St. Louis, Missouri, where he helped mobilize the trade unions in the railroad strike of 1877. He became politically active, getting important legislation introduced on child labor and mine ventilation and convincing legislators to create the state Bureau of Labor Statistics. He became deputy commissioner of this bureau but soon began longing to take part in the labor wars and left his job to fight them.

At the time, the United States was evolving into a more industrialized country where quick work—and quick profits—was what mattered. Employers, once the spiritual partners of tradesmen, forgot about workmanship and grew more distant from them.

In 1882 McGuire realized a dream by creating the United Brotherhood of Carpenters and Joiners of America (UBC); he invited other carpenters to join him at a convention in Chicago at which bylaws were established and McGuire became general secretary. Also in 1882, McGuire came up with an idea for a Labor Day parade and then dedicated himself to making it an annual event.

The year 1886 has deservedly been called the year labor came into its own. Gabriella Edmonston, general president of the UBC, and McGuire proposed that workers all over the country strike on May 1 for eight hours as a show of power. Some 340,000 workers across the country did, marching in parades and sending a message to employers that the time of the worker was at hand. The success of the strike swelled the enrollment of workers in McGuire's union. Within four years, there were more than fifty thousand union members.

As great a figure as he was in the labor movement, McGuire's life ended on a sad, melancholy note. He had a problem with alcohol, and by 1900 he was forced out of the AFL. A year or two later he was charged with embezzling funds from the UBC, a charge that proved false but resulted in his being forced out of his executive position in 1902.

McGuire died in Camden, New Jersey, on February 18, 1906.

24

George Meany

(1894–1980)

The abiding image of George Meany, a seminal force in the labor movement in the twentieth century, is that of a balding, white-haired man with a cigar jutting from his mouth, a man as hard as nails. Meany was, in fact, very tough, and in the decades that he served as president of the AFL-CIO, he proved that over and over again.

In 1957, it was Meany who was the major force in expelling the Teamsters Union from the AFL-CIO because of its mob affiliations. It was Meany who would not tolerate racism and decreed that separate black and white chapters must be merged. And it was Meany's toughness that showed itself most frequently at the bargaining table. Toward the end of his life, in 1976, Meany gave a stirring speech before the American Irish Historical Society, which cut to the core of the man. He said, in part:

Now it may be that the Irish rose to leadership in American labor because of their flair for language and love of the spoken word—

but I like to think that they were equally spurred by the deep, centuries-old indignation which injustice stirred in them. . . .

The yearning for freedom—the insistence on human dignity—are forever enshrined as part of the Irish character. Similarly, they are the wellspring of the American trade union movement. Oh yes, we spend lots of time negotiating for wages and hours and working conditions, but these are simply the material manifestations of the achievement of worker dignity.

Meany was born and raised in the Bronx. His grandparents were from County Longford. His father was a union plumber, a trade in which a number of Meany's relatives had engaged. Meany's father didn't seem to want his son to become a plumber, saying it was "awfully hard work," but by the age of sixteen Meany, a high school dropout, was in the plumbers' union.

After some years working at the trade, he got involved in union politics and gradually rose through the ranks. In 1952 he was elected president of the AFL, and three years later he was the driving force in merging the American Federation of Labor (AFL) with the Congress of Industrial Organizations (CIO). The merger was ironic, because when the CIO had first been formed, it had been composed of young idealists, a number of them with Communist sympathies, who wanted to better not only the employees' lot but the lot of all Americans by changing our way of life. However, Meany stayed a staunch anti-Communist all his life and would not have touched the CIO in those early days.

On the other hand, he used his considerable political weight—a large percentage of registered voters were union members—to get many laws enacted, including ones relating to fair labor practices, Medicare, Medicaid, and Social Security.

He also supported free trade unions behind the Iron Curtain, pouring union money and influence into his efforts. In 1980, shortly after his death, the Solidarity union in Poland was formed. It seems unusual that a young plumber from the Bronx should have had such a profound effect on the world stage, but he did. It was one case of a father's advice to a child being wrong.

James K. Polk

(1 7 9 5 – 1 8 4 9)

When one thinks of great U.S. presidents, the name James K. Polk hardly ever comes to mind. But great he was. During his single term as president from 1844 to 1848, the United States fought and won a war with Mexico. As a result, the nation annexed Texas, added the Oregon Territory, and took all the Mexican provinces that were above 31 degrees north latitude. By the time Polk's presidency was over, the United States extended from the Atlantic to the Pacific Ocean.

Polk was Irish on his father's side. His great-great-grandfather had emigrated from County Donegal in 1690. Originally, the name had been Pollak, but it had been condensed to Polk.

Polk was born on November 2, 1795, in Mecklenburg County, North Carolina, but when he was eleven years old, his family moved to the new territory of Tennessee. Later he returned to North Carolina, became a lawyer, and ran for Congress. He served five terms in the House between 1825 and 1834 and then, in 1835, became speaker, holding this post until 1839.

Polk was well connected politically. He was a confidante of President Andrew Jackson, who greatly respected him. In 1839, with Jackson's help, Polk ran for governor of Tennessee and was elected. His administration was uneventful, but in 1841 he was defeated by someone named James C. Jones, a man who was said by one biographer to rely "more on buffoonery than discussion of political issues."

In the presidential election of 1844, Martin Van Buren seemed a shoo-in for the Democratic nomination, but then he made a mistake: He was opposed to the annexation of Texas. Polk came out firmly for annexation and also for taking the Oregon Territory. He was slipped in as a dark horse candidate for president after a meeting with Jackson at the Hermitage, Jackson's Nashville, Tennessee, residence. On March 4, 1845, not yet fifty years old, James K. Polk was sworn in as president.

He proved to be his own man, disagreeing even with Jackson on a number of points and accomplishing much. He showed himself to be very savvy. It was said that he manipulated Mexico into a position where it had to give up Texas. In the case of Oregon, to which Great Britain had laid claim, while he wanted much more than he got (part of Canada), the territory he did acquire was significant.

Why was Polk not recognized for his achievements? After all, his administration saw five thousand square miles of territory added to the United States, including access to the Pacific. The lack of recognition was probably because of his personality, his preference for secrecy, and his refusal to blow his own horn or get involved in controversy for political gain. He worked very hard as president and, in fact, damaged his health during his term, dying on June 15, 1849, only a few months following his retirement. He was fifty-four years old.

Mother Jones
(Mary Harris)

(1830–1930)

Mary Harris, known widely in the union movements of the 1800s and early 1900s as "Mother Jones," was a small, delicate-looking woman, her image of fragility enhanced by her falsetto voice.

But she was not someone you would want to take on without thinking twice. No less a world-class battler than lawyer Clarence Darrow (who in the twenties fought for the lives of murder suspects Nathan Leopold and Richard Loeb) said in his introduction to her autobiography:

She was a born crusader, a woman of action, fired by a fine zeal, a mother especially devoted to the miners. Wherever fights were fiercest and danger greatest, Mother Jones was present to aid and cheer. She had a strong sense of drama. She staged every detail of a contest. . . . Her personal non-resistance was far more powerful than any appeal to force.

Indeed, her strength shone in her own life.

Mary Harris was born in County Cork, Ireland. When she was five, she emigrated to the United States to join her father, Richard Harris, who had left Ireland to find work. He had gotten a job as a railway construction worker and had sent back money for his family's passage.

Her early years were spent in Toronto, where she received a good education. She taught in Monroe, Michigan, and started a dressmaking business before moving to Memphis. It was there, in 1861, that she married and settled down to the life of a young homemaker, caring for herself, her husband, and the four children she bore.

Then, in 1867, when Mary was just thirty-seven years old, tragedy came: An epidemic of yellow fever killed her husband and all of her children. Suddenly she was alone.

She could not bear to keep living in Memphis; there were haunting reminders of her family everywhere. She moved to Chicago and tried to deal with her loss as best she could.

Then tragedy came again: The great Chicago fire of 1871 gutted her house and consumed all her belongings. But something inside her made her go on.

It was a chaotic and dangerous time: The rights of labor were in diametric opposition to the claims of management. Mary Harris started to attend meetings at the Knights of Labor, an organization that vied for members with the American Federation of Labor. Its philosophy was more cooperative with management than that of the AFL, but one would hardly know this by Mary Harris's activities. She threw herself into the fray—many frays—and was both vocal and tough.

She was particularly concerned with the rights of miners, whose lives were horrendous. Theirs was low-paying, hazardous, backbreaking work. As Mother Jones, she attended rally after rally, exhorting workers to try to better their conditions.

But she did not only make speeches; she organized marches to evoke public sympathy. For example, she led an army of children into New York City to dramatize the exploitation of children in the workforce. She organized miners' wives to march, brandishing their mops and brooms. She also worked undercover, a sometimes dangerous activity, by slipping into an area without identifying herself and learning just how management was exploiting workers.

As the years went by, the tiny woman with the high voice came to be feared by management. Owners and bosses knew that she had great influence with workers.

Though she was arrested a number of times and jailed, undoubtedly her scariest confrontation with management occurred at the 1913 copper mine strike in Colorado, when she was eighty-three years old. She was charged with murder, and a kangaroo court convicted her. But then a special Senate panel convened and found her innocent.

Mother Jones was still going strong in 1923, when she spoke at the AFL convention. In 1930, the year she died, she was still giving interviews and speaking out for the working classes.

She was buried near the mines in Kankakee, Illinois. At her funeral, a speaker said, "Today company management everywhere are breathing sighs of relief . . . Mother Jones is dead."

27

Andrew Jackson

(1767–1845)

By the time he was fourteen, Andrew Jackson, the man whose face adorns the U.S. twenty-dollar bill, was an orphan.

During the Revolutionary War, Jackson's two brothers, who lived with Jackson and his mother at the Waxshaw settlement in South Carolina, were killed by British soldiers (Jackson himself was seriously wounded for defying a soldier and was taken prisoner). A short while later his mother, an immigrant from County Antrim in Ireland, contracted cholera and died. His father had died a year after he had arrived in America, in 1765.

Jackson could be described in one word: tough. As an adult, he engaged in a number of wars, and he was so tough that his troops dubbed him "Old Hickory" after the hardwood.

In 1784 he went to Salisbury, South Carolina, and, with a legal career in mind, apprenticed himself to a law firm. In 1787 he passed the bar; then he headed west to Nashville. He was able to buy a plantation and raise horses, but marauding Indians were very much a problem in the area. Jackson fought them effectively, garnering a well-deserved reputation. In 1802 he married Rachel Donelson Robards.

Jackson was six feet, one inch tall, a thin man, with reddish brown hair and a quick temper, which led him to a number of duels. His most famous—a duel over horses—occurred with a man named Charles Dickinson. Dickinson fired first, thinking with horror that he had missed because Jackson just stood there and fired back—and Dickinson was mortally wounded. However, Dickinson *had* hit Jackson. But Jackson had worn a large, heavy coat that had caused Dickinson to misaim: The coat was so oversized that the bullet hit Jackson below the heart. He recovered from the wound after a few weeks.

During the War of 1812 Jackson became famous for his military prowess. In 1818 President James Monroe appointed him to deal with Indians in Florida, which he did by torching Pensacola and summarily hanging two Englishmen he thought were conspiring with the Indians, an event that caused an international incident.

Gradually, he emerged as a presidential candidate. He ran in 1824 against John Quincy Adams and lost because of what he characterized as a "corrupt bargain" among various people. But in 1828 he won.

During his two terms, Jackson increased the power of the presidency. He used the "spoils system," appointing his own political cronies to office and organizing counties into branches of the Democratic Party so they could deliver the vote more effectively. He also made good use of the presidential veto. He used it a dozen times, more than all other previous presidents combined.

He also put the "pocket veto" to good use: If a bill came to his desk fewer than ten days before Congress adjourned, the law permitted him to put the bill "into his pocket" and turn it down without giving Congress a reason why. For example, Jackson was opposed to the restructuring of the Bank of the United States and used the pocket veto to defeat relevant legislation. Jacksonian scholar Robert Remini wrote that Jackson created a gain in presidential power that did not abate until the resignation of Richard Nixon in 1974.

In foreign affairs, Jackson also achieved much: He revived trade with England, exempting English goods from the harsh tariff of 1828 (the so-called Tariff of Abominations). He also used his influence to help reopen trade with the British-held West Indies. He also succeeded in getting payments for France for the "spoliation," attacks on American ships during the Napoleonic Wars earlier in the century.

One great domestic triumph was the annexation of Texas. Though Jackson wanted to annex it, he did nothing while in office because he feared that the unresolved slavery question could cause problems for the election chances of his handpicked successor, Martin Van Buren. After Van Buren was elected, Jackson supported annexation, which took place in 1845, the year he died.

Jackson liked to give parties, and he was a man of the people— everyone was welcome. At his last party as president, he had a fourteen-hundred-pound cheese brought into the White House, and it was eaten in two hours. The White House smelled of the cheese for weeks.

28

Henry Ford

Legend has it that auto baron Henry Ford had a unique way of firing people: An employee would leave on a Friday and return on Monday to find his office cleaned out and a notice that he was no longer employed by the company.

Three things are known for certain about Henry Ford: He revolutionized the automobile worldwide; he brought into being something called the production line, which revolutionized industry; and he changed the way America lived. Before Ford, there was the horse and buggy. After Ford, there was the motorcar.

Members of the Ford family started to come from County Cork to Dearborn, Michigan, in 1832. William, Henry's father, and a host of uncles and aunts arrived in the area in the 1840s, driven from Ireland by the potato famine.

Michigan was a good place to emigrate to. At the time, anyone could buy an acre of land for the munificent sum of ten shillings, about $1.20 in American money. The immigrants bought every square inch of soil they could afford and then set about farming it. At harvest time, the produce was sold in Detroit, which was not so far away that it couldn't be reached by horse-drawn carts.

Henry, born two years before the Civil War ended, worked on his family's land. But when he was sixteen, he took a part-time job at a machine shop, where he could exercise his interest in inventing and how mechanical things work.

He then went to work for the Detroit Edison Company and, by the time he was thirty, had worked his way up to being chief and was responsible for that city's electricity.

The job allowed him a lot of free time: While he had to be on call twenty-four hours a day, circumstances rarely required his presence. He was able to bury himself in his shop, where in 1893 he constructed a gasoline engine that was an improvement over those that then existed. Three years later he invented an ungainly, spidery-looking thing with four wheels that was part bicycle, part car. He called it the "quadricycle" or "horseless carriage."

Over the next few years, he improved the horseless carriage, and in 1903, he felt he had developed a marketable car. With just $28,000, Ford incorporated the Henry Ford Company.

His company was a success (he publicized it by racing his cars; he himself drove a "999" to a world record, covering a mile in 39.4 seconds) and was almost immediately pounced on by the Licensed Auto Manufacturers, who said he couldn't use the gasoline engine, which, they claimed, had been patented in 1895. Ford disagreed, saying his engine was different from the original. They went to court, and in 1909 Ford lost. But in 1911 he won on appeal.

In 1908 Ford told the world that he would build a car for the masses, and he did. The Model T sold more than fifteen million vehicles, and Ford captured half the world market.

At the core of his success was not just the car, which was well made, but the value consumers received for their money. In 1908 the Model T cost $950, but because of Ford's innovations on the production line and because of his willingness to pay his workers double what other auto manufacturers did and thus encourage them to greater productivity, in 1927 he was able to produce a Model T that sold for less than $300.

To get supplies for his cars, Ford bought the producers—the mines, forests, glassworks, rubber plantations—of the raw materials needed, as well as ships and trains to transport the materials. His cash flow was so great that he could finance these purchases himself.

While Ford had a passion for building cars and other mechanical items, he had a deep interest in other activities as well. One was country dancing, which he remembered fondly from his youth. In fact, he had met his wife, Clara (whom he married in 1888), at a square dance. In 1900 he set about to bring country dancing back into public consciousness.

He also brought it back into the consciousness of his employees, whether they liked it or not. Here, his dictatorial side showed. He made learning square dancing mandatory for his executives, actually curtaining off a large area in one of the laboratories to serve as a dance studio.

He also had members of his company research country dancing

thoroughly to make sure the steps were correct, and he ultimately wrote a book on the subject entitled *Good Morning—After a Sleep of Twenty Years, Old-fashioned Dancing Is Being Revived by Mr. and Mrs. Henry Ford.* Ultimately, Ford would push and support country dancing to the point where it became part of the curricula of many colleges.

Though Ford's car and production line achievement helped eliminate the old ways things were done and the way people lived, he never lost a liking of things from yesteryear. To help preserve those traditions, he built Greenfield Village near Detroit, which sought to reproduce things the way they had been when he was a boy.

And his admiration for Thomas Alva Edison (he once wrote in one of his notebooks, "God needed Edison") was reflected in his Greenfield Village duplication of the Menlo Park, New Jersey, laboratories where Edison had invented so much. Ford had worked for Edison and regarded him as his mentor. Early on, when he had been working on the gasoline engine, Edison had encouraged him to continue, rather than get involved with steam or some other fuel system.

In the 1930s the fortunes of the Ford Motor company declined. The successor to the Model T, the Model A, did not sell as well, and across the 1930s the graph line showing the company's sales continued downward. But when World War II came along, and with it the demand for thousands of new vehicles, Ford rebounded.

Ford was a tough man, but the great sadness of his life, the one thing he could never put behind him, was the death of his son, Edsel, of cancer in 1943. It is said the heart went out of him not only for business but for life itself. Two years after this, he handed the reins (or steering wheel) of the company to his grandson Henry II.

He died four years after Edsel and gave his shares of the company to the Ford Foundation, instantly making it a leading philanthropic organization.

Woodrow Wilson

(1856–1924)

Woodrow Wilson was a bespectacled, ascetic-looking man who resembled a schoolteacher. Indeed, for a good part of his life, he was one. He knew how to exploit opportunity: At one point during his presidency, he had sheep graze on the South Lawn of the White House, selling their wool to raise money for charity.

Both of Wilson's paternal grandparents came from the Strabane area of County Antrim. He was raised by a stern father, Joseph Ruggles Wilson, a Presbyterian minister and theologian, and a mother who was the daughter of a minister in England. Both were of Scotch-Irish lineage.

He was born on December 28, 1856, in Staunton, Virginia, but a year later his family moved to Augusta, Georgia.

He graduated from the College of New Jersey, which later became Princeton, in 1879 and received a Ph.D. in government and history in 1886 from Johns Hopkins University.

He held a variety of academic positions in the years following graduation, including a fifteen-year stint at Princeton, which was capped by his being appointed university president in 1902. Then, in 1910, apparently fatigued by academic life, he entered politics, accepting the Democratic nomination for governor of New Jersey in 1910.

His political beliefs were described by the word "progressivism," and he had a number of goals: to eliminate political corruption, to institute antitrust legislation, and to restructure the election system by using direct primaries. At the time, the last proposal would not have been advantageous for his party and was a courageous move on his part.

He won the election handily, and America began to take notice of him. Two years later, in 1912, Wilson started a run for the presidential nomination. His chief opponent for the Democratic nomination was Champ Clark, speaker of the House of Representatives.

It was a grueling nomination fight, requiring forty-six ballots, but Wilson eventually prevailed.

As it turned out, the election campaign was a cakewalk by comparison. The Republican Party was split between William Howard Taft and Teddy Roosevelt (who was running as an Independent), and Wilson overwhelmed them both.

Once in office, Wilson helped establish the Clayton Act, an amendment to the Sherman Antitrust Act, which strengthened labor's ability to strike, established the Federal Reserve Board to help control the currency, and instituted the income tax.

As dominant as he was in domestic matters, Wilson was even more influential in foreign ones. (He was the first president to leave the United States while president.) During his presidency, the United States became involved in the affairs of a number of countries. Wilson always had a justification for these acts, which is where some historians question his sincerity. Perhaps he was so imbued with righteous indignation that he never realized he could be morally wrong.

The event in which Wilson's lack of moral insight had the biggest impact was World War I. When war broke out between France and Great Britain and Germany, Wilson was at first neutral. In fact, in 1916 he conducted a successful reelection campaign based on the slogan "He kept us out of the war."

In fact, he was hardly neutral. He put the not insignificant industrial might of the United States at the disposal of France and Britain. And he became outraged at the torpedoing of ships with Americans on board. He became more warlike in his pronouncements but swathed them in high-toned rhetoric such as "establishing a peace that will win the approval of mankind" and "an equality of right."

On April 2, 1917, Wilson delivered a speech to Congress with the oft-quoted line "the world must be made safe for democracy." Finally America was in it—and surely a crucial partner for the Allies.

Following the war, Wilson was one of the important architects of the League of Nations, which essentially detailed the rules by which nations would deal with one another. When the League of Nations' charter was examined by Congress, the Senate thought it compromised the United States' sovereign rights and wanted to make changes Wilson found abhorrent. In a cruel twist of fate, Wilson found himself making a whistle-stop tour across the country, urging Americans to pressure their representatives *not* to support it.

It was while he was on this jaunt, in Pueblo, Colorado, that Wilson suffered a stroke that left him temporarily unable to speak. From that time on, his wife, Edith, virtually took over in what was described by cynics as the "petticoat presidency."

His last words to Edith were "Edith, I'm a broken machine, but I'm ready." The day he spoke them was February 3, 1924. He proved to be more popular in death than life.

Sean MacBride

(1904–1988)

Sean MacBride was very much like his fiery parents: a fighter for human rights. But he went about things differently than they did.

He was born on January 26, 1904, the son of John MacBride and Maud Gonne. Both his parents were militant revolutionaries. John MacBride had been a soldier in the Boer War. After his return to Ireland he fought in the Easter Rising of 1916 and was captured and executed. Sean's mother, Maud, had been born in England but spent her entire life fighting for Irish independence, a fight that landed her in jail more than once.

When Sean was born, his parents were living in Paris, and after their marriage ended and MacBride was executed, his mother stayed there. Indeed, Sean's first language was French, but when he was very young, he went to Mount St. Benedict's, in Gorey, Ireland, where he learned English.

Sean gave every sign of being as militant as his parents. Though very young, he joined the Irish Volunteers and saw service in the War of Independence. Like his mother, he opposed the Treaty of 1921. As a member of the IRA, MacBride served several prison terms and was on the run for a time, living in Paris and London, where he worked as a journalist. In 1936 he returned to Dublin as the IRA's chief of staff.

In 1937 he started to change. He had been studying law and in that year became a lawyer. That same year the new constitution of Ireland was enacted, and MacBride had an epiphany: One could pursue one's ends through peaceful means—and succeed.

He quit the IRA and became famous defending Republican prisoners and constitutional issues. In 1946 he founded the political party Clann na Poblachta and became minister for external affairs in the first interparty government.

MacBride brought his influence to bear on a great many important issues. Ireland stayed out of NATO, and on Easter Monday 1948 the Irish government repudiated Britain's External Relations Act—the symbolic declaration of a republic of Ireland.

In June 1952 Clann na Poblachta lost ten of twelve seats, but he kept his. He held on to it again in the 1954 election but lost in 1957 and 1961. He then left politics, returning to the practice of law.

MacBride then became known for his pursuit of human rights and peace. He took on the Lawless case, which was the first case to be heard by the European Commission on Human Rights, and he was a founding member of Amnesty International, one of the most important human rights organizations in the world. He chaired UNESCO's international commission for the study of communication problems. The report on that work was entitled *Many Voices, One World*.

A principle of behavior he espoused and that came to be known as "MacBride's Principle" aimed at stopping discrimination against Catholics by employers in Northern Ireland. He won support for this in the United States.

He died in Dublin on January 15, 1988, and was buried next to his mother and father in Glasnevin Cemetery in Dublin.

Charles Carroll

(1 7 3 7 – 1 8 3 2)

Charles Carroll was the only Roman Catholic to sign the Declaration of Independence, but he was by no means the only important person with that name. In fact, Charles Carroll was just one of the Carroll clan who settled in the thirteen American colonies. The joke at the time was that there were so many Carrolls that he felt constrained to list his address after his name to distinguish himself from the others, even on the Declaration of Independence.

Carroll said that he was descended from Irish princes of the Ely clan and that, until the genocidal activities of Oliver Cromwell in 1649, the Carrolls had been affluent.

The first Carrolls arrived in America in 1688, settling in Maryland. Charles played a major role in the American Revolution, a role marked by skillful leadership and courage. Signing the Declaration of Independence was more than a formality. Indeed, besides being the only Roman

Catholic to sign, he was also the richest signatory. If the revolution were lost, he would lose everything—including his life.

Charles was not involved much in politics either before the revolution or after it. One of his first involvements was to write a series of pamphlets in 1773, addressing the volatile issue of the way the English were taxing their colonies to support the established Anglican Church. He signed the pamphlet anonymously "First Citizen," but it was not difficult to guess who the writer was.

At one point, revolution became inevitable, and the revolutionaries were looking for help. They looked north, to Quebec, hoping that the French would get involved. In February 1776 Carroll, Benjamin Franklin, Samuel Chase, and Charles's cousin John traveled across the frozen land and made their appeal to the French. They were turned down, and in the spring they returned.

If the English did not know about Carroll before his trip, they found out afterward. Upon his return, he guided a resolution through the revolutionary Continental Congress that called for separation from England. On July 4, 1776, the day independence was declared, Carroll became a member of the Continental Congress; a month later (on August 2) he signed the Declaration. He also helped formulate Maryland's bill of rights and its state constitution.

In 1787 Carroll was elected to the Constitutional Convention and supported the ratification of the Constitution. He served as a U.S. senator from Maryland for three years, from 1789 to 1792.

He was involved in politics until around 1800, when he retired and devoted his energy to his businesses; here, too, he exerted great influence. In 1828 he was one of the cofounders of the Baltimore & Ohio Railroad, and he sat on the board of the Chesapeake & Ohio Railroad until his death.

Charles Carroll was the last signer of the Declaration to die, and as such, he was revered as a giant who helped set America free.

Sir Edward Henry Carson

(1854–1935)

In 1900, when Oscar Wilde filed a slander suit against the marquis of Queensberry for remarks he was said to have made about Wilde's sexuality, the marquis chose as his attorney Edward Carson. During the trial, Carson conducted a withering examination of Wilde that, in effect, put Wilde rather than the Marquis on trial. Indeed, when the trial was over, charges were brought against Wilde that resulted in his being sentenced to jail for two years.

In a sense, Carson's actions had an impact on gay sexuality: The entire debacle had clearly illustrated just how far Victorian England would go in suppressing anyone who openly practiced "the love that dare not speak its name."

But the Dublin-born Carson was equally famed for his political activity. Just as there were Irish who were all for making Ireland independent from England, there were Irish who weren't—and Carson was a prominent figure among them. His actions influenced events for many years.

Carson was educated at Portarlington School and Trinity College, Dublin. He was called to the Irish bar in 1877 and the English bar in 1893. In 1900 he joined the Unionist government and was knighted.

Carson was as militant in his quest to keep Ireland part of England as many of his opponents were not to. He consistently fought against the dissolution of ties in Parliament and was not afraid to resort to violence or at least threats of violence to keep the union intact.

When Lord Asquith of England introduced the Home Rule Bill of 1912, Carson was a driving force in the formation of the Ulster Volunteers, a military force that held training exercises in the open for all to see—a clear message that Ulster was ready to fight rather than come under the control of the Irish Parliament, as Asquith's bill would have forced it to do. In support of union, thousands of Ulster residents signed a document titled "A Covenant of Resistance to Home Rule," and about their activities Carson uttered the famous phrase "Don't be afraid of illegalities"—such as shooting people.

In 1914, in an act that was clearly illegal under British law but that had the approval of the Conservatives in the British Parliament, guns for the Ulster Volunteers were landed at Antrim.

Some sort of home rule bill was inevitable, however, and in 1914, one was approved. But it did not go into effect until after World War I. Carson and his cohorts were assured that Ulster would not be included under the bill. Following the Easter Rising of 1916, Carson was again assured that Ulster would be excluded by the Home Rule Bill of 1914, and he took the position of first lord of the admiralty. After the war, he became prime minister of the Dincairn division of Belfast.

Carson had fought to repeal the various home rule acts but at one point realized that this was not going to be possible, and in 1920 he urged the Ulster Unionists to support the Government of Ireland Act of 1920, which would allow Ulster to retain its independence.

In his time, Carson was probably the most influential of all Irish figures in resisting Ireland's independence from England. The British appreciated him. He died on October 22, 1935, and, after a state funeral in Belfast, was buried in St. Anne's Cathedral.

Chester A. Arthur

(1829–1886)

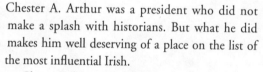

Chester A. Arthur was a president who did not make a splash with historians. But what he did makes him well deserving of a place on the list of the most influential Irish.

Chester Alan Arthur was born on October 5, 1829, in Fairfield, Vermont. His father was an immigrant from Ireland who was a highly respected scholar and became a Baptist minister. He imbued young "Cheaters," as Chester was called, with a love of learning that would ultimately earn him membership in the Phi Beta Kappa Society.

Arthur was a schoolteacher for about ten years, but in 1854 he began practicing law in New York. At one point he and a friend traveled to the West to practice law but returned because the country was so lawless.

Arthur was a staunch abolitionist, and when the Civil War broke out he joined the Union forces. Though he was eager to get into the conflict, his skills were suited more to being quartermaster, and he gradually worked his way up to becoming quartermaster general.

After the war, he became deeply embroiled in politics and in 1871 became chairman of the New York State Republican Party. He was also an outstanding lawyer, and in 1871 President Ulysses S. Grant appointed him collector of the Port of New York—the most prestigious position outside Washington.

He continued to be active in politics and in 1880 went to the Republican National Convention in Chicago and supported Garfield. In a political compromise, he was nominated for vice president on the Garfield ticket.

At the polls in November, the Garfield-Arthur ticket sneaked in. But on July 2, 1881, a deranged office seeker named Charles J. Guiteau shot Garfield. He lingered for eighty days before dying; now Chester A. Arthur was president.

The nation was in shock and afraid that Arthur, a machine politician, would somehow hand the country over to his party. To allay the fears, Arthur publicly dissolved his relationship with Senator Roscoe Conklin, who headed the Republican Party.

Arthur's presidency was surprisingly successful. He organized a program of trade agreements with various countries, developed America's first steel navy, prosecuted people who defrauded the postal service, and vetoed the Chinese Exclusion Act. Possibly his greatest achievement was the passage of the Pendleton Act, which became the foundation for civil service reform.

Additionally, though they were not decided during his presidency, Arthur brought up the issue of statehood for Alaska, the question of a building for the Library of Congress, and laws concerning the counting of electoral votes.

Despite his achievements, he was unsuccessful in obtaining the party nomination in 1884 and retired.

He died at his home in New York City on November 18, 1886.

Ronald Reagan

(1 9 1 1 –)

In 1984, while running for president, incumbent Ronald Reagan visited the beaches at Normandy, where forty years earlier the Allies had invaded Europe. From there his helicopter carried him across the sea and set down in the little town of Ballyporeen, County Tipperary, Ireland. Almost a hundred years earlier, his great-grandfather had left this little town forever, and standing there Reagan said:

Although I've never been a great one for introspection or dwelling in the past, as I looked down the narrow main street of the little town from which an emigrant named Michael Reogan had set out in pursuit of a dream, I had a flood of thoughts. . . . I thought of Jack [the president's father] and his Irish stories and the drive he'd always had to get ahead; I thought of my own childhood in Dixon [Illinois], then leaving that small town for Hollywood and later Washington.

Great-grandfather Michael had first gone to England, where he met Katherine Mulcahy, whom he married. Originally, the name was spelled "Reogan," but when he signed the ship's manifest, he dropped the "o" for an "a," perhaps because the name was easier to spell.

The young couple then emigrated to America, and in 1883 Ronald's father, Jack, was born. Jack lost both his parents when he was a little boy and was raised by a maternal aunt. In 1904 he was married to Nelle Clyde Wilson.

While Reagan has always maintained he is a Presbyterian, his brother Neil is a Catholic. Why Ronald was never baptized has not been explained.

Jack Reagan was a shoe salesman with big dreams for success in business and, it is said, "a big thirst." Ultimately, he was fired from his job for drinking, and with it went his dreams of glory.

But Reagan said he was proud of his father—and his mother. His mother instilled in him the values of a lifetime by being involved in charitable causes for others, and his father taught him the importance of treating everyone the same. He is particularly proud of what his father did one night in a hotel in a small town. Jack had been on the road all day, he was cold and tired, and he had stopped at the hotel to get a room. After looking at his name, the clerk said he should be particularly happy: Jews were not welcome. Jack stormed out of the hotel, first telling the clerk that they probably wouldn't like Catholics either, and spent an uncomfortable night in his car.

Jack Reagan moved his family a number of times, always following work, but finally settled in Dixon in 1920. But young Ron was a boy with wanderlust, and he decided he wanted to be an actor.

In the 1930s he got a job in radio, announcing sports results, which he read off a Western Union ticker; later he headed for Hollywood. In 1937 he was introduced to an agent, who got him a screen test—and a salary of two hundred dollars a week. As an actor, Reagan was competent, appealing—and successful. He also was active in the Screen Actors Guild, fighting for actors' rights.

His road to the presidency was long and winding, and almost a fluke. After Jack Reagan was fired from his job in 1931, he changed course and started to fight for the election of Franklin Delano Roosevelt in 1932. When FDR won, Jack was rewarded by being made the head of the local welfare office. Young Ronald, or "Dutch," as he was nicknamed, followed his father's politics, but as time went by he became more and more conservative.

In 1960 he came to the attention of Republican Party bigwigs—and clearly revealed how far to the right he had traveled—by giving a stirring speech calling for the 1964 nomination of Barry Goldwater for president.

The bigwigs, hungry for viable and vibrant candidates, settled on Reagan, and in 1962 he ran for governor of California—and surprised everyone by winning handily. He won again four years later and in 1980 ran for president and won. He served two terms.

Reagan accomplished much as president, but he seemed to be some-one who was either revered or reviled. The reality is that Reagan, like most people, was neither John Wayne nor the Devil incarnate, but somewhere in between, a good person who was not perfect.

In the mid-1990s Reagan's family revealed that he was suffering from Alzheimer's disease. He was, as he said, "in the twilight of his life." It is surely a life that will be remembered.

James Larkin

(1 8 7 6 – 1 9 4 7)

If one's image of a union leader and organizer is that of an aggressive firebrand, James Larkin fills the bill perfectly. His labor life could be described as tumultuous, and sometimes confining: He spent several years in jail.

Larkin was born to poor parents on January 21, 1876, in Liverpool, and when he was a child, he lived with his grandparents in Newry, County Down. As a young man, he returned to Liverpool, got a job as a seaman, and was eventually promoted to foreman. But one day the men under him staged a strike, and when Larkin joined them, he was fired from his job. He then obtained a job as an organizer for the National Union of Dockers.

Larkin's talents as a labor leader were demonstrated during the labor strife of 1907 in Belfast, when he introduced the strategy of "blacking," which meant declaring a business or industry subject to boycott by trade union members. Larkin was also charismatic enough so that he engineered a strike by local police.

In 1909 he formed his own union, the Irish Transport and General Workers Union. In its ranks were unskilled workers such as carters, laborers, and factory hands. These people lived in horrific conditions in the slums of Dublin, which one biographer said were at the time "among the worst in Europe." Big Jim Larkin was a powerful orator and persuader, and soon he had thousands of members in his union.

In 1913 William Martin Murphy, an employer, informed his workers in Larkin's union that they were to resign from it. When they refused, Murphy locked the employees out. Other unions rallied behind Larkin, and the event developed into a major confrontation: One hundred thousand workers were involved. The struggle lasted eight months, during which some workers literally starved. When the strike ended, it had not been a resounding victory for the workers, but they emerged with defined rights that they did not have before.

After the strike, Larkin traveled to America to raise funds for his union. To his surprise, he found U.S. employers even more hostile than those in Ireland.

While in the United States, Larkin was arrested and sentenced to a ten-year prison term for "criminal syndicalism." His sentence was commuted by Governor Al Smith three years later.

Larkin returned to Ireland a virtual hero, but in his absence the committee that had overseen his union while he was gone had expelled him from his own union. He immediately formed another, the Workers Union of Ireland.

He also became a member of the government. He became a Dublin city councillor and a deputy member of Dáil Éireann from 1927 to 1932, again in 1937 and 1938, and in 1943 and 1944.

In 1940, Larkin led a campaign against the Wages Standstill Order and was able to effect changes. And later he was instrumental—after leading a fourteen-week strike—in gaining a two-week leave for workers.

Larkin's impact on labor, particularly manual laborers, was great, and he is still remembered with affection and respect by workers and with irritation by employers. Said one, "For years this lad was a big pain in the arse."

36

Grover Cleveland

(1 8 3 7 – 1 9 0 8)

The influence of Grover Cleveland cannot be specifically tallied though his impact on the economy was significant. But his greatest influence was as a person of courage and integrity, a president who was very unlike the image many cynics have in mind when they think "politician." It was a clean, strong, honest image Americans needed during a particularly dishonest time.

Stephen Grover Cleveland was the fifth of nine children born to Ann Neal (her grandfather was a Niall, a famous Irish name, and had immigrated from Ulster) and Richard Falley Cleveland whom she had married in Baltimore in 1829; he was a tutor there. The family lived in several towns in New York State, particularly in Fayetteville, where Cleveland spent most of his youth.

For a while Cleveland lived with his uncle on a farm; he then studied law and became a lawyer. He was also attracted to politics and, while still in his late teens (1856), got involved with the Democratic Party in Buffalo.

He worked ward politics for the Democrats, and when he was twenty-five, he was made a ward supervisor. He also dabbled in law enforcement, becoming an assistant district attorney for a while.

Cleveland impressed his Buffalo colleagues with his hard work, attention to detail, and great energy. Most of his spare time was spent with friends fishing, hunting, or having a drink at a local saloon.

Following the Civil War, Cleveland briefly took a job as sheriff of Erie County in New York and demonstrated his cast-iron integrity: Two criminals were sentenced to be hanged, and Cleveland volunteered to pull the lever. His reasoning was that if he supported the death penalty, he should be willing to go all the way.

When the Republicans put up a "ring" (machine) candidate for mayor of Buffalo in 1882, the Democrats searched for someone who was clean. They found Cleveland. The people liked what they saw. At the age of forty-four, Cleveland was elected mayor.

That same year, the New York governor's race was on, and Cleveland was brought in to run against the Republican candidate. Again he succeeded in convincing the voters that he was honest and was elected.

His gubernatorial administration was known for its honesty, openness, and solid appointments and values as well as for Cleveland's courage in dealing with Tammany Hall, putting the needs of the people ahead of political concerns.

In 1884 he was selected to run for president against James G. Blaine, who had been tainted since he had been part of the Ulysses S. Grant administration. Blaine then immediately unearthed a fact that had until then been buried: Cleveland had fathered an illegitimate child. Blaine and cohorts circulated a rhyme that went "Ma! Ma! Where's my pa? Gone to the White House. Ha! Ha! Ha!"

Cleveland's response was to tell the truth, which made him look even better than expected. It turned out he had acted honorably toward the woman who bore his child.

Cleveland won the election. Two years after he had been elected mayor of Buffalo, he was president of the United States.

As president, Cleveland's character continued to shine through. He used his veto power more than three hundred times, striking down special-interest bills.

Domestically, he worked to reduce the tariff, civil service, and he was instrumental in getting the Dawes Act, which guaranteed American citizenship to Indians, passed and the Interstate Commerce Commission formed.

One issue on which he was greatly pressured, particularly by fellow Democrats, was support of the silver standard. But Cleveland resisted, and ultimately the gold standard was passed. Many economists attribute Cleveland's fortitude in holding out for the gold standard to be crucial to the United States' being able to stay on an even keel.

Cleveland's term was not trouble-free. A financial deal he made with a large bank, which he said would help the country, was widely viewed as a fiscal sellout. He also used federal troops to suppress a strike by workers at the Pullman Company and sent them against unemployed demonstrators.

Cleveland ran for president again in 1888 but lost to Benjamin Harrison; Cleveland won the popular vote, but Harrison captured enough electoral votes to unseat him. However, Cleveland recaptured the presidency from Harrison in the 1892 election, becoming both the twenty-second and the twenty-fourth presidents of the United States.

He declined to run for a third term in 1896, preferring to settle down with his wife, Frances, the twenty-two-year-old daughter of his former law partner, whom he married in the White House in 1896.

Cleveland wasn't particularly popular when he left office, but his goodness and courage helped restore his image.

Douglas Hyde

(1 8 6 0 – 1 9 4 9)

It's hard to conceive of a more memorable position than being the first president of Ireland, but Douglas Hyde, a teacher and scholar before he became a politician, did even more: He brought back the Irish language, and he was a great promoter of Irish culture. He was an inspiration to Lady Gregory, W. B. Yeats, and others who were major figures in promoting Irish culture.

Hyde was born in Castlerea in County Roscommon on January 17, 1860, the son of a rector. After distinguishing himself in grammar school and high school, he went to Trinity College, Dublin, where he became proficient in a dazzling array of languages, including Latin, Greek, Hebrew, French, German, and Irish.

Hyde loved old Irish tales, and he spent much time gathering Irish poems and stories from the people who lived in the countryside around his father's rectory. Based on what he learned, he published *Beside the Fire* in 1889. Later, in 1893, *Love Songs of Connacht*, which contained his own verse translations, came out.

In 1893 Hyde started the Gaelic League, serving as its first president. By 1905 there were 550 branches of the league. At its heart was an encouragement of Irish dances and games.

In 1905 Hyde traveled to America on a fund-raising tour for the league. He found a very responsive Irish America.

In the early 1900s, when National University was put together, Hyde and his supporters lobbied for Irish to be part of the entrance requirements, and when the institution opened its doors in 1908, it was. In 1909 Hyde became the first professor of Modern Irish at University College, Dublin.

It was Hyde's belief that the Gaelic League should be kept nonsectarian and that the Irish language and political matters be kept apart. But as the language became more and more a symbol of one's political stance, language and belief soon became inseparable.

Hyde would have none of it. In 1915 he resigned the presidency of the league and focused his energies on teaching.

Hyde was characterized by one person as the "kind of chap who doesn't make enemies." He was nonconfrontational. So when the constitution of 1937 was created, he was the unanimous selection of all parties to be president of Ireland.

Two achievements he cherished were the facts that his play *Casadh an Tsugain* was the first play ever performed in Irish on a professional stage and that he had been one of the major forces in keeping the Irish language alive. He richly deserves to be included as one of the most influential Irish of all time.

William McKinley

(1 8 4 3 – 1 9 0 1)

Even though William McKinley is not usually placed on most historians' lists as a great U.S. president, the influence he had both in the United States and overseas is irrefutable and important.

McKinley was born of Scotch-Irish stock (his father's family came from Dervoch, County Antrim) in Niles, Ohio, but he called Canton, Ohio, home.

He was raised by highly religious parents. His father, William Sr., was an iron founder in both Pennsylvania and Ohio, and did not do very well. Because the family's funds were limited, McKinley completed only one year of college.

When the Civil War broke out in 1861, McKinley joined the Union troops. He distinguished himself in a number of campaigns and was discharged as a major when the war ended in 1865. A key contact he made while in the army was Rutherford B. Hayes, who was impressed with McKinley's administrative abilities. (Hayes would be elected president himself in 1877.)

Following the war McKinley attended law school in Albany, New York, and then returned to Canton. There he met and married the well-off Ida Saxton in 1871, but two years later Ida fell victim to a severe nervous affliction and remained an invalid for many years. McKinley always remained compassionate and caring towards her.

McKinley's political career started in the House of Representatives, where he spent fourteen years (1877–1883 and 1885–1891). He became deeply involved in tariff questions; his most significant achievement during his years in Congress was the McKinley Tariff, which allowed goods from some foreign countries to be imported without any tariffs; American sugar refiners were subsidized for any loss they might incur. The bill created a furor among the American public, but it didn't politically hurt McKinley, who ran for and was elected governor of Ohio in both 1891 and 1893. He had been primed to run for president in 1892, and Republican politicos had exhorted him to do so, but McKinley had declined, saying the party should stand behind Benjamin Harrison, the incumbent president.

But he did run for president in 1896 against firebrand William Jennings Bryan, a contest the entire country watched with interest. In the campaign, Bryan came across as a demagogue, while McKinley seemed balanced and sane, a much better candidate. Bryan did endless whistle-stop tours, while McKinley simply went out onto the porch of his Canton home and spoke calmly with supporters and reporters. McKinley won handily.

Undoubtedly, his greatest influence was in foreign affairs. It was through his efforts that the United States annexed the Hawaiian Islands in July 1898 and got involved in the rebel uprising in Cuba. Since Cuba was so close to the United States, McKinley—spurred on by the "yellow journalists" of the day—involved America in a war with Spain and quickly defeated it. When a peace was negotiated in Paris, the U.S. negotiators, at McKinley's behest, persuaded Spain to give up not only Cuba but also Puerto Rico, Guam, and the Philippine Islands.

McKinley was easily reelected in 1900 on the slogan a "full dinner pail," which referred to the good economic times that had come again.

McKinley's life was ended by an assassin named Leon Czolgosz, who shot him on September 6, 1901; he died on September 14, 1901.

Cuchulain

According to some sociologists and historians, the Irish suffer from a kind of mass inferiority complex. Because of this, they have needed heroes in their lives, characters they can look to, dream about, and draw strength from. And none is greater than Cuchulain (pronounced coo-KUL-in), whose exploits have been told and retold down the centuries.

As with most ancient figures, Cuchulain and his exploits are part legend and part fact. The name Cuchulain is said to have resulted from an event that occurred as Cuchulain approached the house of Culain. He was attacked by a vicious dog. Cuchulain, then named Setanta, killed the hound with his bare hands. This caused great grief to Cuchulain. The young boy who saw the incident told Setanta that from that time on as penance for this deed he would be "Culain's hound"—or *cú Chulainn* in Irish.

Cuchulain was the foster son of Conor MacNessa, a great king of the time. He first noticed the young Cuchulain playing a game. The king asked who he was, and Cuchulain told him that he was his foster son, son of Sualtim and Dectaire, "your sister."

From that moment on the king paid special attention to him, and at one point Cuchulain decided to take up the profession of arms, to become a warrior.

On the day this was to occur, the Druids, who used omens to predict the future, said that it was not a good day, that if he took arms, he would achieve great fame, but that his life would be short.

But Cuchulain didn't care. "I care not if I die tomorrow," he said, "if only my deeds live after me." His words were to be prophetic.

Of all Cuchulain's heroic stories, no doubt the most famous is the *Táin Bó Cuáilnge* (The Cattle Raid of Cooley).

It starts with simple jealousy. Queen Maeve of Connaught, who had been married to Conor MacNessa, was now being courted by King Ailill. Part of the process was to compare their worldly possessions. King Ailill had a bull that was superior to any in Queen Maeve's possession, and this made his worldly wealth greater than Queen Maeve's.

She had heard of a bull owned by the chief of Cuáilnge, and she sent a courier to ask if she could borrow it. She said that she knew he would not want to let his precious bull out of his sight, so the courier was to tell him that she would invite him to her court and that he would be entertained as long as the bull stayed there.

The request was granted, but the courier made the mistake of getting drunk and telling the chief of Cuáilnge that if he had not loaned the bull to Queen Maeve, she would have come with her troops to wrest it from him forcibly. The chief told the courier to leave immediately—without the bull. Once she learned of this, Maeve became enraged. She assembled a huge army and marched on Cuáilnge.

One part of the queen's army was headed by Ferdiad, who was a close friend and foster brother of Cuchulain. And it so happened that Cuchulain was aligned with the chief, so this would pit him in battle against his friend.

Cuchulain was said to be a sentimental and loving friend, and he importuned Ferdiad not to fight, but Ferdiad said that the fight must go on. Cuchulain refused, but Ferdiad goaded him with taunts, and finally they began, casting spears at each other.

The battle raged for days. In the middle of the fourth day, when Cuchulain was getting the worst of the fight, a friend named Laeg came to the rescue, goading him to rally. He soon delivered a killing blow to Ferdiad. Then, running to him, Cuchulain grasped his friend as he lay dying, and Cuchulain fainted himself.

After years of bloody hostilities, Maeve got the bull. Yet the wars extracted a terrible price of death and blood—and finally she had to return the bull.

The story goes that Cuchulain died in battle while refusing to lie down, leaning against a tall rock that jutted from the ground. Though he was dead, his enemies did not approach him until the vultures started to peck at him. And that rock still stands to this day.

Joseph R. McCarthy

(1 9 0 8 – 1 9 5 7)

Even now, decades after he began his investigation into Communist infiltration into the U.S. government, Joseph McCarthy's name still generates strong feelings. Some view him as a dangerous demagogue who destroyed innocent lives. Others think of him as a martyr to the anti-Communist cause.

Joseph Raymond McCarthy was born on November 8, 1908, in a farming community near Appleton, Wisconsin, one of five children of Tim McCarthy, of German-Irish heritage, and Bridget Tierney McCarthy, who had been born in Ireland.

He quit school at fourteen and tried his hand at business when he was sixteen, opening a chicken business. At the age of twenty, he got a job in a grocery store, where he did very well. While not an intellectual, McCarthy had a great memory and was able, while working as a grocer, to earn his high school diploma, cramming four years of schoolwork into one. He then went to Marquette University, majoring in law.

In college, McCarthy held a variety of jobs and became adept at poker. He was also an amateur boxer. He graduated in 1935.

In 1939 McCarthy ran for circuit court judge in a vicious campaign. He was accused of using dishonest tactics, a charge that would be repeated later in his life. He was elected. He was still a judge when he entered World War II. Later he would trumpet his military accomplishments—he called himself "Tail Gunner Joe"—but just how extensive his combat experience was remains open to question.

In 1944, while still in the army, he returned to Wisconsin to run as a Republican for Robert La Follette's Senate seat. He was defeated. But when he was discharged from the army, he ran again in 1946 and, in a squeaker, won.

The events which were to make him famous—or infamous—occurred a few years later. Most Americans feared being engulfed by a Communist wave. The United States and the Soviet Union were at odds, but the core of their animosity was a fundamental disagreement about the correctness of their political systems: democracy and communism. And it seemed as though the Communists might win. They had moved into China, expanded into Eastern Europe, and were moving into Korea. They had the atomic bomb. The trials of Alger Hiss and Julius and Ethel Rosenberg for spying had generated a feeling in many Americans that the Soviet Union was dangerous.

By 1949 Joseph McCarthy had been in the Senate for three years and was looking for a cause. In a conversation with a Catholic prelate, Father Edmund Walsh, founder and regent of the Washington,

D.C.–based Georgetown University School of Foreign Service, it was suggested that he might profit by unearthing Communists in government. In 1950 McCarthy made a speech in Wheeling, West Virginia, charging that there were 205 "card-carrying" Communists in the U.S. State Department.

President Harry S Truman's administration challenged the charge, and the Senate Foreign Relations Committee investigated it. No Communists were discovered, but the charge was repeated many times in other settings. It characterized the Democratic Party as the "party of treason." Americans, particularly Irish Catholic Americans, began to listen. Priests and members of the Catholic hierarchy, such as Cardinal Francis Joseph Spellman, archbishop of New York, supported McCarthy. So did the Kennedys, particularly Joe Kennedy but also Robert Kennedy, who was working for the committee as an investigator. In addition, much of the Catholic press was also behind him, though there were some publications, such as *America* and *Commonweal,* that deplored the methods used in investigating people. McCarthy was soon made head of a Senate investigating committee and began calling witnesses. The hearings were broadcast on TV, and all America watched, arguing their merits.

It was a time when people were reduced to the essence of their courage: If you believed that McCarthy was wrong, you could stand up to him. But it might well turn out that you would lose your livelihood if you did, because the assumption would be that you were a Communist or a "pinko," sympathetic to the Communist cause.

It was also possible that you would lose much even if nothing was proven against you. Many people who had liberal or Communist affiliations—often as the result of misguided idealism—lost their jobs, and there were some suicides.

Critics say that this occurred with President Dwight D. Eisenhower. McCarthy branded war hero George C. Marshall, who had been Truman's secretary of state, as being "soft on communism," while Marshall's war comrade, Eisenhower, remained mute. In 1951, Eisenhower said that in America there was "a conspiracy so immense and an infamy so black as to dwarf any previous venture in the history of man."

The Republicans, in part because McCarthy's backing helped win them the 1952 presidential election, stayed on the sidelines. But as time wore on, McCarthy did not let up, and the Eisenhower administration came to regard him as a liability. He simply was not producing proof of any Communist infiltration. He answered criticism by his fellow senators and press people, such as Drew Pearson, by making stronger accusations. There came a time when both politicians and the public demanded that McCarthy produce proof.

In 1953 television hearings began, with McCarthy as the inquisitor, first on the Voice of America, then on *The Overseas Library Program.* Nothing was proven in these hearings, though McCarthy leveled charges ranging from "un-Americanism" to "subversion." But in 1954 he held hearings on Communist infiltration of the army, the so-called Army-McCarthy hearings.

As the world watched, McCarthy came across as a bully who could not back up his accusations. His popularity plunged. There was one transcendent moment when army counsel Joseph N. Welch looked across the smoky, crowded hearing room and said, "Until this moment, Senator, I think I never really gauged your cruelty or your recklessness. . . . Have you no sense of decency, sir, at long last? Have you left no sense of decency?" McCarthy, smiling and looking very uncomfortable, did not respond.

The hearings ended, and in December 1954, McCarthy was censured by the Senate in a vote of 67 to 22. The censure seemed to break his spirit. He lost interest in politics and began to drink more heavily. His health failed completely, and he died on May 2, 1957.

For some people, McCarthy's existence was a reminder that tyranny is never far from one's doorstep. For others, it proved that communism was alive and well in America. And for yet others, it showed how weak we all can be. As Edward R. Murrow said, quoting Shakespeare at the end of his exposé broadcast of McCarthy, "The fault is not in the stars, dear Brutus, but in ourselves."

Cyrus McCormick

Cyrus McCormick invented a machine that came to be called the McCormick reaper, and a case could be made that it was as important an invention as the automobile. It had a revolutionary effect on the way we live, was a factor in helping the Union win the Civil War, and helped usher in the Industrial Revolution.

McCormick was born on February 15, 1809, in Walnut Grove, Virginia, the eldest of eight children. His parents, Robert and Mary Ann McCormick, were both Scotch-Irish and highly religious.

McCormick ascribed his success in business, in great part, to his physical condition—which, in turn, fueled a large amount of energy. He neither drank nor smoked nor partook of any other activity that might be described as sinful. Once he described his physical appearance as a young man: "My hair is very dark brown—eyes dark, though not black, complexion fresh and health good, 5 ft. 11 ½ inches high, weighing 200 pounds." It was later said that just keeping up with him was a job in itself.

In 1857, at the age of forty-eight, he slowed down enough to marry Nancy Fowler. They were married for twenty-six years and had seven children.

The device he invented was designed to cut and store grain more quickly. At the time, the following method was used for cutting grain: Men with sharp scythes sliced it down, and then women and children picked it up and tied it in sheaves to dry. The average man could cut two to three acres per day. Using the McCormick reaper, one man could cut *twenty* acres of grain a day.

McCormick's reaper, which was an improvement on one his father had been working on for twenty years, was a large metal contraption with reciprocating cutting blades that were shielded by metal fingers, a reel to bring the grain against the blade, a divider to isolate the grain to be cut from grain not to be cut, and a platform onto which the cut grain could fall. It was heavy, and horses were required to pull it.

McCormick patented the reaper in 1834 and started manufacturing it in 1840. He started selling the machines in the Virginia area, but there were problems that made it seem as though the device wouldn't make it. Pulling the reaper exhausted the horses, and it was constantly breaking down. In fact, it had so many bugs that for the first few years of its manufacture, many farmers still relied on the old method—sheer physical labor of a lot of people—to harvest the grain.

Then McCormick had a bright idea. In 1844, with sales sluggish, he visited the northwestern section of the country to see how the reaper might perform. What he saw under the big sky was endlessly flat fields of grain, a far cry from the hilly, rocky patches of ground in Virginia. He figured that his reaper would perform much better in this type of environment, and he was right. He moved his operation to Chicago, and in 1847 he began manufacturing reapers in his own factories.

Any good moneymaking idea is sure to be challenged in a variety of ways; the McCormick reaper was no exception. He had patented his reaper in 1834, but a New England man named Obed Hussey had patented his own successful reaper the year before. This was to lead to innumerable court battles and bitterness between the two men. Additionally, McCormick had to contend with patent rip-offs: Someone would steal McCormick's basic design, add a mechanical flourish here or there, and then patent the result as a new machine.

But Cyrus McCormick was not only a creative inventor but a creative marketer, and that was one big reason why he succeeded. In 1856 he was selling four thousand reapers annually by using another innovation: the installment plan. Farmers who might not ordinarily be able to buy one now could. McCormick knew that farmers had money only after harvest time, so he would take $35 down in the spring (the reaper cost $100) and allow the balance to be paid in December.

If something went wrong with a reaper, McCormick or his workers would fix it immediately. He also knew that farmers would want to be able to fix their own reapers, so he published a how-to manual. In addition, McCormick and his brother had a habit of showing up at harvest time just to make sure things went right.

By the eve of the Civil War, McCormick was reaping huge profits. By then there were between eighty thousand and ninety thousand reapers in use, most on midwestern farms.

And, as mentioned earlier, the reaper helped win the Civil War. For one thing, it enabled northern farmers to produce much more grain for horses and other livestock as well as for men than the Confederacy could, and the machines freed more men to become soldiers: Two men operating one reaper could do as much work as ten or twelve men with scythes or cradles. Additionally, it influenced the Industrial Revolution, allowing more people to leave farms to work in factories.

McCormick's inventive mind also came up with a two-wheeled mower with a movable or flexible cutter bar that could adjust to terrain and allow easy moving over bumpy terrain.

McCormick never forgot his Calvinist roots. All his life he was a religious man and contributed heavily to the support of the Presbyterian Church; his main preoccupation was a desire to keep the old dicta in place. And when the war was over, he worked hard to ensure that the South and North would once again be joined, at least when it came to religion.

It can be fairly said that Cyrus McCormick revolutionized farming in America; indeed, his invention enabled America to move closer toward its potential as a farmland.

McCormick died on May 13, 1884. At harvest time you can still see his basic machine doing what it has been doing for more than one hundred years. Today, the company he founded is called International Harvester.

42

Father Edward Flanagan

(1886–1948)

The 1938 movie *Boys Town* appears to be one instance where Hollywood got the reality right. The movie portrayed Father Flanagan (played by Spencer Tracy, who got an Academy Award for his work), head of the real-life Boys Town in Omaha, Nebraska, as a loving, caring person with a deep understanding of the troubled young men who came to his facility. And that was just what he was.

Edward Flanagan was born in County Roscommon, Ireland. He became a priest there and, after emigrating to the States, was assigned to a parish in Nebraska.

Right from the start, Father Flanagan was interested in troubled people. At first he was involved in helping unemployed farm laborers. In 1913 he opened the Workingman's Hotel in Omaha; there men could find a clean bed for a night and get help locating jobs. And then young boys started to show up, and Father Flanagan started to let them in.

In those days, the social machinery for helping the less fortunate was not in place, so early in December 1917 Father Flanagan established his own shelter for such kids: Father Flanagan's Boys Home. He started with five boys, and by Christmastime he had twenty more. By the end of January 1918 he had taken in fifty boys. It wasn't long before Father Flanagan's Boys Home was forced to open larger facilities outside Omaha; in 1922 the name was changed to Boys Town. In time even those facilities proved inadequate, and a number of new ones were opened all over the state.

While Boys Town was not a country club for boys—rules and discipline were strict—the feeling was that the staff, following Father Flanagan's lead, truly cared for the young people. Caring was what troubled boys needed more than anything else; and for many, this was the first time anyone had ever cared for them. The caring grew out of Father Flanagan's deeply held belief—a belief he would often articulate in court—that "there's no such thing as a bad boy."

The vast majority of the children who went to Boys Town grew up to be accomplished, responsible adults, successful in every walk of life from athletics to medicine. In 1979, Boys Town also became Girls Town, when troubled young women were first admitted.

There is no question that Father Flanagan's pioneering work with troubled boys was a catalyst for the opening of many other facilities throughout America and in other countries and the implementation of a new attitude toward wayward boys, based on caring rather than punishment.

Father Flanagan died in Berlin while on a promotional tour for the U.S. government, and his body was taken back to the United States. Two services were conducted—one private, for his boys and staffers, and another, opened to the public, which attracted more than twenty-five hundred people.

Following Father Flanagan's death, Boys Town went out of the public limelight, but it kept going and today is still very active.

Father Flanagan, as was his request, was buried near the facility, near his "boys." On his tombstone is his epitaph, which sums up his life perfectly: FATHER FLANAGAN, FOUNDER OF BOYS TOWN, LOVER OF CHRIST AND MAN.

Amen.

43

John Carroll

Like his cousin Charles, John Carroll was an American hero, but a man of peace—and a priest. He could easily have joined his cousin in the Revolutionary War because he was very sympathetic to the colonists' cause. On the other hand, he was a man of God and would not take another person's life no matter what the stakes. He did fight a war—for Catholics— but did so peacefully.

He was born in 1735 in Upper Marlboro, Maryland, and both he and Charles attended the same school, Bohemian Manor on the Eastern Shore of Maryland, where they were taught by Jesuits. Then both went to France for their higher education at Collège Saint-Omer in France. John, who intended to become a priest, could not get the ecclesiastical training he needed in the colonies. He was ordained a priest in 1767 and stayed in Europe until 1775.

Upon his return to the United States, in his one direct involvement in the revolution, he accompanied his cousin and other revolutionaries to see officials in Quebec to ask for their help in the coming hostilities. But the officials refused, partly because England had promised them that their own language and religious freedom were to be guaranteed.

The war changed Catholicism for the colonies. There had not been a lot of colonial Catholics (only about thirty thousand), but the conflict severed their tie with the vicar apostolic in England. An American Catholic church was formed, and Carroll was involved in it, including writing a plan of reorganization for the church, which he pushed for passage of to Pope Pius VI. In 1785 he was named prefect apostolic by the pope.

Then, in 1789, he did something that was to have a profound effect on education—as well as those who wanted to be priests. His family owned a large parcel of land near Georgetown, at the time the only town along the Potomac River, a place kept alive by the main commodity of both Maryland and Virginia: tobacco. Carroll, well aware of the difficult and sometimes hazardous journey priests had to make to Europe to be ordained, used the land partly to establish Georgetown University, a Jesuit institution that is still one of the best universities in the country.

His work did not go unnoticed by the Papal See. On August 15, 1790, he was consecrated a bishop—the first Catholic bishop in the United Sates.

Carroll continued his good works, settling long-standing disputes between Germans and Irish Catholics in Philadelphia and erecting new churches. His greatest triumph—though he died before it was completed—was the construction in Baltimore of the Basilica of the Assumption of the Blessed Virgin Mary, a huge, three-domed structure that was the first cathedral built in America (and perhaps the only one designed and built free, thanks to world-class architect Benjamin Latrobe). It was completed in 1818.

In 1808 he was made an archbishop. Though a peaceful man his entire life, he was also a patriot, and when the War of 1812 erupted, he supported the United States openly.

44

St. Colmcille

(ABOUT 521–597)

S t. Colmcille—St. Columba in English—is one of the most revered Irish saints, a man who was dealt in middle age what could have been a death blow, but rose above it, ultimately achieving sainthood.

Colmcille was descended from kings in the line of O'Neill in the principality of Tir-Conaill, what is now Donegal, and when he was a very young man, he left the area to be educated and to become a priest.

He returned home in 544 because of a pestilence that had driven him from the area where he had been studying. A close friend gave him a tract of land in Derry, where he founded and built a monastery. Early on, Colmcille was said to have been ecologically alert and to have had a reverence for all living things. This concern showed when he was building the monastery. The site, on the river Foley, was near a stand of oaks, and Colmcille had the monastery built so that its chancel was toward the east and thereby did not interfere with sunlight getting to the trees.

He continued to build monasteries all over Ireland—at Drumcliff, Kells, Swords, Drumore, Kilgas, and elsewhere. By 562, at the age of forty-one, he had built at least thirty. Then his troubles began.

One day Colmcille was in his monastery when an agitated young man named Curan asked to be let in and given sanctuary. He explained to Colmcille that at a game he had accidentally struck the king's son, who had then died. The king would have him killed unless Colmcille protected him.

Colmcille gave him sanctuary—but that didn't stop the king. The enraged King Diarmuid sent his soldiers into the monastery—an outrage and a sacrilege. They hauled the young man out and summarily executed him. Colmcille was furious, but his own survival hung in the balance. He was able to slip out of the monastery and make his way back to Tir-Conaill. There he told his friends and relatives what had occurred, and they assembled a force to punish King Diarmuid. Ultimately, there was a ferocious battle between them and the forces of King Diarmuid at a place called Cuildremne. When it was over, there were three thousand dead.

Colmcille was blamed for the deaths by the Church hierarchy, although it had not been his idea to mount a military force. Various penalties were considered, including excommunicating him. He did feel responsible for the deaths, and the only way for him to rid himself of his guilt was to go to confession and perform a penance.

The penance had to suit the gravity of the crime. Thus, Colmcille was sentenced to banishment: He was to leave Ireland and never set eyes on it again. He was directed, moreover, to bring Christ to as many people as had been killed at Cuildremne.

With terrible sadness, he at first sailed to one of the Hebrides, intending to settle there, but it was not suitable: Far in the distance across the sea he could still see Ireland, and being so close—yet so far—was something that he knew he could not endure. He and his party got into their boat and sailed away, this time leaving Ireland far behind.

They landed on the island of Iona in pagan Scotland, which was ruled by King Conal of the O'Neill family, a relative of Colmcille. They started to build more monasteries and to go about the business of bringing the gospel to anyone who would listen.

Years passed, and then Colmcille received some very bad news: Irish poets, who had been revered for years, had come on hard times. In part as a result of their own arrogance and slovenliness, they were on the verge of being banished from Ireland by King Aedh. In order to pass a legal decree, Aedh had called all nobles, scholars, and ecclesiastics to gather at Drimceatt, which was near the town of Limevada in Derry.

Colmcille was a member of this poetical society, and he vowed that he must try to do something. He must go to the meeting and make himself heard. But how was he to do so? His penance had clearly stated that he was never to set eyes on Ireland again. He decided that he could go with a blindfold over his eyes—and he did.

His reputation as a holy man was well known in Ireland, and when he arrived he was greeted by most people with love and adulation. Then there came the moment when he was to speak at Drimceatt. In a sense, he was speaking for the future of poetry in Ireland.

He must have been an imposing figure, as he was described by one biographer, Adamnan, as a man "of well-formed and powerful frame, his face broad and fair and valiant, lit by large gray luminous eyes; he had a large and well-shaped head crowned with close and curling hair—except where he wore his frontal tonsure."

And his voice was surely heard. Adamnan continues: "His voice was clear and resonant, so that it could be heard a distance of 1500 paces, yet was sweet and more than the sweetness of birds."

He carried the day, and while the rules that the poets were required to function under were changed, the poets were not banished. Then he returned to Iona.

He spent the rest of his life doing what he had done before: building monasteries, doing good works, copying sacred texts in his fine calligraphy. At his monasteries, he demanded that monks separate their days into thirds: one third for praying, one for good works, and one third for reading or writing.

He was proud of what he had accomplished at Iona and elsewhere, but there was a certain emptiness inside him. Shortly before he died, he ascended a hill called Cnoc-na-Carnan, which, as Seamus McManus writes in *The History of the Irish Race,* "arose above the monastery . . . and took a last long look over land and sea—and we may be sure a fond, fond look towards the western horizon below which lay the land of his heart."

Colmcille was a builder of monasteries and in his time helped save poets. But he has also been in the hearts of many Irish for many centuries, an influence that cannot be measured but is surely significant.

45

Sean Lemass

(1 8 9 9 – 1 9 7 1)

While most teenage boys were doing what teenagers do, Sean Lemass, fifteen years old, was fighting in a revolution, the Easter Rising of 1916, under Captain Eamon de Valera, as well as in the general post office with other Irish Volunteers.

When the rising was put down, Lemass was one of the lucky ones: He escaped execution as well as deportation. When he was eighteen, he went to work in his father's drapery shop in Dublin. But inside he was more a revolutionary than a draper's helper, and he was soon back as an officer in the Irish Volunteers. He was captured in 1920 and spent a year in prison at Ballykinlar.

Following the treaty of 1921, he took the antitreaty side. He was captured again and sentenced by the British to the ill-named Mountjoy jail for a year, until December 1923. While he was in jail, he made good use of his time, reading every book on history and economics he could get his hands on. Upon his discharge from prison, he started his political rise, which began when he was elected a member of Dáil in 1925 and culminated in 1969, when he retired from politics.

His career in Irish politics was filled with achievement, and he had great influence not only in that area but in a number of others, including the development of the infrastructure of Dublin. He was a founding member of Fianna Fáil and became minister of industry and commerce under de Valera.

Lemass was a man of great drive and energy. He built up Ireland's industry behind what one biographer called a tariff wall. He appointed state boards to develop turf resources *(Bord na Mona)* as well as starting a shipping company named Irish Shipping, and an Irish airline, Aer Lingus.

Lemass also helped to bridge the gap between north and south with a number of steps. In 1965 he established free trade with England, viewing this action as a prelude to England and Ireland entering the Common Market. The same year, he took the unusual step of visiting Terence O'Neill, the premier of Northern Ireland, who was in Belfast, and went a long way toward mending fences.

46

Richard J. Daley

When John F. Kennedy was elected president of the United States by the narrowest margin ever in the twentieth century, there was a sour Republican joke going around that quite a few of those votes had come from voters in cemeteries in and around the Chicago area, where Democrat Richard J. Daley was mayor. Daley himself admitted that he had played a most influential role in the election of Kennedy, that at one point Joseph Kennedy had "sat down" with him and they had planned it out.

While Daley had an effect on the Chicago vote, his influence by no means stopped at the Cook County line. He knew mayors, governors, and other politicos in other states, and he wasn't shy about calling these folks and twisting arms.

Just how Richard J. Daley conducted himself in Chicago is the subject of some debate. In his book *Boss,* Chicago newspaperman Mike Royko skewered Daley. Others have been kinder. Some say that Daley ruled by consensus—that before he made a decision on something, he would consult with the parties whose self-interest was involved and make a decision based on this feedback. That seems logical. If he had been a total tyrant, it seems unlikely that Chicago would have run so smoothly during the years he was mayor. He was proud to advertise Chicago as the "city that worked."

Certainly, to many people, Daley had the image of a tyrant. This was precipitated by what came to be described as the Battle of Telegraph Hill, the place where the Democratic National Convention was held in 1968. During the convention, the protests of antiwar activists in the street turned into a riot, complete with baton-wielding cops; the debacle was televised worldwide.

The irony of 1968 is that by this time Daley himself believed that America should get out of Vietnam. But he kept this view to himself out of loyalty to the president, Lyndon Johnson.

Daley was born in a brick house on South Lowe Avenue in the Bridgeport section of Chicago. An Irish enclave that had started to develop in the 1830s, it was unaffectionately known as "Cabbagetown" by Chicago denizens because there was a cabbage field on one corner.

Daley's parents were second-generation Irish, his father a member of the sheet metal workers union, which eventually got him involved in the area's politics. His mother, Lilac Dunne, was about eight years older than Daley's father, Mike, and quite an impressive woman. She was a suffragist and frequently had Richard by her side as she marched in demonstrations in downtown Chicago. She also, Daley said, taught him valuable lessons on how to accomplish things, lessons that he applied all his life, particularly in running Chicago.

Daley followed his father into politics at the age of twelve, becoming a gofer and doing odd jobs for the Eleventh Ward in the Democratic organization.

Following graduation from high school, he got a clerical job in the stockyards. He then went to DePaul University Law School at night. It took him a decade before he was admitted to the bar. Meanwhile, he continued his political links with Eleventh Ward politicos, including becoming a member in a club called the Hamburg Social Athletic Club, whose chief task was to get out the vote and act as enforcer when that was required.

Eight years after he entered politics, Daley was working in Eleventh Ward councilman Joseph McDonough's office. The councilman got him a job in the Chicago treasurer's office, and Daley rose through the ranks to the highest administrative post in the treasurer's office. In 1936 he ran for state representative—and won. He was on his way up the political ladder. And in 1955 he ran for mayor and was elected.

Revered by many and reviled by others, Daley was a colorful character. Like his contemporary of the time in New York City, Mayor Robert F. Wagner Jr., Daley was a master of the malaprop. Perhaps the most famous instance of this was his comment during the 1968 riot: "The policeman is not there to create disorder," he said to an appreciative crowd, "but to preserve disorder."

Daley was also Irish through and through. He always made a super event of the St. Patrick's Day parade, which including dyeing the Chicago River green.

Despite the bad press from the 1968 convention and charges that Daley was racist, Chicagoans, including minority groups, continued to support him. He regularly garnered 70 percent of the vote—black and white. Nonetheless, he did suffer the ignominy of having his own delegates supplanted at the 1972 convention by a group led by the Reverend Jesse Jackson. But he remained a true party man, supporting Jimmy Carter in 1976.

That was the year he died. Just as he had requested—an Irishman to the end—Daley was buried while the Shannon River Pipe Band keened the strains of his favorite marching song, "Garryowen," across the cemetery.

Conn of the Hundred Battles

(LATE SECOND–
EARLY THIRD CENTURIES)

His name is descriptive of how the man lived his life, and though, as Seamus McManus points out in *The Story of the Irish Race,* there were "worthier men," his life exerted great influence: For a thousand years after Conn died, many noble families took great pride in tracing their heritage to him.

Conn's most famous battles were against Mogh Nuadat of the southwestern province of Munster. The battle really started about a half century before the Christian era, when some of the warlike Earnaan people, driven out of the north of Ireland where they lived, settled in Kerry, part of the province of Munster. When King Duach, who had given them the settlement, died, the Earnaan, aggressive and warlike, became rulers of the province.

They ruled for some two hundred years, when Mogh Nuadat, an Eberian ruler, rebelled against them. Conn sided with the northerners, but despite his intercession Mogh Nuadat was able to conquer the province.

Mogh Nuadat, inspired by his victory, then drove against Conn, but lost badly and was forced to flee to Spain. He stayed there nine years and married Beara, a daughter of the Spanish king of the castle they lived in, Heber Mor. His father-in-law, in turn, allowed Mogh Nuadat two thousand Spanish troops to aid him in invading Munster.

Mogh Nuadat engaged in ten pitched battles with Conn. Finally, Conn was forced to capitulate partially, giving Mogh Nuadat the southern half of Ireland. But Mogh Nuadat was bitter when he reflected on what had happened and regretted allowing Conn to escape with half the land. Moreover, the Spanish warriors with him had a bellicose temperament and were only too willing to go to war again quickly. A huge battle erupted, capped by what was regarded by some at the time as outside the rules of chivalrous behavior: Conn attacked Mogh at night. Only one of his officers, Gioll, refused to join in.

But Mogh held out. As dawn broke on the battle, Conn's army was starting to fade, when something happened that turned the tide of battle: Gioll slew Mogh Nuadat. This took the heart and fight out of Mogh's army, and they retreated.

In victory, Conn was farseeing. He did not glory over the vanquished, and he worked to get their allegiance, even going so far as to have his daughters marry not only the leader of Mogh's army, but also Mogh's only surviving son. Moreover, because he had attacked at night, he also gave the losers an eric, or find, which consisted of his carved brooch, gold ring, shield and sword, two hundred horses and chariots, two hundred cows, and two hundred slaves.

Conn continued to fight battles with a number of enemies. His life came to an end at Tara, where he was tricked by fifty men who came to his castle dressed as women. They killed him before he realized what was happening.

Joseph Medill

(1823–1899)

In 1884, when unemployment was rampant in Chicago, an editorial in the pages of the *Chicago Tribune* had a rather radical solution: murder. "The simplest plan, probably," the paper said, "when one is not a member of the Humane Society is to put arsenic in the supplies of food furnished the unemployed or the tramp. This produces death in a short time and is a warning to other tramps to keep out of the neighborhood."

It sounds bizarre, but the paper, and the man behind it, Joseph Medill, meant every word. Indeed, Medill's probusiness stance resulted in his backing a variety of causes that today would sound nothing short of criminal. For example, during the railroad strike of 1877 in Chicago, the *Tribune* demanded that strikers, whom they described as the "scum and filth of the city" who refused to take pay cuts and dismissal notices "get out of the way. . . . If they will not step out voluntarily, they must be made to by force."

The man behind the police, Joseph Medill, represented the best and worst in journalism, and during his long career at the helm of the *Tribune* he used the newspaper with a lack of objectivity that was laughable. On the other hand, Medill did some very good things with the influence the paper had, including going a long way toward getting Abraham Lincoln elected president and founding a publishing dynasty that exists to this day.

Joseph Medill's forebears were Scotch-Irish, a long line of shipbuilders from Belfast. Medill was raised in Canada, where he was born, and then his family—father William and mother Margaret as well as three brothers and two sisters—moved to Massillon, Ohio.

When he was twenty-one, Medill studied law in Canton, Ohio. There was little business, however, and he tired of it. He preferred to hang around and help—by setting type—at the local newspaper offices and to write an occasional editorial.

He found himself interested in the newspaper business. In 1850 he bought the *Coshocton Democratic Whig* and renamed it the *Republican*, giving rise to a rumor that Medill had also named the Republican Party.

Medill had married Katharine Patrick, the daughter of a small publisher, and she encouraged him to pursue a newspaper career. He did, buying an interest in a small daily in Cleveland and renaming it the *Cleveland Leader*.

He did a successful job editing this publication, and in 1854 he was invited by the owner of the *Chicago Tribune,* J. D. Webster, to edit the *Tribune.* The paper was in tough shape and housed in a dilapidated building, but when Medill went to see it, he was very impressed with something else: Chicago. The city had a raw vitality, and though Cleveland was bigger and more sophisticated in every way, Medill could see Chicago's potential, particularly since he was able to learn that the city was destined to become a big rail terminus and that immigrants were pouring into the city. He dropped the Cleveland paper and headed for Chicago, where he bought a controlling interest in the *Tribune.*

He was, of course, right about Chicago: It boomed. Though Medill's ostensible editorial philosophy was objectivity (it was "the organ of no man"), he used it to flail, whip, excoriate, and do mayhem to his enemies and the issues as he saw them. He was very antilabor, and he mounted virulent attacks against labor unions and anything else that suited his fancy. He blended in a bit of eccentricity—he believed "microbes" were the controlling units of the world—and supported the abolition of slavery. In sum, he developed a formula that added up to a thriving newspaper.

And he was a political animal through and through. His greatest achievement, he once said—and it is probably true—was to help get his friend and fellow Illinoisan, Abraham Lincoln, nominated for and elected president of the United States.

During the Civil War, Medill and his partner Charles H. Ray often went to the front to report, and the public lapped up the stories. The paper continued to grow.

At one point Medill was elected mayor of Chicago. Nevertheless, until his death on March 16, 1899, in San Antonio, Texas, he held to his antilabor and anti-immigrant stance. (His last words were supposedly "What is the news today?")

In addition to influencing many people with his views through the newspaper, and being an important factor in Lincoln's election, Medill started what is truly a dynasty in publishing. His grandson Robert R. McCormick continued as publisher of the *Tribune.* Another grandson, Joseph M. Patterson, went on to found the *New York Daily News.* Medill's granddaughter, Eleanor Medill "Cissy" Patterson, published the *Washington Times Herald,* and his great-granddaughter Alice Patterson Guggenheim founded the dominant Long Island daily, *Newsday.*

Charles J. Feeney

(APPROX. 1931–)

Until the story broke on the front page of the *New York Times* a few years ago, no one knew who he was, and Charles Feeney worked at keeping things that way. But what he did was eye-opening and automatically put him on any list of the most influential Irish who ever lived: He gave more money to charitable causes than perhaps any Irishman ever—and perhaps the vast majority of others as well. By late 1992, Feeney had donated some $600 million—and that over the relatively short period since 1982.

Why all the secrecy?

Feeney is a man who wants to protect his privacy. He told *Times* reporter Judith Miller that he wanted to go through life without being asked for money: "There are people who want and rightly deserve recognition for giving, but in our case it wasn't important." Besides the $600 million, Feeney, who sold a chain of shops in which he had an interest, put $3.5 billion into his charitable foundations.

Why does Feeney do it? His own answer is that he doesn't need a lot of money. In fact, one of his administrators, Harvey Dale, says, "He doesn't own a house. He doesn't own a car. He flies economy, and I think the watch he owns is worth about fifteen dollars."

Feeney's personal fortune, which could have been billions, is estimated to be about $5 million after his donations. Asked how the giving has affected his lifestyle, he says, "Occasionally someone else picks up a restaurant tab."

But he adds in all seriousness, "It [money] doesn't drive my life. I'm a what-you-see-is-what-you-get kind of guy."

Feeney's foundations have given to a wide variety of organizations, both in the United States—such as Mount Sinai School of Medicine in New York and the University of Pennsylvania—and in Ireland—the Union Hall Library in Northern Ireland and the Disability Foundation of Ireland. Some 47 percent of the money has gone to higher education. The largest single grant at one time was for $30 million, but the recipient's name was not revealed.

Feeney has also given personal contributions that are not routed through his foundations. Among these is Sinn Féin, the political wing of the IRA. Feeney says that the money is carefully monitored so that it is used for peaceful purposes.

One of the foundation's presidents, Frank H. T. Rhodes, president emeritus of Cornell University, says that the foundations are scrupulous in not telling recipients how to use the money. Recipients are examined closely before the grant is made, but once the money is given, that's it. Mr. Dale says, "We let good people do good things. We oversee, but we don't interfere."

50

Jonathan Swift

(1667–1745)

It sometimes seems required that if you have great ability, you should *not* show it early. Hence, we have people such as Albert Einstein failing mathematics in grade school, Eugene O'Neill being tossed out of college, and F. Scott Fitzgerald on the verge of the same. And then we have Jonathan Swift, who needed special exemption to graduate from Trinity College and about whom Henry Boylan writes, in *Dictionary of Irish Biography:*

Swift was one of the most commanding intellects and the greatest writer of his day. His prose is unmatched for simple strength and clarity. His satire was savage in its mockery, overpowering in its sheer force of intellect. His letters are among the best in English literature, and show an ease and lightness that carry the reader along in sheer delight.

For hundreds of years, other writers have learned from and imitated Swift, and readers have delighted in *Gulliver's Travels,* but he was much more than a writer.

Swift was born in Dublin on November 30, 1667. In 1689, when he was twenty-two, he took a job as secretary to Sir William Temple at Moor Park, Surrey. In 1694 he took holy orders and became "porebend" of Kilroot, County Antrim. But it was a wild and lonely place, and he soon tired of it. He returned to England to work for Sir William and while there tutored the young Esther Johnson, known later to his readers as "Stella," who was the daughter of a companion of Temple's sister. Stella was to become a great love of his life.

In 1704 Swift published *A Tale of a Tub,* which displayed something that ran through all his writing: honesty. In this case, he satirized religious cant. Like most of his writing at this time, it was published anonymously.

In 1701 he was appointed vicar of Laracor near Trim, County Meath, and over the next ten years or so he divided his time between there and London, where he did some work for the bishop. In London he became known for his witty conversation, and he and the literary lions of the day, such as William Congreve and Joseph Addison, were perennial companions in the coffeehouses and clubs.

He also had become known for his potent pen, and the Tories sought its services. He joined them, flaying the Whigs in pamphlets and lampoons for their war policies, and he contributed to the overthrow of the duke of Marlborough in 1711. He described his activities of these years in the delicious book *Journal to Stella.*

After all his efforts, he thought he would be appointed bishop by Queen Anne, but she was afraid of giving that much power and influence to a man who could pen something like *A Tale of a Tub* (it had become known that Swift was the author). He was assigned to St. Patrick's Cathedral in Dublin, which looked to him like exile rather than reward.

It is not certain if he ever married Stella, but it is known that at this time another woman entered his life, the beautiful Vanessa, the twenty-year-old daughter of Ester Vanhomrigh, a rich widow with property near Dublin. Vanessa was smitten by Swift, though from his writings of the time it seems he regarded her as more a friend than anything else.

Living in Ireland had its effect on Swift. This was the 1600s and early 1700s, a time when the Irish were treated in particularly inhumane and vicious ways by the English, and Swift flayed the English with his pen. He also gave money to build a mental hospital and performed many good works for the poor.

In 1720 Swift produced a pamphlet that recommended that the Irish boycott English linen, and in 1724, in *Drapier's Letters,* he succeeded in derailing an English scam involving foisting a new copper currency on the Irish.

The year 1726 saw the publication of *Gulliver's Travels,* which became a children's classic even though it had not been intended to be that, as well as "A Modest Proposal," which has been hailed as perhaps the finest satire ever written in English. In the essay, Swift suggests that the poverty of the Irish people could be alleviated if they were allowed to sell their many children to the rich as food—in other words, be paid by cannibals.

While he viciously attacked the English, he maintained friendships with Alexander Pope, John Gay, John Arbuthnot, and other luminaries because he had a capacity for friendship that was able to get around deep differences.

In 1728 Stella died. At the time, Swift was sixty, and her death seemed to have a traumatic effect on him. The last seventeen years of his life were marred by increasing giddiness and deafness; he was in terror of going insane. By 1742 he had slipped into such a lethargy that he could not even speak. Three years later he died and was buried in St. Patrick's Cathedral.

He was wickedly funny, but his tombstone bears the words that truly define him: FIERCE INDIGNATION CAN NO LONGER TEAR HIS HEART.

51

Bishop George Berkeley

(1 6 8 5 – 1 7 5 3)

He was a born teacher, an idealist, and a dreamer. His big dream of a university for all people did not come true, but as a teacher once said of him, "He had a passion of higher education and helped other people to have dreams that would come true."

Berkeley was born to a well-off family in Kilkenny, Ireland, on March 12, 1685. He was extremely bright and at the age of ten went off to Kilkenny College, a very special private school that still stands to this day. Born a Protestant, Berkeley (pronounced BARK-lee) went on to Trinity College in Dublin, where he taught logic, philosophy, theology, and Hebrew for twenty years.

He was a brilliant writer and when he was only twenty-three brought out one of his most famous works, "An Essay Towards a New Theory of Vision," which discussed whom we see as opposed to how we think we see. It was in perfect harmony with the inventions of the period—eyeglasses, telescope, microscope—which, in fact, enabled people to see better.

His writing gave him entrée to all kinds of places, and in the early 1700s he traveled extensively in Europe, lecturing and teaching. But he was appalled by what he saw in Europe: Industrialization had started, and with it seemed to come a concomitant moral decay.

He had a vision: to start a new school, which would be known as St. Paul's University, in the New World (America), where spiritual values could be taught. And in Berkeley's scheme of things, everyone would be welcome, including blacks and Indians, whom he considered savages.

He showed the courage of his convictions in presenting his ideas to the English Parliament. Some people thought the idea harebrained. But he persisted, and some important people such as Jonathan Swift endorsed his idea. He was able to persuade Parliament as well as King George I to back his proposal.

Berkeley extracted a promise that he would receive twenty thousand pounds to fund the school, which he calculated would best be built in Bermuda, where it would be between the northern and southern colonies. He then left for the New World, arriving in Newport, Rhode Island, in 1729 with his new wife and family in tow.

The school, he knew, would need food. He bought a ninety-six-acre plot in the town of Middletown to farm, his purpose being to grow food for the school there. He called it Whitehall Farm, after the street on which Parliament was located. Then he waited for the money to arrive so he could begin construction.

He waited two years and then was notified by one of the members of Parliament that the money would not be arriving. With that his dream died.

While he was in America, Berkeley was a frequent speaker at Trinity Church in Newport, and the parishioners tried to convince him to become their pastor. But his main concern was the school; when that didn't come to pass, he left America forever, going back to Ireland and settling in County Cork, where he became bishop of Cloyne.

Though some thought of him as English or American, he was Irish through and through, and he empathized closely with the suffering of those in his parish at Cloyne. Eamon de Valera used to refer to his writings frequently, and in 1985 Ireland issued a stamp in his memory.

Though his dream for a university never came true, his passion about higher education, as expressed in his speeches and writing, went a long way. It was recognized in a place, California, that Berkeley saw, when a school there was named after him.

52

John P. Holland

(1840–1914)

The scenario is unlikely but true. An Irishman named John P. Holland, a schoolteacher in Paterson, New Jersey, uses his spare time to invent a submarine or, at the very least, to put it on track to becoming a practical—indeed, deadly—weapon of war.

Holland was born in Liscannor Bay in County Clare in 1842. He was educated at the Limerick Christian Brothers School, and he originally intended to be a Christian Brother, to which end he took vows in 1858 and over the years taught in a number of different places. He also wanted to go to sea, but his poor eyesight prevented him from doing so.

In 1872 the family emigrated to the states, but before leaving Holland was released from his vows.

Holland, the son of a coastguardsman in Ireland, had no formal engineering education, but he started educating himself in engineering and drafting when he was very young and showed a brilliant aptitude for it. He had always been interested in submarines. After all, at the time the British navy was formidable, and Holland looked on the sub as a way of sneaking up unseen and sinking its ships.

In 1874 and 1875, when Holland was trying to first interest the U.S. Navy in his submarine, the idea was not new. Indeed, using a submarine to sink a warship had been demonstrated in the Civil War by the Confederate sub *Hulney*, which had succeeded in its attack on a warship but sunk in the process. And one hundred years before that a submarine invented by a man named David Bushnell had tried to sink a British ship during the Revolutionary War.

The navy thought the idea a bit preposterous, in part because Holland was not a sailor; this idea, of course, was also preposterous, as if only a sailor could invent a seagoing craft.

But the Fenians were interested. Though they had been dealt a serious blow in the war against England because of their defeat in Canada in 1866, a number of them had reassembled, and Holland presented his idea to them. He impressed them enough to invest some sixty thousand pounds from their "skirmishing fund" for him to build the real thing. He did, and one day the Fenians and Holland assembled on the banks of the Passaic River and the fourteen-foot craft was launched.

It didn't even float, quickly filling up with water and sinking to the bottom. But it was raised, and after an examination it was discovered that one of the workman had failed to install a pair of screws, which had left an opening for the water to pour in through.

The submarine was drained, the screws were installed, and Holland himself took it out. It floated, it dived, and—surely much to the relief and joy of Holland—it resurfaced.

Holland set about fine-tuning the craft. The plan for mounting an attack against British ships was already settled. Holland was well aware of the power of their ships, which made a direct confrontation foolhardy. Sneakiness would be the key. His plan involved launching the sub from a trapdoor in the side of an innocent-looking ship that would anchor near the British craft. It was a plan, indeed, that modern navies would use over and over again.

Then, in 1883, the Fenian organization abruptly started to deteriorate. One night a group of Fenians took the sub, which was anchored in New Jersey, hauled it up to New Haven, Connecticut, and tried to launch it. They didn't succeed, and they abandoned the craft at a nearby brass factory. Holland was incensed, and the great scheme was abandoned. Holland and the Fenians never communicated again.

Holland was truly ahead of his time. His theory about the submarine was that the best possible shape would be that of a cigar. But the soundness of this idea did not emerge until the 1950s, long after Holland was gone.

He never made any money from the submarine, and as time went by he started to be deeply concerned about the havoc a sub could wreak. The validity of his concerns was borne out particularly in World War II, when German "wolf packs" roamed the Atlantic, sending thousands of tons of materials and thousands of people, many of them civilians, to the bottom of the ocean.

Philip Sheridan

Wars are won by men who can be ruthless, who can make decisions where the end justifies the means, no matter how horrific. And certainly this is an apt way to describe Civil War soldier Philip Sheridan, general of the Union army and a man famed for his take-no-prisoners conduct of the war. His actions in the Civil War influenced not only its outcome but the simmering attitude of southerners long after the war.

Sheridan seemed incapable of showing mercy. He stood five feet four inches and was known as "Little Phil." But he certainly didn't seem so small to the Confederate armies who opposed him. At the end of the war, Abraham Lincoln, as reported by John A. Byrne in *Irish-American Landmarks,* said, "When this particular war began I thought a cavalryman had to be at least six feet four inches high, but I have changed my mind. Five feet four inches will do in a pinch."

Sheridan was raised in the little town of Somerset, south of Columbus, Ohio. Originally, his parents, both Irish immigrants from County Cavan, had gone to Albany, New York, at the behest of an uncle of Phil named Gainor. But employment opportunities were limited, and Sheridan's father, John, traveled to Ohio to get work on the railroad, which was pushing west.

Little Phil, one of six children, always seemed entranced by the military. He was in awe of local veterans. Supposedly, a blacksmith forged a little sword of tin for him when he was a boy, and he delighted in leading the other boys around.

He matriculated at West Point, but it was not easy going there. At the time the Irish, who were pouring into America, were not held in high regard, nor was Catholicism, both of which characteristics Sheridan possessed. Sheridan found himself the butt of all kinds of jokes and negative attitudes.

But he had a nasty temper, and one day early in his senior year, Sheridan did something that almost ended his military career—and the life of a fellow cadet. The cadet and Sheridan were marching in a parade, and the other cadet kept harassing him. Finally, Sheridan lost control, screamed that he would "run him through," and lunged at him with his bayonet, which was mounted on his rifle. The authorities didn't take kindly to attempted murder. Nevertheless, Sheridan got off lightly. The event got him suspended from school for nine months. He returned and finished his senior year, graduating in the bottom half of his class.

When the Civil War broke out, Sheridan joined the cavalry. He first came to the attention of General Ulysses S. Grant when he led a ferocious charge over the crest of Missionary Ridge in the battle of Chattanooga. Against the objections of others in the cabinet, Grant put Sheridan at the head of all Union cavalry troops, and his judgment proved sound. Sheridan won a number of important victories, one of which was a battle with the Confederate cavalry lead by the dashing and until that time invincible J. E. B. Stuart. Sheridan and his troops soundly trounced the Confederates and in the process inflicted a dispiriting blow: They killed Stuart.

But Sheridan's greatest renown came from his actions at Cedar Creek, called Middletown by the southerners, in the Shenandoah Valley. The valley, stretching 150 miles from the Blue Ridge Mountains on the East to the Alleghenies on the west, was like one big larder for the South, a place where the southern forces got all kinds of supplies, not the least of which was food grown on the farms.

Said Grant to Sheridan, "Eat out Virginia clear and clean, so that crows flying over it for the balance of the season will have to carry their own provender with them."

Sheridan followed Grant's instructions: He and his army charged across the countryside, burning everything in their wake—houses, crops, farm buildings—and in the process driving out the Confederates, who controlled the valley. Later, southerners would simply describe this action as "the Burning," and everyone would know what they were talking about.

But partway through his devastating action, Sheridan stopped and returned to Washington for a conference with the secretary of war. He figured the Confederates were on the run and would not counterattack. He was wrong. Jubal Early, the Confederate commander, waited until the Union soldiers were settled into their camp. Then he swept down on them, driving them back and taking thirteen hundred prisoners.

Sheridan, meanwhile, was on his way back. While eating breakfast some distance from the fighting, he heard the sound of gunfire, got onto his horse, and galloped toward the sound. He was shocked to meet his retreating, bedraggled, and routed troops. Sheridan screamed at them to stop, turn, and fight, and he was able to reorganize them into a counterattack.

Early and his men, sifting through abandoned Union supplies and equipment they sorely needed in what was to be the last year of the war, were caught by surprise and routed. It was a key defeat, and from that time on, the Confederates never returned to the valley.

After the war, Sheridan was sent to do battle with Mexico. For a while he was military governor of Louisiana and Texas, but his policies were so harsh that after six months he was dispatched out west to do what he did best: fight, in this case Indians. He engaged in battles that were little more than ruthless massacres. Attributed to him is the famous line "The only good Indian is a dead Indian."

Sheridan's rise through the ranks paralleled that of William Tecumseh Sherman. When, after the war, Sherman was named commander of all forces, Sheridan was promoted to lieutenant general. In 1884 Sheridan took Sherman's position as commander of all forces.

There are many statues to Sheridan, but the best known is in Sheridan Circle in Washington. Standing about nine feet taller—fourteen feet high—than he did in life, Sheridan is shown on his horse Rienzi in the Battle of Cedar Creek.

Sir Roger Casement

(1864–1916)

Sir Roger Casement is another of the revolutionaries involved in the Easter Rising of 1916, about which Hollywood is sure to make a movie one day. It was an event filled with passion, heroics, and dark intrigue.

Casement was born in Sadycove, Dublin County, on September 1, 1864, and educated at Ballymena Academy. He seemed to be a man who identified with those who were victimized. After serving in Africa in 1884 as part of the British Colonial Service, he made a significant report on the terrible treatment given workers in the Belgian Congo. He also traveled to South America, where he investigated the treatment of people working at the Peruvian Rubber Plantation on the Putamayo River, and his report created a worldwide sensation when it was published in 1912.

He was such a servant to the Crown that in 1911 he was knighted for his service: The same year that his rubber plantation report was published, he retired from public service.

Despite his service to the Crown, Casement was always a person who yearned for Irish independence; he was a person who identified with the oppressed and downtrodden. In 1914 he traveled to Berlin to try to get Germany's backing in gaining Irish independence. He also tried to assemble a brigade composed of Irish prisoners but did not succeed.

In April 1916 the Germans finally sent help—a boatload of arms that landed at Banna Strand, Tralee Bay, to be used in the Easter Rising. Casement followed in a submarine.

But disaster struck. The British discovered the shipment, seized the ship—the *Aud*—and blew it up. Casement was captured and put on trial for treason. His trial was covered worldwide. He was found guilty and sentenced to be hanged.

The sentence triggered a flurry of pleas by influential people trying to save his life. There was a very strong sentiment in America that he should not die.

He might have been saved because he had public opinion on his side, but then there emerged copies of the so-called black diaries kept by Casement, who was a homosexual. One of his biographers, Rene Mac-Coll, says that the diaries were legitimate. Nevertheless, using them in the trial was a devious stratagem that helped turn public opinion against Casement. (The British government reputedly distributed them.) Like other patriots of the Easter Rising, Casement was executed, he on August 3, 1916.

His contribution to Ireland was never forgotten. In 1965, fifty years after he had been killed, his remains were returned to Ireland and were later buried in Glasnevin Cemetery after a state funeral.

Oscar Wilde

(1854–1900)

In his time, Oscar Wilde was famous for three things. One was his quick wit, which he showed early. Once, biographer Mark Nichols says of him, Wilde, all of sixteen, was at a grand party and had the temerity to ask one of the unmarried titled ladies to dance. She looked down her lorgnette at him and said, derisively, "Do you think I'm going to dance with a child?" Wilde snapped back, "Madam, if I had known you were in that condition, I never would have asked you!"

Wilde was also known for his writing, including the play *The Importance of Being Earnest,* and his witty poems such as:

Humanity takes itself too seriously.
It is the world's original sin. If
the caveman had known how to laugh,
history would have been different.

But Wilde has become most famous—or infamous—for a celebrated court case in which he was tried for his homosexual activities, or as people called them back then, "the love that dare not speak its name."

Wilde was born in Dublin on October 16, 1854, the son of Sir William Wilde and Jane Francesca Elgee. He was educated at the Portora Royal School and Oxford, where he excelled. He won the Newgate Prize for Poetry in 1878, graduated first in his class with honors in classics and humanities, and became well known for his conversation and repartee. In 1882 he toured the United States, laying out his aesthetic philosophy, the core of which was "art for art's sake."

Returning to London, he spent the next six years reviewing books. In 1884 he married Constance Lloyd and spent the next two years editing a journal, *Woman's World.* He started his literary career with the publication, in 1888, of *The Happy Prince and Other Tales,* a collection of delightful fantasy stories. In 1891 he produced his only novel, *The Picture of Dorian Gray*, which was poorly reviewed. Years later the book was made into a mesmerizing movie of the same name.

He had dabbled in drama before this time—unsuccessfully—but when his first comedy, *Lady Windermere's Fan*, was produced in 1892, it garnered raves and was a hit with the public. Three more comedies followed: *A Woman of No Importance* was produced in 1893, and 1895 saw two of his plays hit the boards, *An Ideal Husband* and *The Importance of Being Earnest.*

All his comedies reflected the witty Wilde, their lines epigrammatic and sharp. Of all the plays, *The Importance of Being Earnest* is considered his masterpiece and is periodically revived.

While some critics think him inconsequential in terms of literature, that is not a universal opinion. No less a giant of literature than George Bernard Shaw thought Wilde's work substantial and influential.

In his private life, Wilde apparently periodically picked up what would today be characterized as "rough trade" (professional sexual predators) for sexual dalliances. But his decline and fall began with his relationship with Lord Alfred Douglas, whose father was the marquis of Queensberry. The marquis, who had formulated rules for boxing, played by no rules when it came to his son.

The marquis disapproved mightily of Wilde and Douglas's being together—they flaunted their relationship in public—and he started a campaign of harassment against Wilde, including publicly characterizing Wilde as a "sodomite."

Spurred on by Douglas, Wilde sued the marquis for libel. However, the trial in 1895 turned into an indictment not of the marquis, but of Wilde. Under a withering cross-examination by Edward Carson, who would go on to become prime minister of Ulster, seamy details of Wilde's life were unearthed, actions that at the time were criminal offenses to the Victorian mind. Following the libel suit, which he lost, Wilde was arrested.

Wilde was tried and convicted of criminal offenses. The judge, after he had issued a declamatory harangue about how evil Wilde was, completed his thoughts by saying, "People who do these things must be dead of a sense of shame, and one cannot hope to produce any effect on them. It is the worst case I have ever tried."

Wilde was pilloried not just because he was homosexual. As writer Michael Musto points out in an article for *Interview* magazine in July 1996, Wilde's homosexual activities

> were not the only aspects of his personality that made him anathema to the Victorian middle classes. In fact, during the course of the trial Wilde symbolized a much broader spectrum of perceived decadence and degeneration that to late Victorians threatened cultural collapse as the century drew to a close. In short, Wilde functioned as a cultural lightning rod for an anxious fin de siècle England.

Wilde served the maximum sentence—two years—in Reading Gaol, and it was a bitter, humiliating, and life-sapping experience that broke him. Three years later, in 1900, he died of cerebral meningitis, after receiving last rites from a Catholic priest. His wife had died in 1896, while he was in prison; he was survived by two sons.

Wilde is often held up as a symbol of gay courage, but anyone who knows the details of the case knows that is not true. Indeed, in 1905 his posthumous apology in effect for being gay, *De Profundis*, was published. Wilde's real problem was very simple, though: He was born about a hundred years too early.

56

Anne Sullivan Macy

(1866–1936)

Six months after she was born in 1880 in Tuscumbia, Alabama, Helen Keller said her first word, and she was walking by her first birthday. Her parents, Captain Arthur H. Keller, an ex–Confederate soldier, and her mother, Katherine Adams, a beautiful belle from Memphis with relatives in the famous Adams family of Massachusetts, were very happy with their bright, energetic child.

Then, in February 1882, little Helen became desperately ill. She ran a terribly high fever, and the doctor who came by diagnosed her condition as "brain congestion," which in modern parlance might be encephalitis. She hovered between life and death, and then somehow the fever subsided and she survived. This was the first of a number of miracles, but her parents were horrified to find out that the illness had left her both deaf and blind.

For the next six years her parents, feeling terrible about what had happened to their baby, indulged her, and Helen gradually made their lives miserable: She was unruly and angry, with no table manners or indeed any manners at all. She was a terrible burden.

In desperation, Katherine Keller contacted Dr. Alexander Graham Bell, inventor of the telephone, who was in Washington, D.C., working on developing a device for the deaf. Bell couldn't help her, but he referred her to the Perkins Institution for the Blind in Boston, where he knew of a Dr. Samuel Howe who had succeeded in communicating with a deaf and blind girl by tapping on her hand.

On March 3, 1887, Anne Sullivan, twenty-one, the daughter of impoverished Irish immigrants from County Limerick and with limited sight herself, met Helen. It was a momentous meeting: Years later, Helen would identify that day as the day her soul was born.

The two women were together for fifty years, even after Sullivan was married to John Macy. In the beginning, and for many years, Annie Sullivan was Helen Keller's conduit to the world.

And in the beginning, it wasn't easy. Annie Sullivan had ways to teach Helen to communicate, but before she could do that she knew she had to teach the child discipline. She and Helen moved into a small cottage on the Keller property and started their work.

The struggle of Annie Sullivan and Helen Keller was magnificently portrayed many years ago in a play, *The Miracle Worker.* It was a long, hard struggle, but eventually Sullivan won the day, and for the first time since she had been stricken by the illness, Keller was able to communicate.

The method Sullivan used was to spell words in Keller's hands. When Sullivan first started doing this, Helen was able to repeat the words easily, but she didn't know what they meant. Then one day, Helen had her hand under a stream of cold water near Sullivan. Suddenly she connected the stream of water with the symbols for "water" being drawn in her hand by Sullivan. From that moment on, she couldn't learn enough.

Keller and Sullivan's hand language became quite extensive and sophisticated, and Keller also learned to read Braille. To sharpen Keller's abilities even more, Sullivan started taking her to the Perkins Institution, where she could read many Braille books and use a variety of teaching aids.

The great thing about Keller was her spirit. Though she had been robbed of two precious senses, she remained undefeated all her life. She was an upbeat person, cheerful, witty, eager to be liked—and pretty, with sparkling blue eyes, brown hair, fine features, and a trim figure. Annie Sullivan was like Keller in many ways, particularly in terms of her spirit.

Over the years, with Sullivan as her constant companion, Keller increased her communication skills. Indeed, it took her twenty-five years, but ultimately she was able to speak in a way that people could understand. Speaking was not her only achievement; in 1899 she took the entrance exam for Radcliffe College, Sullivan by her side tapping the various questions into her hand.

Anne Sullivan passed away in 1936. It wasn't until 1968 that Keller died.

57

Edmund Burke

(1729–1797)

Edmund Burke was a writer and orator of great skill, and he was to have a significant influence on the independence not only of Ireland but of America. He was one of the greatest thinkers the British Isles have ever known.

Burke was born during the height of the Penal Laws, on January 12, 1729. His father was a Protestant lawyer—which was what he wanted Edmund to be—and his mother a Catholic.

He entered Trinity College, Dublin, in 1744. After graduating, he entered the Middle Temple, London, where he studied law. Unfortunately, he failed to become a barrister, a circumstance that estranged him from his father.

In 1757 he married Jane Nugent, the daughter of his Irish Catholic doctor. To support his family, he took a job as editor of the *Annual Register,* a publication he would be associated with for thirty years.

Burke was not a smooth orator. He had a harsh voice and was given to awkward gestures. (In fact, he was so bad a speaker that people would sometimes leave during his speeches.) But he was brilliant, and his power was created by the potency of his ideas: They made people think.

Eventually, Burke found himself in politics, becoming secretary to Lord Rockingham, the new prime minister, and entering Parliament as member for Bristol in 1765.

One of England's problems at the time was America. The colonies were becoming more and more difficult to manage, and the problems were starting to build to the breaking point. Burke, speaking in Parliament, advised conciliation rather than more violent methods and was able to persuade enough of his colleagues to his point of view. He wrote a number of speeches and pamphlets that received a wide readership: The speeches "American Taxation" and "Conciliation with the Colonies" came out in 1774 and 1775 respectively, and the pamphlet "Letter to the Sheriffs of Bristol" came out in 1777—all conciliatory, liberal, and brilliant. They had a wide audience and were much discussed.

Burke also fought for conciliation and intelligence in dealing with Ireland. In three letters, penned after the colonies had achieved their independence, he laid out a simple yet powerful point to his colleagues in Parliament: Stupidity had lost the colonies, and the same kind of stupidity would lose Ireland. He advocated conciliation and legislative independence.

The reaction was to accuse him of Catholicism, and he was voted out of his seat in Parliament, which he never regained. However, he was able to win the seat at the borough of Malton, and in 1782, when Rockingham returned to power, Burke was appointed paymaster and privy councilor. He immediately endeared himself to his colleagues by reducing his own salary from twenty thousand pounds a year to four thousand and effecting reforms that affected other public officials.

As Burke grew older, he grew more conservative, and in the 1780s he opposed Pitt's measure for free trade with Ireland and the so-called Commercial Treaty with France. In 1790 he wrote his acknowledged masterpiece, "Reflections on the French Revolution," which strongly encouraged rulers to resist revolutionary activity. In a number of publications that followed, Burke even encouraged rulers to suppress free opinion.

Burke's ideas were to exert an influence long after he was gone. For example, his ideas were instrumental in the formation of the Canadian government. And his thoughts, along with Benjamin Disraeli's, were to become the foundation of modern conservatism. Historians acknowledge that his philosophy had a large impact on the politics of a variety of nations, including Russia.

58

Thomas Murray

(1860–1929)

His name is not a household name like Edison's or Bell's, but Thomas Murray was an inventor on a prodigious scale. He held patents on more than eleven hundred items, most safety devices, and only Edison has more.

Murray was born in Albany, New York, the son of John Murray and Anastasia McGrath. When he was nine, his father died, necessitating his going to work. The jobs he got would prove to serve an inventor such as himself quite well. While attending night school, he worked in the drafting room of local engineers and architects. He also worked in a variety of machine shops for four years.

In 1881 Murray got a job supervising the power station of the Municipal Gas Company in Albany. He rose quickly and soon was involved in a variety of other properties owned by the company, including the Troy Electric Light Company and the Kings County Electric Light and Power Company. He was also involved in helping to form the Edison

Electric Illuminating Company, which came to be known as the Brooklyn Edison Company.

In 1895 Murray was given a large assignment in New York City, managing the consolidating electric companies, and within five years he was general manager. As time went by, he rose to greater importance in the power industry in New York. He also supervised or designed various power stations that supply the city's neighborhoods, such as Hell's Gate, East River, and Williamsburg. Murray also went upstate and out of state to design power plants. For example, he designed a hydroelectric power plant in Chattanooga, Tennessee.

While Murray was working, he was also inventing. Many of his early inventions were in the gas appliance and electric fields. He invented water wall furnaces for steam boilers, copper radiators, cinder catchers, pulverized fuel equipment, automatic welding equipment, and electrical protection devices. One of his inventions was important to the U.S. armed forces: Under tests, it was found that only Murray's method of welding 240-millimeter mortar shells was viable.

He also worked with Thomas Edison on a number of Edison's electrical projects. When it came to inventions, Murray's family thought he was the greatest inventor ever, even greater than Edison. One of his grandchildren said in *Real Lace: America's Irish Rich* by Stephan Birmingham, in speaking about the lightbulb:

Thomas Edison's invention may have been more spectacular and showy, with the incandescent bulb. But Grandpa Murray [a name everyone commonly called him] virtually invented everything but the light bulb—the circuits, switches, dynamos, and power systems that got electricity to the bulb. In my opinion, it was a more important contribution. After all, if there hadn't been a way to get power into the bulbs, how would the bulbs light up?

Murray was indeed an almost compulsive inventor. At night he kept a pile of thin copper plates and a metal stylus near his bed. If an idea struck him, he would get up and immediately sketch it out on the copper.

He could also invent on the spot, as it were. When he had accumulated considerable wealth, he and his family took a home in Southampton on Long Island—he had nine children, and ultimately was to have thirty-seven grandchildren, almost all of whom would gather every Sunday for dinner at the house. He built two pools fed by saltwater from the sea. The problem was that the sand from the bottom of the ocean would also flow into the pool. Grandpa Murray broke out his stylus and copper plate and invented a filter to keep the sand out.

Murray was a staunch Catholic and believed in "corporal works of mercy." He would always use what eventually was vast wealth to help the needy.

Murray was a lover of yellow taffy, and he would hand it out to whoever would want it. But taffy turned out not to be too good for him. In July 21, 1929—in those preinsulin days—he contracted diabetes and died later at the age of sixty-nine.

Perhaps the most amazing thing about Murray's life is that except for the in-depth coverage given him in Birmingham's 1973 book, little has been written about him, and he tends to get overlooked even in roundups of inventors and scientists. He shouldn't be. He was truly an important figure.

59

Robert Fulton

(1 7 6 5 – 1 8 1 5)

Many people think that Robert Fulton invented the steamboat. In fact, variations of a steam-powered boat were on the scene (and in the water) before Fulton. His achievement was to show that a properly made steamboat was technically achievable and could be a viable mode of transportation.

Fulton was the son of Robert Fulton, a leading citizen of Lancaster County, Pennsylvania. Early on, Fulton showed a remarkable ability to draw, and when just a teenager, he was employed by local gunsmiths to draw designs for their guns.

His abilities were so good that when he was seventeen he left Lancaster County for Philadelphia and set himself up as a portrait painter and miniaturist, an artist who painted miniature pictures on cameos and the like. Deciding to advance his painting education, after four years he left America for England, intending to study under the painter Benjamin West.

But he was not prepared for what greeted him in England. The Industrial Revolution was in full swing, with canals, factories, mines, bridges, and all kinds of new equipment coming into play. Fulton was enthralled with it all, so much so that he switched careers, putting aside painting for engineering.

When he was just fourteen years old, Fulton had designed a steamboat powdered by paddle wheels. Now he wanted to put his design into action. He appealed to the British government to let him buy a steam engine and ship it to America. The government at first refused his request, having put a ban on this practice.

Fulton kept trying for three years, but he was by no means idle meanwhile. He designed and patented a variety of devices, including one for hauling canal boats over difficult terrain, dredges for canal work, and a machine that could twist hemp into rope.

But the British were adamant about shipping the engine, and after a while Fulton gave up. He went to France, where he tried unsuccessfully to interest people in his inventions. He also conducted tests on a submarine, called the *Nautilus*, that he had invented as well as fitting steam engines on ships.

Then an event occurred that eased the way. He met Robert Livingston, who had been a partner in another steamboat invention and American minister to the French government. In 1803 the two men importuned the British government again, and this time they were able to buy an engine from the firm of Boulton and Watt. Still, they had to wait another three years before they could get authorization to ship it to the States.

In New York City, Fulton and Livingston set about the task of making the idea work. Livingston favored a rear paddle, while Fulton favored a paddle wheel on each side, the design they eventually chose.

They installed a twenty-four-horsepower steam engine into the hundred-foot-long *Clermont,* and on August 17, 1807, it made its first voyage up the Hudson River, traveling about five miles an hour.

The trip was successful, and a few weeks later the boat made its first commercial run. Only a few hardy souls got on, but as the *Clermont* kept to its regular schedule, more and more passengers used it. By the time the operation was closed for the winter, a small profit was being turned.

Because it could give such a smooth ride (if the water was smooth, as on the Hudson or Mississippi), Fulton was able to install furniture, and thus he introduced American to luxury steamboating. He built twenty more boats, each fancier than its predecessor, and steamboats spread across the country.

When the War of 1812 broke out, Fulton was focused on designing submarines and warships. He was in the midst of building a huge steam-powered ship with great destructive capacity when he died of a respiratory ailment on February 15, 1815, shortly before news of the war's being over reached America.

Father
Theodore M. Hesburgh

(1 9 1 7 –   )

The distinguished writer and priest Andrew Greeley stated in his 1981 book *The Irish-Americans: The Rise to Money and Power* that the most influential "Irish priest in America, both inside and outside the Church, is Notre Dame's President Theodore M. Hesburgh."

Theodore Martin Hesburgh had a father who was of German heritage and a mother, Anne Marie Murphy, who was Irish. He was born in Syracuse, New York, and dates his desire to be a priest from the ripe old age of four.

A Jesuit priest who was a friend of the family tried to get him to become a Jesuit priest, but instead, after graduating from high school in 1934, he matriculated at Notre Dame and entered the Holy Cross Order. He got his B.A. in 1940, and studied theology at Holy Cross Seminary in

Washington, D.C. He was ordained a priest on June 24, 1943. He volunteered to be a missionary but was instead assigned to Notre Dame in 1945 as a teacher and chaplain to the World War II veterans on campus.

When Hesburgh arrived on the campus, the students were subject to a wide variety of arbitrary, rigid controls, including having to attend mass three times a week and being subjected to bed checks as well as lights out at midnight. Hesburgh became a student advocate. The president of the university, Father John J. Cavanagh, recognized the need for someone like Hesburgh and named him vice president. When Cavanaugh retired in 1952, Hesburgh became president.

During his time as president, Hesburgh made vast changes. The curriculum was enlarged and deepened, and the school became coeducational. Because of outstanding fund-raising activities, Hesburgh was able to add nine buildings, new staff, and more students to bring the university up to the level of an Ivy League university.

Father Hesburgh has been outspoken in his criticism of Rome (for example, he told Pope Paul VI that he thought the pope's 1968 encyclical on birth control was a mistake and he supported the right of Father James T. Burchaell to question the same document).

At the height of the Vietnam War, Hesburgh was also involved in a worldwide controversy. When antiwar disturbances were at their zenith in 1969, he issued an ultimatum on campus:

> Anyone or any group that substitutes force for rational persuasion, be it violent or nonviolent, will be given fifteen minutes of medita-

tion to cease and desist. They will be told that they are, by their actions, going counter to the overwhelming conviction of this community as to what is proper here. If they do not within the period cease and desist, they will be asked for their identity cards. Those who produce these will be suspended from the community as not understanding what this community is. Those who do not have or will not produce identity cards will be assumed not to be members of the community and will be charged with disturbing the peace on private property and treated accordingly by the law.

The memo succeeded in quelling the disturbances, but also achieved a reputation for Hesburgh as a hard-liner. He hardly was or is. Indeed, following this incident he wrote to the White House suggesting that it would be wrong to come down too hard on students protesting the war.

While he has made a huge difference in the university, it is on the outside where his greatest influence has been felt. Over the past forty years or so, he has walked the corridors of power in this country and elsewhere. As Greeley details, Hesburgh has "represented the Church in Washington and in United Nations meetings, at the Rockefeller Foundation, in Antarctica, in organizing and promoting the Green Revolution, on the United States Civil Rights Commission, at world conferences, in the councils of the mighty and poor parishes in Mexico." Indeed, a campus joke used to be: "God is everywhere; Father Ted is everywhere but Notre Dame."

Alfred Thayer Mahan

(1840–1914)

Some books and some writers have a profound effect on what happens in the world, and many times the writers are well known. But sometimes, even though a work has a profound effect, the writer may remain in relative obscurity. Such a writer was Alfred Thayer Mahan, who wrote about naval warfare and whose writing was one of the driving forces behind America's assembling the most powerful navy in the world.

Mahan's father, Thomas, an Irish immigrant who had fled from Ireland after the unsuccessful rising of 1798, was a teacher at West Point and a distinguished author himself. For example, he had written the military classics *Complete Treatise on Military Fortifications* and *Course of Civil Engineering,* which were to influence generals on both sides in the Civil War.

But his son Alfred felt the call of the sea, and he graduated first in his 1859 class at Annapolis. He served in the navy during the Civil War and also became an instructor at Annapolis.

Alfred had always been interested in naval warfare, and he studied its history from ancient times to his day. This study was to lead to the central insight of his life: Whoever controls the sea controls the war. He wrote, "All at once I realized that control of the sea was an historic factor which never had been systematically appreciated and expounded."

Mahan gave numerous examples to prove his premise. About the Peloponnesian War, for example, he wrote: "It struck me how different things could have been if Hannibal could have invaded Carthage by sea . . . or, after arrival, been in touch with Carthage by water."

Mahan first expounded his theories in a series of lectures in front of the Naval War College in Newport, Rhode Island, where he had become an instructor in 1885, and in 1890 a collection of these lectures was published under the title *The Influence of Sea Power upon History, 1660–1783*.

It was read assiduously by a military audience, who were stunned by its brilliance. But the most important reader was Theodore Roosevelt. He had written a book on sea power based on the War of 1812, but he read Mahan's book straight through and pronounced it a naval classic. Its influence was felt a decade later; when Roosevelt set about the task of converting the American navy from a glorified coast guard into a world naval power, *The Influence of Sea Power upon History* was his blueprint.

Several of Mahan's other books were also published, including *The Influence of Sea Power upon the French Revolution and Empire, 1793–1812* (1892) and *The Interest of America in Sea Power* (1897).

Thomas Burke

(1849–1925)

The cliché goes that the Irish are a bigoted, narrow-minded people who are unfailingly intolerant of the rights of others. At times, the Irish have been like that, and there have been some shameful moments, such as the Irish stoning of blacks in the 1800s to drive them off their jobs in New Orleans.

However, many of the biographies in this book put the lie to that presumption. On the contrary, having been oppressed by conquerors themselves for so many years, the Irish are generally tolerant and liberal-thinking, and many have conducted themselves that way in the face of harsh opposition, even the threat of death. One of these was Thomas Burke, a son of Irish immigrants known out West as the "Man Who Built Seattle."

During his time, Seattle, Washington, was tough, raw, and undeveloped, and was deeply involved in building railroads. It also seemed to have a bottomless supply of Chinese laborers. But the Chinese had problems. They were not allowed to become citizens nor to bring their wives to live in the area. Starved for female companionship, they frequently got into trouble with the law because of their involvement with the many prostitutes who worked the area.

In 1886 the pent-up rage of the population overflowed against the Chinese, but Burke took their side. By then an attorney in Seattle for eleven years, he maintained that they had a right to citizenship and all the rights enjoyed by everyone else. The result was that Burke literally had to run for his life; a crowd of rabble-rousers just missed hanging him.

Burke had traveled a winding road from his home to Seattle. He was born in upstate New York in December 1849, the child of Irish immigrants who had fled from the potato famine. But the early death of his mother uprooted the family, and they settled in Iowa and then went to Ypsilanti, Michigan.

Burke worked and continued to go to school, ultimately graduating from Ypsilanti Academy. He then went on to become a lawyer, studying for two years at the University of Michigan. In 1873 he was admitted to the bar, and that same year he was appointed city attorney of Marshall, Michigan.

But being city attorney did not totally satisfy him. He wanted to be part of big business, so he looked west, where business was booming—in Seattle—and in 1875 headed out there. It didn't take him long to get somewhere. In 1878 and then again in 1880 and 1882, he was elected probate judge.

No city can thrive without transportation, and Burke was just what the city needed. He turned out to be a railroad man through and through. He became general counsel to the Great Northern Railway and convinced its chief executive officer, J. J. Hill, to use Seattle as the terminus of the railroad, which began in Minneapolis. He also worked at and succeeded in getting railroads such as the Walla Walla and the Seattle, Lakeshore, and Eastern Railway to link up with the Union Pacific. And he did other good works, most related to the enhancement of the city.

The one thing he didn't seem able to achieve was high public office. In the late 1880s he ran for Congress with negative results. He also tried to get elected to the U.S. Senate in 1910, by which time he had switched his party allegiance from the Democrats to the Republicans, but lost. His skills were appreciated at the highest levels, though, and at one point President Theodore Roosevelt offered him an ambassadorship to China, which he declined.

He died in 1925, a revered member of the community and one who had helped bring a great city into being.

Edward M. "Ted" Kennedy

(1932–)

For many people, Ted Kennedy will forever be the man who in 1969 drove a car off a bridge into a river connecting Martha's Vineyard with the island of Chappaquiddick. In the vehicle with him was a pretty young woman—not his wife—who drowned while, many speculate, he fled the scene and chose not to report the accident for ten hours. That single event, which sullied Kennedy's reputation beyond redemption, killed all hopes that Kennedy would one day be president.

To other people, Ted Kennedy is a beefy-faced man who likes to drink and carouse, the perfect butt of jokes by early-morning and late-night comedians.

And to yet others he is the proverbial bleeding-heart liberal who will, as one politico once said, "cry at the drop of a welfare check."

But these nasty clichés hardly define the real person. Nowhere does Kennedy the person shine more than in his work as a senator. For more than thirty-five years he has been at the forefront of legislative change, his eyes always on bettering the lives of the less fortunate among us. His influence can be seen on almost every bill that has been passed relative to health care, the handicapped, or the young. Even Republicans describe Kennedy as a "workhorse," as Donna Cassata said in the July 13, 1994, issue of *Congressional Quarterly Weekly Report,* "who crafts bipartisan legislation, deftly negotiating with skills honed through more than three decades of service." Indeed, his work has won the grudging, on-the-record admiration of more than one Republican.

"Republicans lack anyone like him," said Paul M. Weyrich, president of the conservative Free Congress Research and Education Foundation. "He is willing to do whatever it takes to win. He has a lot of Republicans on the run. He's much more liberal than the rest of the country. He comes from a state out of touch. He represents a failed ideology . . . but by sheer will, he makes those Republicans run. I admire it."

Kennedy is highly regarded for his efforts in the peace process in Ireland. It is known that he was instrumental in getting President Clinton involved in negotiating a peace treaty between the Republic of Ireland and Northern Ireland, and he is in close touch with the situation. Indeed, the Irish regard him very highly.

Niall O'Dowd, publisher of *Irish America Magazine,* wrote, "He has led the cause of Ireland on Capitol Hill for over a generation now and has often received little recognition in return. I am convinced that when the history of the era is written, however, that he will loom largest of all. He deserves the gratitude and respect of every Irish American for what he has done."

And Ted Kennedy is a man with an ability to win elections, even when those around him are buried. In 1994, for example, many predicted that Ted Kennedy, after decades in the Senate, would be swept out of office by a Republican tidal wave. The wave came and did sweep many Democrats out of office; but though battered, Kennedy, much to the consternation of his Republican foes, was still standing.

Born to privilege, Ted was subject to the same kind of dominance by his father, Joseph, as the other Kennedy boys were. It would have been very hard to predict that he would achieve what he did.

He was always regarded as the lesser Kennedy even by those in the Kennedy clan. But in 1962 it was decided he should run for the congressional seat in Massachusetts that his brother John had held. His opponent was Edward McCormick, son of the speaker of the House and not a lightweight by any stretch of the imagination. In fact, the Kennedys reportedly offered to put McCormick into a position where he could acquire work that would net him more than one hundred thousand dollars, which happened to be what he owed at the time, plus other perks, but McCormick refused. He thought he could beat Kennedy.

The Kennedys did too. McCormick challenged Ted to a televised debate. Beforehand the Kennedys, including John, who was president at the time, got Ted into a room and peppered him with possible questions, telling him to memorize his answers and not to lose his temper.

Kennedy won the debate not so much because of what he said but because of what he didn't say. McCormick ripped into his inexperience and his heavyweight political baggage, and Kennedy stood mute.

McCormick's attacks backfired; voters identified with Kennedy, and he won the election.

His stints in Congress were followed by his defeating George Lodge—another Boston Brahmin—in the Massachusetts senatorial race and he was poised to run for president in 1972. Then, on July 11, 1969, came Chappaquiddick.

Kennedy stayed out of the limelight and was expected to be trounced in the next senatorial election, but pundits were wrong. The people of Massachusetts had forgiven if not forgotten, and he went back to office with an overwhelming mandate—78 percent of the vote.

In 1980 he made a run for president, and when he started, he was leading Jimmy Carter for the Democratic nomination by an astonishing two-to-one margin. But Carter wrested the nomination away, and Kennedy's presidential aspirations evaporated.

Nevertheless, anyone who expected Ted Kennedy simply to lick his wounds and hide in a corner was in error. He stood before the convention and delivered an electrifying speech that defined his life and the dreams of his party for all: "The work goes on," he said. "The dream shall never die."

As history would prove, this was not just verbiage to excite a partisan crowd. Kennedy meant it, and he lived it. He cared deeply for others, putting his heart, mind, and strength to the task of making life better, particularly for the less fortunate. And in the end, what he has achieved makes him the greatest Kennedy of all.

Mary Robinson

(1944–)

A few years ago a staff member at Washington's Blair House, where visiting heads of state often reside, knocked at the door of one of the suites and handed the morning newspapers to a woman in hair curlers and bathrobe who answered the door, telling her that it was very important that the Irish president, who was a guest, read them, as they contained stories on the president's visit to the United States. The woman thanked the staffer, told her she would do so, and closed the door.

And so she would, because she was Mary Robinson, the president of Ireland herself.

Her appearance in the doorway in hair curlers and bathrobe is in perfect keeping with the image Robinson projects—and lives. She is a woman of the people, unassuming, down to earth, and possessed of a personality in which pose and pretension have no place.

Robinson is much more than plain and personable. She has also made a career of being controversial, speaking her mind about and backing such issues as gay rights, legal divorce, and contraception. And as if to emphasize her views, Robinson, a Roman Catholic, is married to a Protestant.

She truly seems to be concerned more with what is right than what is politically expedient. Conciliation, fair play, and reaching out are quintessential components of her personality. So is the courage of her convictions. In November 1985, when Robinson was a member of the Irish Labour Party, the coalition government in Ireland signed an agreement with England on Northern Ireland. But she didn't; instead she resigned, because she felt that the pact was unfair to the province's Protestant majority.

Mary Bourke was born on May 21, 1944, in Ballina, County Mayo, the only girl among five children. Extremely bright, she obtained a B.A. in French from Trinity College, where the faculty and students are largely Protestant, and obtained a law degree from Dublin University. She then went to graduate school in the United States, at Harvard, and had the chance to observe the turmoil over the Vietnam War up close. She considered it "very refreshing . . . that everything was up for examination."

Back in Ireland, she married Nicholas Robinson, a lawyer she had met at Dublin University. She was a constitutional scholar and senator by the time she was twenty-five—and a woman possessed of fiery oratorical skills.

She haunted the courts in Ireland and abroad, fighting against discrimination against gays; for gender equality in social welfare benefits and taxation; and against discrimination against women in the jury system. She championed the rights of single mothers and the right to contraception, and the opposition played very dirty: One morning when she went to her mailbox, she discovered it full of condoms—used.

But partly as a result of her efforts, there have been vast changes in Ireland. Gays have far more rights, and divorce is legal, as is contraception. She made much more of the office of president, which until her election was widely viewed as just ceremonial.

Her achieving the presidency of Ireland was almost a fluke. In 1990, Dick Spring, who at the time was leader of the Labour Party and Ireland's foreign minister and deputy prime minister, proffered her as candidate for president. While Spring was totally aware of her independence of mind, which had caused friction with Labour Party politicos, he also calculated that her beliefs might allow her to capture independent voters in parts of Ireland where the party had previously not garnered many votes.

Spring's analysis was right, but it was Robinson who brought out the vote. She understood the power of local communities, and for six months she traveled all over Ireland—to housing projects, rape crisis centers, and agricultural cooperatives. She even crossed choppy seas to visit people living on islands off Ireland's western coast. She spoke one-on-one and to small groups, trying to be, as she told a reporter, "conscious of the opportunity to reconcile differences . . . rather than to confront and challenge, to draw out people's fears and hopes and aspirations."

And she encouraged Irishwomen, who had long been out of the mainstream of Irish politics—in fact, the 1937 constitution had established homemaking as their primary role—to get involved.

During her campaign, Robinson became well known, as did her message. Indeed, in one advertising billboard for her, a huge black-and-white photo showing a group of women sitting around talking, Robinson is there but not even identified. The only writing, across the bottom, stated, "You have a voice. I will make it heard."

She was elected president and was very popular—she earned a 93 percent approval rating in 1995. She held the office until 1997, when she took on the office of high commissioner of human rights at the United Nations.

William Randolph Hearst

(1863–1951)

There seems little doubt that the character played by Orson Welles in the movie *Citizen Kane* was based on William Randolph Hearst. Hearst himself gave credence to this view by mounting a punishing attack on the film in his newspapers. The result was that one of the greatest motion pictures ever made did not turn a profit.

Hearst was one of the most influential publishers of the twentieth century, and a publishing empire that bears his name still exists. The publications have, however, been considerably sanitized from the days in the early 1920s when Hearst was in power. Indeed, in the kind of journalism he produced, anything went as long as you pandered to your readers.

Hearst started life with silver—and copper—spoons in his mouth. The Hearsts (originally spelled Hyrst, which means "thicket" in Scottish) were Scotch-Irish and had emigrated from Ireland to America around 1680. His father, George, a geologist—a lucky one—had settled in California during the Gold Rush of 1849, and he was one of the relatively few who had hit it big, being in on the Comstock Load of silver in Colorado and the Anaconda copper mine in Wyoming.

George Hearst was so successful that Randolph grew up essentially without him. George was always preoccupied with business meetings and had little if any time for Randolph. He was also politically ambitious and was elected senator from California. In fact, to further his political goals he bought a small, struggling newspaper, the *San Francisco Examiner*.

Randolph's education was chaotic. He went to Harvard but was expelled because of his penchant for practical jokes: He had sent silver chamber pots to his professors with their names inscribed on the inside! He never completed college.

George wanted young Randolph to go into business with him, but Randolph had his eye on the *Examiner,* and after a number of requests, his father allowed him to run it.

Just as the character Charles Foster Kane made the fictional newspaper boom, Randolph Hearst made the *Examiner* explode. He gave it a fresh and exciting face, running exposés and sensational stories that grabbed readers. The paper butted heads with such powerhouses as the Southern Pacific Railroad, big business that sought to control utilities, and more. It was war—and the public ate it up.

George Hearst died in 1891, when Randolph was only twenty-eight. Rather than take over from his father, he set out to conquer the world of New York journalism.

The opposition was formidable, mainly *The World,* published by Joseph Pulitzer. Pulitzer had built up his paper with the same techniques—sensational stories, exposés, causes, gripping design—that Hearst had used to build up the *Examiner*. Hearst launched the *Journal* and the war was on.

The war brought, someone once said, "the newspaper industry to new lows."

When Hearst wanted something, it was always on an "I-need-it-last-Thursday" basis. Anxious to grind Pulitzer into a paste, he increased his paper's size, lowered its price, redesigned it, filled it with sensational stories (usually on crime, sex, and corruption), and hired many of Pulitzer's staff away with generous pay packages.

It was during this time that the term "yellow journalism" was born. Hearst hired away a cartoonist who drew a strip called *The Yellow Kid*, and Pulitzer hired another "Yellow Kid" to take the place of the one that had been filched.

The most famous—and yellowest—story the *Journal* was involved in was Cuba. Day after day, the *Journal* ran stories on Cuban heroics and the atrocities of the Spanish occupying force, making the American public more and more angry. In particular, Hearst attacked President McKinley for not doing anything; one of Hearst's acid-tongued writers even hinted outrageously that it was time for McKinley to be assassinated. (McKinley eventually was assassinated, though over a different issue.)

Hearst also sent artist Frederic Remington to Cuba to draw the war that was going on. When Remington reported that nothing was happening, that there was no war, Hearst made his oft-quoted reply: "You furnish the pictures, and I'll furnish the war." When the battleship *Maine* was sunk, reportedly by the Spanish (though that was never proved), Hearst finally had his Spanish-American War.

Hearst's yellow journalism paid big dividends. By 1903 he had seven daily U.S. papers, and his flagship *Journal* had a circulation of more than one million. But that was only the beginning. Like his father, Hearst was also politically ambitious. In 1902 he ran for and won a congressional seat, winning reelection in 1904 and 1906.

In 1906 he ran for governor of New York and with the support of his papers was on his way to victory when President Roosevelt threw his weight against him, reminding New Yorkers of the attacks Hearst had so callously waged on President McKinley. Hearst lost.

Later, he strove for the presidential nomination and came close to getting it. But he was beaten in a bitter struggle with Governor Al Smith of New York.

Hearst bought more and more newspapers, and his power and influence spread throughout the country. In addition to his own money, he had access to the Hearst fortune, which his mother, Phoebe, had inherited. He also started a lifelong habit of collecting that could fairly be described as crazed. He indulged in such extravagances as shipping entire rooms from European Renaissance manor houses to his estate at San Simeon, California. Sometimes he would just buy things and never uncrate them. The most important thing seemed to be simply to collect.

At his zenith, William Randolph Hearst owned twenty-six daily newspapers; he also had interests in radio stations and newsreel stations. When he met Marion Davies in 1915, when she was eighteen and he fifty-one, he got interested in movies, trying to find starring vehicles for his paramour. While conducting this affair he remained married, and though he never divorced his wife, he remained devoted to Marion his entire life.

The Great Depression shook Hearst's empire, almost bringing it down. He was forced to slow down, curtail his free-spending ways, and stop collecting. But after the war Hearst was able to make a comeback, taking control of what was now a media empire—newspapers, TV, radio, and so forth.

He died on August 14, 1951.

Michael Cudahy

(1841–1910)

For years, the meat industry was a winter-season business only; butchers couldn't keep meats fresh year-round because there was no effective means to preserve them. Meats were given some preservative treatment by being liberally salted, which, in light of modern medicine, is not a very healthy way to go. Michael Cudahy changed all that.

Cudahy was a native of Ireland, born there on December 7, 1841, in Callan, County Kilkenny, the son of Patrick and Elizabeth Shaw Cudahy. He emigrated from Ireland to Milwaukee in 1849 in the midst of the Great Famine.

Cudahy quit school at the age of fourteen and entered the employ of Layton & Plankinton, meatpackers. His rise through the firm was rapid, and he eventually left it to work for another firm. He then returned in 1866 as a meat inspector for Layton & Co. and in 1869 was promoted to superintendent of the entire packing house of Plankinton & Armour in Milwaukee.

In 1875 he was offered a partnership in the firm of Armour & Company of Chicago. Only thirty-four years old, he took charge of the company's plant operations at the Union Stock Yards.

It was around that time that he married Catherine Sullivan of Cedarsburg, Wisconsin, and developed what one biographer said was "epoch making." It had never occurred to anyone that meat could be eaten year-round, but Cudahy recognized that with the invention of refrigeration, this was highly practical. His role was to apply the technology to meat-packing.

First developed were "coolers"—cold-storage warehouses where the meat could be stored ready to be shipped. The meat was then loaded into refrigerated trucks, and shipped to various destinations. This process is something we take for granted today, but it created a revolution in meat consumption by enabling people to eat meat year-round. This resulted in a great expansion in consumption and a huge increase in the workforce, not only in the meat industry itself but in companies that served the industry and in those that made foods that went with meat.

To expand domestically and help meat realize its potential—particularly meat of hogs, which were very plentiful—in the mid-1880s Cudahy, Philip D. Armour, and Cudahy's younger brother, Edward, scouted around for a suitable location for a new meatpacking plant. Omaha, Nebraska, intrigued them. There wasn't much competition there, only two small packinghouses that sold only to Britain. In 1887 the men bought a small packing plant there and developed not only a large domestic market but a foreign one as well.

In 1890 Cudahy sold his interest in Armour & Company, and bought Armour's interest in the Armour-Cudahy packing company, which was eventually renamed Cudahy Packing Company.

Cudahy remained company president for another twenty years, until his death on November 27, 1910. During his life, Cudahy, a Roman Catholic, gave much back to the community, becoming widely known for his philanthropic and civic activities.

67

William F. Buckley Jr.

(1925–)

Noted historian and liberal writer Arthur Schlesinger Jr. has called him the "scourge of American Liberalism," and there is little doubt that that is true. For years, in his magazine *National Review;* in his books, starting with *God and Man at Yale;* on his television show, *Firing Line;* or whenever he has a public forum, Buckley's rapierlike wit and insight are much in evidence; indeed, there are many liberals who will not appear with him in any public forum because they're afraid of being embarrassed.

But while one does sense a combativeness in Buckley, one doesn't sense cruelty. He simply believes passionately in what he says and will run through anyone who dares to challenge him.

He describes himself as a conservative, but his is a conservatism that is not rigid or fanatical, such as, say, that of the John Birch Society, a group that *National Review* attacked as being extreme and dangerous. President Richard Nixon said that Buckley had taken away the society's respectability, and no one else could have done that.

Buckley was born in New York City on November 24, 1925, the sixth of ten children. His paternal grandfather had emigrated from Ireland to Canada. William was educated in foreign countries and had the best of everything, but his father, a rough-and-ready oilman (when he died in 1958, he was estimated to be worth more than $10 million), raised his children so they would not be "effete," even importing broncos for them to ride.

Buckley went to private schools in England and New England, then went on to Yale, an institution that was not famed for its right-wing policies and where Buckley did not fit in. He graduated from Yale with honors in 1950, and in 1951 *God and Man at Yale: The Superstitions of Academic Freedom* was published. It is a savage polemic that suggests that Yale professors who teach things against the "public welfare" be terminated. The book created a furor, attracting both praise and pans.

Following this, he was convinced to take a job with the CIA in Mexico, where his control agent was none other than E. Howard Hunt of Watergate fame. He lasted in that job for a year. This experience came in handy later, when he started writing espionage thrillers.

Buckley published more books, coauthoring with his brother-in-law, lawyer L. Brent Bozell, *McCarthy and His Enemies.* This publication also created considerable heat, its central point being that despite its excesses, McCarthyism was "a movement around which men of good will and stern morality can close ranks."

The perception of Buckley and other conservatives was that it was necessary to "revitalize the conservative position." To that end, in November 1955, Buckley founded *National Review.* Originally geared toward top-ranking conservatives who were in a position to change policy, the magazine turned out to have a much broader appeal to a wide variety of intelligent conservatives who were not necessarily policy makers. Planned to have fifteen or sixteen thousand readers, it ended up with many more than one hundred thousand.

National Review and Buckley himself have influenced more than people's thoughts; they have affected presidential elections and were thought to play an important role in the landslide victory of Ronald Reagan over Jimmy Carter in 1980. (After the election, *Review* staffers, long used to being the opposition voice, now quipped that they were toiling for an "establishment organ.")

Buckley is a man with a strong sense of justice. This led him to back Edgar Smith, a man who was in jail for a murder committed in the 1950s. When Smith got out, he kidnapped a girl and admitted to the murder that he had denied to Buckley for so long. Buckley admitted his mistake and said that Smith should be kept in prison for the rest of his life.

In 1961 Buckley's friends persuaded him to run for mayor of New York. He lost, but his presence made it a much livelier campaign. He has also written some well-received espionage novels and taken some celebrated sailing trips, which he has recorded in books.

Buckley has been one of the most powerful voices of American conservatism in this century, and his influence is likely to continue for many years.

68

James Joyce

(1882–1941)

Of all the writers in the twentieth century, few have created more controversy than James Joyce. The publication of his novel *Ulysses* in Paris in 1922 set off a firestorm of praise, damnation, and censorship; a number of countries, including the United States and Great Britain, refused to allow the book in because it was said to be pornographic. The virulent feelings *Ulysses* generated can be seen in a comment critic James Douglas made in the British newspaper *Daily Express*:

> It is the infamously obscene book in ancient or modern literature. The obscenity of Rabelais is innocent compared to this with its leprous and scabrous horrors. All the secret sewers of vice are canalized in its flood of unimaginable thoughts, images and pornographic graphic words.

Besides notoriety, one thing *Ulysses* achieved for its author was solvency: Between the copies smuggled into various countries and those sold in Paris, Joyce made a lot of money, something that he had not done until then. Indeed, like his American contemporary F. Scott Fitzgerald, he was always borrowing from friends and relatives to keep afloat.

Ulysses and his other works established Joyce, in many critical circles, as a genius; some even went so far as to say that his was the greatest voice since Shakespeare's.

James Augustine Joyce was born on February 2, 1882, in Dublin, one of eleven children, most of whom died fairly young. He carried on a love-hate relationship with his father most of his life. But when his father died, Joyce suffered "self-accusation" because he had been out of the country and had not seen his father in eleven years. He said that the guilt bothered him more than the death. For his part, the father, John, was a wife abuser and drinker. Always in one kind of debt or another, John was evicted from his home quite a few times.

Early on, the younger Joyce also rebelled against school and Catholicism—and by extension the Ireland he was raised in. In his senior year, for example, he refused to take the exam in Catholic studies, and the priest who was in charge of all the exams, including the interdenominational ones, which those who wished to go to college had to take, was incensed and refused him permission to take them. But at the last moment, his French teacher interceded with the priest and he was allowed to take the test, which he passed.

He went to University College, Dublin, and there continued his acting, singing, and writing. He also developed a great admiration for the great Norwegian playwright Henrik Ibsen, who, though an old man at the time with a considerable body of work behind him, was not well known outside his own country.

Joyce was very active sexually. At one point, it hardly seemed to matter to him whether a woman was a pickup or a prostitute. But late in college he tired of prostitutes, longing, as biographer Stan Gebler Davies wrote in *James Joyce: A Portrait of the Artist,* to be with someone he could love: "Whores," Joyce said, "were bad conductors of emotion," and Davies said, Joyce longed to copulate with a soul. He meant he wanted to be in love with a woman who would be in love with him. But he would have to wait three years after college for that to happen.

Joyce had written poetry, plays, and songs and had started a novel called *Steven Hero* during his college days. He had also written for such publications as the *Daily Express* and the *Irish Times.*

His abilities as a writer were also starting to be known, and at one point he met W. B. Yeats, the great Irish poet who later won the Nobel Prize for literature. Far from being awed, Joyce treated Yeats with a certain haughtiness, as he did most people.

When Yeats suggested that he submit some of his work to the Irish Literary Theatre (later the Abbey Theatre), which he had helped form, Joyce's response was to ask him if the theater would be producing foreign plays, such as Ibsen's. When Yeats said no, Joyce declined to submit.

Three years after he left Trinity College, Joyce had a fateful meeting. It started out like so many of his other meetings when it came to women. Joyce had spotted her, a pretty woman with a mane of gorgeous reddish brown hair, walking down a street in Dublin. He approached her, started a conversation, and learned that her name was Nora Barnacle, and after a while he succeeded in getting her address. He wrote to her, hoping that she hadn't forgotten him. She hadn't, and soon they were seeing each other.

She would become the great love in his life—as it happened, just as he became famous. She was one of the few people who never seemed too impressed by that. To her he was always Jim, not James Joyce. They would have two children together (Giorgio and Lucia) but not be formally married until 1931.

Joyce had always wanted to leave Ireland, and in 1904 he left, Nora with him, landing in Trieste, Italy, where he supported himself as an English teacher at a Berlitz school. From there he and Nora traveled to a variety of places, occasionally returning to Dublin but always essentially expatriates in other lands. And Joyce was always writing.

As one critic has written, Joyce is arguably the greatest modernist writer, a comic genius, an innovator, and a poet of Irish life and language. In his work, he pioneered the use of inner monologue and stream of consciousness and made brilliant use of such devices as pastiche and parody.

In 1914 Joyce published *Dubliners*, a collection of fifteen short stories that were linked predominantly by situation, symbol, and atmosphere. That same year, he also started a novel, *Portrait of the Artist as a Young Man* (published in 1916), which explored the development of a writer in hostile surroundings.

His great work, *Ulysses* (1922), which describes one day in the life of Dublin, is an exploration of the meaning of ordinary lives.

His last book, the transcendent *Finnegans Wake,* is really Joyce's attempt to pack the experience of life itself between the pages of a book. He took many years to write it, it is filled with all kinds of literary and other allusions, and it is virtually impenetrable.

Joyce had trouble with his eyes all his life and had them operated on quite a few times. Davies feels that this eye trouble may have been the result of venereal disease passed on to Joyce by his father. He was also a drinker, frequently impoverished, and attacked by uncomprehending readers and savage critics. But he was a committed artist and saw it all through.

His influence on other writers is impossible to measure but profound. Certainly, any list of whose he affected would have to include T. S. Eliot, Ezra Pound, William Faulkner, Vladimir Nabokov, and Irish novelist Flann O'Brien.

He died of stomach trouble in Zurich on January 13, 1941.

69

George Bernard Shaw

(1856–1950)

The defining trait of George Bernard Shaw in most people's minds is probably his wit. There is plenty of it in evidence. A typical Shavian response was given to a critic who said his plays were too "talky." "It is quite true," he said, "that my plays are all talk, just as Raphael's pictures are all paint, Michelangelo's statues are all marble, Beethoven's symphonies all noise . . ." But a close look at his life reveals much more than wit, and perhaps his defining trait was not wit but courage, of which he had a considerable amount.

Shaw was born at 3 Upper Synge Street, Dublin, on July 26, 1856, to a failed wholesale wine merchant who liked to "tipple" his wares and a mother who was a singer. They shared a house with his music teacher, George Vandeleur Lee, and in the summertime would all go to Lee's vacation home in County Dalkey, Dublin.

Shaw grew up shy, poor, and lonely, and he used to haunt the National Gallery in Merrion Square. It was there, he would later say, and in his home listening to music, that he had received his real education, rather than that at Wesley College, which he had attended.

In 1872 Shaw's mother, tired of the endless difficulties brought on by her husband's drinking and their lack of money, went away, taking their two daughters with her to make a better life for herself but leaving Shaw behind to fend for himself with his father.

Four years later, in 1876, Shaw, now twenty, joined her, and he had a clear goal in mind: He wanted to be a writer. With her money and a small legacy he received, they were able to survive.

He started writing novels, and he continued for nine years with little or no success. But he did not give up. He also joined the Fabian Society, which would require him to speak publicly, something he was very afraid to do. But he focused on the task and went on to become one of the most effective speakers in the country.

Shaw held a variety of jobs. Then one day in 1885 he met a drama critic named Joseph Archer in the reading room of the British Museum, and they struck up a conversation. Archer was impressed with Shaw's wit, intellect, and erudition, and through contacts, got him jobs as a book reviewer for the *Pall Mall Gazette* and art critic for the *World.* Then, in 1888, he got a job as music critic, writing under the pen name Corno di Bassetto. The prose was classic Shaw—clear, lively, witty (and still so today)—and Shaw's name started to filter into literary circles.

But he still had a way to go. He started penning plays. His first, called *Widowers' Houses,* was about evil slum landlords; it was produced in London in 1892. It was followed by *The Philanderer, Arms and the Man, Candida,* and *You Never Can Tell.*

If Shaw had expected the world to fall down before him in adoration, he was disappointed. None of the plays was a resounding success; indeed, Shaw felt he was just as much a failure as a playwright as he had been as a novelist. But he kept going.

Meanwhile, he got back into criticism. He took a post as drama critic at *The Saturday Review,* in the United States, which was under the editorial tutelage of Frank Harris, who was to become famous for his autobiographical books on his sex life. (About him, Shaw said, "He is neither first-rate nor second-rate nor tenth-rate. He is just his horrible, unique self.")

Then success came—from the United States. His play *The Devil's Disciple* received great praise when it was produced in New York, and he made a good deal of money.

In 1897 overwork led to a collapse from exhaustion, and he was nursed to health by Charlotte Paine-Townshend, a wealthy English woman he had met at the Fabian Society. They fell in love and married in 1898, and from that time on not a year went by that Shaw didn't pen another play.

In 1904, under the aegis of Harley Granville-Barker, a brilliant producer at the Royal Court Theatre, where Shaw's new plays were produced, London discovered him for the genius he was. They were treated to plays such as *Man and Superman, The Doctor's Dilemma,* and *John Bull's Other Island.* W. B. Yeats had asked for the last be written for the Irish Literary Theatre. It didn't work, however, because Yeats and company didn't have the technical virtuosity to produce the play and Shaw was not in tune with things Celtic.

By 1914 Shaw was the leading dramatist in England and a renowned wit. Then he fell from grace, not only because he had the courage to tell the truth about war in a pamphlet, "Common Sense About the War," but also because of his defense of Ireland after the 1916 rising and his equally spirited defense of the Irish patriot and known homosexual Sir Roger Casement. And his antiwar play *Arms and the Man,* produced in 1919, was greeted less than enthusiastically by British military veterans.

In 1920 *Heartbreak House,* which Shaw considered his best work, was produced in New York, while in 1924 *Saint Joan*, which many critics consider his best, won rave reviews when it opened in London. He was catapulted into the lofty position of being considered the world's leading dramatist. In 1925 he was awarded the Nobel Prize for literature.

Shaw continued to write. His most famous play is probably *Pygmalion,* which became *My Fair Lady* first as a theatrical musical comedy and then on film. He enjoyed good health into his nineties, something he attributed to not smoking, drinking—or eating meat. He had become a vegetarian in 1881 after reading a book by Shelley called *A Vindication of Natural Diet* (1913).

Shaw's works were as courageous as the man. He covered topics such as war, economics, prostitution, and religion that had previously been covered only in conversation or from the pulpit. His plays were, in fact, "talky," filled with sparkling wit and fresh ideas; he stimulated emotionally but also intellectually. His influence as a writer on other writers and the effect his ideas had cannot be measured.

70

John McCormack

(1 8 8 4 – 1 9 4 5)

Of all Irish singers, undoubtedly the most popular who ever lived was John McCormack. It was not just, critics say, that he had a powerful voice and an unmatched ability to interpret lyrics; he was able to get inside the words, inside the feelings, and when he sang, it was as if the "Common Man," as Brian Kellow, managing editor of *Opera News,* characterizes him, were singing. He gave voice to what was in the hearts of ordinary Irish, and extraordinary ones as well.

McCormack, a tenor, is known primarily as a concert singer. And as long as there are Irish in the world, one should not take bets against his recordings of such songs as "Terence's Farewell to Kathleen," "The Garden Where the Praties Grow," "The Bard of Armagh," and his signature song, "I Hear You Calling Me" not lasting forever. Less well known is that he was first an opera singer. In fact, no less a talent than Enrico Caruso said, "His was the voice of the century."

McCormack was born in Athlone, County Westmeath. He first gave signs of talent when, at the age of eighteen, he won first place in the "Feis Ceoil" singing contest in Dublin. McCormack realized that he could go somewhere with his voice, but he needed training. Then, as now, it was difficult to find professional voice training in Ireland, so he went to Italy, the home of grand opera.

He auditioned for Maestro Vincenzo Sabatini in Milan. When he was finished, Sabatini reputedly said, "I can do little except teach this boy how to use his voice properly. God has done all the rest."

In January 13, 1906, at the age of twenty-two, McCormack made his debut at Savona, Italy, in Pietro Mascagni's opera *L'Amico Fritz*. He didn't leave the audience prostrate in the aisles, but he was regarded as competent. This was because, Kellow says, writing in *Irish America* magazine and quoting from McCormack's wife's memoirs, *I Hear You Calling Me*, "I think Italian audiences like a more robust voice than John's."

He continued his voice training, singing in other operas in Italy, and then returned to London with his wife, made his operatic debut in Covent Garden as Turiddu in *Cavalleria Rusticana*, then crossed the Atlantic and appeared as Alfredo in *La Traviata* in the United States.

He sang with other companies fairly successfully, but deep down opera fundamentally troubled him: He did not find it real or true enough. Said his wife of what McCormack thought, "At a vital moment the soprano will wrench herself from the arms of the poor tenor and leave him standing inanely while she rushes to the footlights to tell her troubles or ecstasies to the world." Also troubling him was his lack of belief in his own acting ability, but subsequent work in a movie would prove that anxiety unfounded.

Around 1923 he decided to devote all his energies to concerts. Once he began these, McCormack kept busy—to say the least—averaging almost one hundred concerts a year during the period of his peak popularity. What made him great, aside from his voice, which was like a precision instrument, was his feeling: He was able to sing from his heart right into the hearts of his listeners. He was more concerned with substance than with style; style tended to distract the listener, while substance didn't.

While he performed Irish ballads, he also sang great pieces from opera. And he continued to perform in some operas (he performed Don Ottavio in *Don Giovanni*). Opera was where he showed his vocal power, indicating, as Brian Kellow says, "phenomenal breath control." He could hold a note seemingly endlessly. He also sang American songs with the same beauty and power he demonstrated in singing other pieces.

In 1919 McCormack became a U.S. citizen, saddening his British fans, but he never really stopped singing the songs that everyone loved. His final U.S. appearance was on St. Patrick's Day of 1937, and he made his farewell appearance in London at the Royal Albert Hall in November 1938.

One might think that the example that John McCormack set as a singer would inspire many other Irish singers to follow suit, but this was not the case. There have been very few tenors who followed in his footsteps, and none has equaled his popularity. More than eight hundred recordings were made of his singing, most still surviving, and a goodly number have been made into CDs.

But McCormack had great influence. For decades he made the Irish feel good about themselves and their lives and let them touch things inside that needed touching. "It's easy to believe, listening to these songs," says Kellow, "that America's ongoing love affair with the Irish is in great part due to him."

William Butler Yeats

(1865–1939)

William Butler Yeats is regarded as one of the greatest poets of the English language, and the world paid homage to his genius in 1923, when he was awarded the Nobel Prize for literature.

Yeats was born in Sandymount, a seaside suburb of Dublin, County Sligo, but he lived there for only the first three years of his life. Then his father, John, an esteemed portrait painter and teacher, moved the family to England, both to attend classes and to conduct his business. There were his mother, Elizabeth Pollexfen; his brother, Jack, who was to become the most famous Irish artist of his generation; and his sisters Susan, known as Lily, and Elizabeth, who was always called Lolly.

The move set a pattern for future moves, with the Yeats family moving back and forth between Ireland and England as circumstances dictated. When grown, Yeats himself would follow suit, spending periods of his life in England as well as Ireland. But he was an Irishman through and through and was dedicated to the cause of Irish nationalism, one of the themes well-reflected in his poetry.

There are mysteries in Yeats's life that even he could not explain. Though he commented more than once that he had no reason to be unhappy—"No one was unkind," he told one of his biographers—he felt a generalized sense of unhappiness as a child, and when he looked back, he always seemed to focus on the unhappy parts of his life. He also sometimes thought he was wicked, even though he was not.

Throughout his life, Yeats was virtually obsessed with the unknown; he believed in astrology, the mystical, even ghosts—what he called the "Unseen." It was as though if he could only see the unseen, he would be able to answer every question he had and be at peace.

His interest in poetry must have been in part fostered by his father, who most days would read poetry aloud over the breakfast table. His first verse appeared in 1885 when he was twenty, two poems in the *Dublin University Press.* That same year, he met Fenian leader John O'Leary, "the handsomest old man." In *W. B. Yeats,* by Michael Macliammoir and Eavan Boland, Yeats is noted as saying that from his conversation with O'Leary, a true Romantic, coupled with the books the old man gave and lent him, "has come all I have set my hand to since." Many years later, in the poem "September 1913," Yeats wrote:

Romantic Ireland's dead and gone,
It's with O'Leary in the grave.

In 1893 another important event occurred: Yeats met Douglas Hyde and John Taylor. Hyde had founded the Gaelic League to preserve and increase the use of the Irish language, which had fallen into disuse. Taylor, who would go on to become a major political force in the Irish nationalist cause and a spellbinding orator, would often quote from Yeats's poetry. Preserving and promulgating Irish writers and writing was to be one of Yeats's lifelong goals. The poets, dramatists, and patrons of the arts were important allies, not only emotionally but sometimes also fiscally.

Yeats's early poems were wistful, mysterious, and heavily dependent on pre-Raphaelite imagery—dreamy sojourns through an unreal world filled with gods and goddesses, priests, peacocks, and more, the stuff of nineteenth-century Romanticism. But there is also a voice that is distinctly Yeats, language suffused with a sense of loss and the unattainable.

In 1889 Yeats met Maud Gonne, who was, to a large degree, to be the great—unrequited—love of his life. He was stunned by her statuesque beauty (she was almost six feet tall and George Bernard Shaw called her "outrageously beautiful") and sensuality and the fire inside her. Though born in England, she was a fierce fighter for Ireland's freedom.

He supported her to some degree in her political activities and at one point asked her to marry him. She refused, begging that they remain friends. They did, but later in his life, when they were both middle-aged, he again asked to marry her, and again she refused. At one point, he even fell in love with Maud's daughter, Iseault, and asked her for her hand in marriage—and was turned down. His poetry is full of his aching love for a woman who is clearly Maud Gonne.

Over the years, Yeats and his great literary patron, playwright Lady Gregory, strove to promote Irish literature, founding a number of clubs and theaters, including the Abbey Theatre. Yeats himself wrote plays that were performed there, as well as keeping up a steady outpouring of poetry.

In 1917, at the age of fifty-two, Yeats finally married an English-woman, Georgie Hyde Lees, and with her had two children.

Yeats was famous for a number of verse collections, including *The Wild Swans at Coole* (1917), *Michael Robartes and the Dancer* (1921), *The Tower* (1928), and *The Winding Stair* (1929).

As time went on, his poetry changed. He developed a new, austere style that was much like the man. Indeed, it is hard to believe that Yeats, a reserved man who looked and acted more like an investment banker, was capable of writing such beautiful, acute, and lyrical poetry. But he was, and he loved doing it. His final poem was written just two days before his death.

On his grave in Sligo are etched the words he requested:

No marble, no conventional phrase;
On limestone quarried near the spot
By his command these words are cut:
Cast a Cold Eye
On Life, On Death.
Horseman, pass by!

Lady Gregory

(1 8 5 2 — 1 9 3 2)

Of her, W. B. Yeats said in his *Memoirs,* "She has been to me mother, friend, sister and brother. I cannot realize the world without her—she brought to my wavering thoughts steadfast nobility." And at one point in her life, George Bernard Shaw called her "the greatest living Irishwoman." You would have had trouble getting anyone to disagree with him.

Lady Gregory was born Isabella Augusta Persse at Roxborough House, County Galway, on March 15, 1852, into a nonliterary, gentleman farmer family. As a playwright, essayist, poet, translator, and editor, she could not have differed more.

Isabella married Sir William Gregory, of neighboring Coole, when she was twenty-eight. He was thirty-five years her senior. William had retired as governor of Ceylon but was keenly interested in tenant rights. Her married life consisted of travel between Ceylon, London, and Coole. Their only child, William Robert, was born in London in May 1881. They had a short but good life together; Sir William died in March 1892.

Lady Gregory had long been interested in literature, particularly Irish tales, and Sir William encouraged her. She had also long been interested in helping the Irish achieve whatever was possible, but in editing her husband's autobiography and selections from Sir William's grandfather's writings during his years as undersecretary for Ireland (*Mr. Gregory's Letter Box, 1813–1830*), she became even more focused on the task of freeing Ireland from England's "overgovernment."

She saw this essentially in terms of reestablishing Irish pride. Since the Great Famine, the Irish language had slowly gone into disuse. To use it was a sign that you were inferior because at one point only the "famine Irish" used it.

In the 1890s she assembled and had published a series of folktales of Galway. Ironically and almost laughably in light of what was to occur, the original motive for her assembling the tales, says one biographer, was jealousy over collections of tales of Sligo by W. B. Yeats (*The Celtic Twilight*)—the same Yeats, of course, who was to become such a great friend and collaborator.

She met Yeats about three years after her husband's death. Then she, Yeats, and Edward Martyn assembled an Irish literary theater, which would ultimately become the Abbey Theatre. Still in existence today, the theater was devoted to presenting Irish plays, both those in Irish and those in English, and encouraging Irish playwrights.

In pursuit of this, Lady Gregory devoted a great deal of time and money of her own and others. She was a gifted fund-raiser, able to pry money even out of her English friends with the warmth and charm of her personality.

After her husband died, she kept her estate at Coole Park, a pleasant, bucolic place that became the center of the Irish literary renaissance. It was also a place where Yeats was to write much of his poetry and where he felt very much at peace.

While most people think of her as a driving force behind the Abbey Theatre and a champion of Irish culture and literary efforts, as well as a translator and gatherer of Irish tales, Lady Gregory was far more than this. At the age of fifty, she discovered that she could write plays, and she wrote a large number, most of them being what are known as tragicomedies.

But she was a woman with great courage. She would defend works such as John Synge's *The Playboy of the Western World* and George Bernard Shaw's *Shewing-up of Blanco Posnet* that attracted hails of criticism.

She was also a complex woman; defining her is not easy. One thing was constant. She was a caring, giving woman who helped countless people, many of them artists (such as Sean O'Casey) who otherwise might not have been discovered. Wrote one of her biographers, "like her hero Patrick Sarsfield of *The White Cockade* (1905), her name too should be set 'in clean block letters in the book of the people.'" She died on May 22, 1932, at Coole Park.

Thomas Moore

(1779–1852)

The irony of his life was that he spent most of it in England, yet he wrote some of the most revered Irish tunes ever. He reinforced for the Irish a positive sense of identity and gave them immeasurable peace in times of travail. The words and music are still very familiar. When Irishmen gathered round a fire, sipped a Guinness, and heard the words "Believe me, if all those endearing young charms," "The Last Rose of Summer," and "The harp that once through Tara's halls," life was good and pain was banished—at least for a time.

Thomas Moore was born in Dublin in 1779, the son of a prosperous wine merchant. He was writing verse and singing songs at a very young age, and his talents did not go unnoticed. He was a friend of some of the greats of the time, including Robert Emmet, but in 1800 he went to London to study the law and was not involved in the turbulence at home.

In 1807 a publisher who wanted to come out with a book filled with Irish tunes asked Moore if he would write the lyrics. He agreed, and the result was very successful; the book was to go to ten volumes and a supplement, in the process making Moore a rich man.

Most of the tunes were taken from *The Ancient Music of Ireland* by Edward Bunting. Bunting had been able to attend the last meeting of the Irish Harpers in Belfast and had transcribed the melodies; up to that time, they had been passed down orally. He had then arranged them for the piano with only minor changes. Although Moore acknowledged where the melodies had come from, Bunting was not amused.

The music in the volumes was arranged by two different people. The first seven volumes, from which most of Moore's most popular tunes came, were done by organist-composer Sir John Stevenson. They were modeled on the work of Haydn. The other three volumes were done by Sir Henry Bishop, and they were more operatic.

Moore's tunes are still popular, and they greatly influenced some American composers. Musicologist Charles Hamm has shown that American composer Stephen Foster was heavily influenced by Moore's work.

While he is famed for his songs, Moore was really more a poet and writer than exclusively a tunesmith. For example, in 1800 he published the pseudonymus *Poetical Works of the Late Thomas Little,* and in 1806 he published *Odes, Epistles and Other Poems.*

Moore was also a novelist. In 1812 a publisher offered him £3,000 to write an Oriental romance. He wrote *Lalla Rookh,* which on its publication in 1817 got good critical notices and sold well.

In Moore's day, there was such a thing as debtor's prison, and Moore almost spent some time in it. He had been appointed registrar of the

Admiralty Prize Court in Bermuda, but the seclusion of the islands didn't appeal to him and he appointed a deputy. In 1818 the deputy absconded with £6,000, for which Moore was held responsible. He avoided prison only by living abroad for three years.

Moore's latter years were awash with sadness. Two of his sons died, and he was said to be suffering from mental illness. He died on February 25, 1852.

74

Bobby Sands

(1954–1981)

Sunday 1st
I am standing on the threshold of another trembling world. May God have mercy on my soul.

Thus begins the diary of IRA prisoner Bobby Sands on the first day of his hunger strike against the British in March 1981. Bobby Sands was born in Belfast, which has been characterized as the most violent city in Ireland. At fifteen he quit school and took a job as an apprentice coachmaker, but he (or the family) was constantly harassed by loyalists—people who wanted Ireland to stay part of England—and in 1972 he and his family moved to Twinbrook in West Belfast. That year he also joined the IRA and became an active operative in the war against the British.

In 1973 Sands was arrested for gun possession and sentenced to five years. He served his term as a "special category" (political) prisoner in Maze prison. Six months after his discharge from prison in 1974, he was arrested again, but this time for a more serious offense: the bombing of a furniture factory. In September 1977 he was found guilty and sentenced to fourteen years in prison.

Sands and other IRA members viewed themselves as political prisoners and wanted to be recognized as such in prison. But when Sands was placed in the new H blocks in Long Kesh prison without any political status, such as permission to wear civilian clothes and other considerations, he and the IRA protested. The British remained adamant on the issue, and the IRA decided to fight back by having prisoners fast.

On Sunday, March 1, Bobby Sands began his fast, and his diary shows that he was a young man very much tortured by what he was doing to his family.

> My heart is very sore because I know that I have broken my poor mother's heart, and my home is struck with unbearable anxiety. But I have considered all the arguments and tried every means to avoid what has become the unavoidable: it has been forced upon me and my comrades.

Negotiations continued, but the British remained implacable on the issue. Three weeks after Sands started his fast, another prisoner started one, and he was followed by more.

As the strike went on, tensions in Northern Ireland rose in all six counties and riots erupted in Derry and Belfast. Then Sands took an unusual step: He ran for public office as member of Parliament for Fermanagh-Tyrone, against straight Unionist Harry West—and was elected. But the sides could still not get together; even though he was an elected official, the British still counted him as a nonpolitical prisoner.

Sands gradually declined. Events surrounding the fast were portrayed in the film *Some Mother's Son,* where at least one of the mothers had her son force-fed. But Sands continued to fast, until finally, on May 5, the sixty-sixth day of his fast, he went into a coma and died. Then another IRA member died, and another, until finally the strike ended on August 20, when the tenth and final prisoner died.

The implications of Sands's fast and death, and the death of the others, have yet to play out completely. Certainly, at the time, these deaths focused world attention on the conflict and showed just how implacable both sides were. Margaret Thatcher, the British prime minister, could have saved the lives of the prisoners but chose not to. So, too, the IRA could have called a halt.

According to John Feehan, author of *Bobby Sands and the Tragedy of Northern Ireland,* the consequences of the death of Bobby Sands for the British government were farther-reaching and more damaging than most observers had anticipated: "Like bolts of blinding fork-lightning, Sands's death struck the whole political world, not once but again and again in quick succession so that the powerful British propaganda machine crumbled before it in almost every country."

The memory of his death is not the kind of thing that people can forget easily, even though it has been almost twenty years since he died.

75

Eugene O'Neill

(1 8 8 8 – 1 9 5 3)

Alfred Hitchcock once said, "Art is emotion." The statement is as terse as it is true. If we do not feel when we watch a movie, look at a painting, or read a book, all the sound and fury, the celluloid, the paint, the verbiage will signify nothing. It is also true, generations of artists have said, that for the perceiver to feel, the creator, the artist, must truly feel; the process does not allow for lying.

Picture, then, Eugene O'Neill, one of the greatest American playwrights, a towering figure of twentieth-century world drama, sitting in front of an old Remington typewriter in his house in California writing *Long Day's Journey into Night,* the story of his own tortured and emotionally wrecked family life, and having difficulty seeing the page because tears were streaming down his face.

But that could not have been the only time he wept. Because in a career that included four Pulitzer Prizes and, in 1936, the Nobel Prize for literature, O'Neill's plays explored the dark sides of the human soul, experiences, biographers say, that arose from his own experiences and were not only to affect his work but to infect his life. He had three wives, a son who committed suicide at forty, and another who died young as a heroin addict. He suffered estrangement from his children and profound mental distress, including a full-blown nervous breakdown in 1951.

O'Neill had a simple explanation for it all: Writing to his son in 1945, he said, "The critics have missed the important thing about me and my work. The fact that I am Irish."

O'Neill was born in a Broadway hotel room on October 16, 1888, and his mother, Ellen, almost died giving birth to him. To help her survive, her doctor prescribed morphine, on which she would become dependent. *Long Day's Journey,* whose action starts at eight-thirty in the morning and goes to midnight, is about a theatrical family, the Tyrones, that comes apart. The wife and mother character is depicted as a woman who lives in a haze of drugs, the son as needing a mother who is not there for him. There are also an alcoholic older brother and a father. The four are bound together by guilt, recrimination, and a variety of other negative feelings, but there is love, too. Ultimately, though, the play is classic O'Neill, his view of life dark and despairing.

O'Neill's father, James, was a great actor who had immigrated to America from Kilkenny. Besides having an impressive lineage in acting, his family could be traced back to Hugh O'Neill, who mounted an uprising against England in 1598 that came closer to winning Ireland's freedom than anything until the Easter Rising in 1916.

As a teenager O'Neill drifted for a while, but his father was a success in America. He was able to afford private boarding schools for Eugene, as well as sending him to Princeton. O'Neill spent a year there, but his academic achievement was hardly remarkable. His most notable accomplishment, friends said, was one day hurling a rock through the office window of the university president, Woodrow Wilson.

After being expelled from school, he went to sea, drinking heavily and entering into a depression so deep that at one point he attempted suicide.

In 1912 he contracted tuberculosis. While he was recuperating, he did some soul-searching and realized his calling: not to perform on the stage like his father but to write the plays that are performed. Indeed, he viewed his father as a sellout. Instead of taking a chance with different roles, his father had toured the country for years playing in *The Count of Monte Cristo* a nauseating number of times, getting rich but prostituting his art.

O'Neill's first play, a short piece called *Bound East for Cardiff*, was produced by the Provincetown Players, a group of highly talented amateurs on Cape Cod. It was a success.

O'Neill's plays were decidedly different from the fare currently in vogue, which featured ostentatious oratory, high melodrama, and various other theatrical excesses. His work was lean and mean. Many of the themes came out of Greek tragedy, such things as matricide, patricide, miscegenation, and Oedipal fulfillment. For example, *Desire Under the Elms* portrays a father who is lust-filled and a woman who murders her infant daughter.

O'Neill was also a bold experimenter. Just as in Greek plays, sometimes characters, as in *Strange Interlude,* would speak directly to the audience. In one play, *The Great God Brown,* the characters wore masks to express various emotions, also as in Greek plays.

All of O'Neill's plays except one had dark themes. (After viewing his first success, *Beyond the Horizon,* his father asked him what he was "trying to do? Make the audience go home and commit suicide?") The one play that was not dark was *Ah, Wilderness!* It was a comedy, but there was a river of longing beneath it—that the little boy could have a different family, one whose members were normal and did not rip one another apart.

O'Neill's influence on drama and the actors who performed it was profound. Generations of young playwrights emulated him in both style and substance, and some succeeded very well.

O'Neill could not have been easy to live with. He was a slim, dark-haired, handsome man with a melodious voice, about five foot, eleven inches tall, and with a watchful, morose temperament. His third wife, Carlotta, said of him that he was a "tough black Irishman . . . who cared only for his work."

In 1951 both he and Carlotta suffered mental breakdowns, and he also had physical problems. From 1943 on, he had suffered from Parkinson's disease and tragically—for both him and the world—was unable to write. He tried dictating, but that didn't work either.

For the last two years of his life, he lived in the Hotel Shelton in Boston so he could be near his doctor. Close to death, he was heard to utter that he had "been born in a hotel room and . . . Goddamn it . . . I'm going to die in one." And he did.

76

Elizabeth Gurley Flynn

(1890–1964)

The essence of the life of Elizabeth Gurley Flynn might be summed up as follows: She fought for those who did not have any rights or whose rights were being trampled. The only problem was that one of the organizations that she joined and became a high-ranking member of was the Communist Party, which advocated the overthrow of the United States.

Looking at her background, it's simple to surmise how she came to do what she did. She was born in Concord, New Hampshire, to an engineer father who was a socialist and a mother who was an Irish nationalist and feminist.

When she was ten, her family moved to the south Bronx, where there was an enclave of Irish families. She was only sixteen when she gave her first speech, to the Harlem Socialist Club, entitled "The Subjection of Women Under Socialism." Flynn was an excellent speaker, as well as pretty, and the crowd was enthralled by her. The same year she started to speak, she quit school and joined the International Workers of the World.

Two years later she married a miner named John Jones and had a son and daughter by him. But soon the marriage was in disarray, and she returned to the IWW. There was an attempt by governmental authorities to ban IWW members from speaking at public gatherings, but Flynn led several fights against the bans. These were successful, and in 1910 she started organizing strikes.

During this time she became romantically involved with Carlo Tresca, a relationship that would last until 1925 but to which she would remain emotionally tied for many years.

In 1917 she almost went to jail. She had vocally opposed World War I, and the government indicted her, along with other IWW leaders, for espionage. But after a while charges were dropped. After the war, the government undertook a purge of radicals, but Flynn had helped found the Worker's Defense Union to help defendants. The government's task was not so easy.

In 1920 she became a founder of one of the most important U.S. organizations, the American Civil Liberties Union, which, ironically enough, was to expel her in 1940 for her Communist affiliations.

She dropped out of the revolutionary scene in 1926 because of illness, but before doing so, she applied for membership in the Communist Party. Ten years later she was healthy enough to return and was accepted into the Communist Party. Ultimately, it was an affiliation that would lead to prison.

Flynn continued to do what she always did: lecture and write, the latter chiefly in the Communist newspaper *The Daily Worker*. She demanded parity in pay as well as protective legislation for the party. And, of course, in general she angered a lot of people.

Just as the United States became involved in World War II in 1941, she was elected to a post on the party's Central Committee, and in 1942 she ran for Congress, with predictable results—she lost. Following the war, she established part of the women's delegation to the Women's Congress in Paris.

Meanwhile, the Cold War in America was soon in full swing, and anti-Communist sentiments were building. Flynn organized defenses for radicals, but in 1951, she was arrested for advocating the overthrow of the United States and sentenced to jail time.

She served time in prison and upon her release showed that she had not changed. She continued to work for the party and in 1961 became its first national chairwoman.

In the early sixties she visited the Soviet Union and eastern bloc countries and finally moved to Moscow. She died there of gastroenteritis.

George M. Cohan

(1878–1942)

George M. Cohan started his show business career
young: His mother carried him onto the stage to
join his parents' vaudeville act when he was only
four months old.

George's father, Jeremiah, or "Jerry," was born in
Ireland. He passed up the opportunity to become a har-
ness-maker offered to him by his father and in the 1840s emigrated to America. Upon arrival, he simplified the name he was born with,
Keohane.

In New York he met Nellie Costigan of Philadelphia. They formed an
act that would involve the whole family in vaudeville, a potpourri of song,
dance, animal, and acrobatic acts that dominated American theater for
roughly fifty years, from about 1875 to the coming of radio in the mid
1920s.

By the early 1920s the four-member Cohan troupe (mother, father,
George, and sister Josephine, a tap dancer) was getting top billing and top
dollar. George had dropped out of high school early, and at sixteen he

penned his first song, "Why Did Nellie Leave Her Home?" And it was George who ended each show with the lines, which were to become famous, "My mother thanks you. My father thanks you. My sister thanks you. And I thank you"—lines that he had first used in response to an audience's calls for "Speech!" after one of the Cohan performances.

From vaudeville, George naturally gravitated into the musical comedy theater, but his first efforts were not successful. Then he teamed up with Sam Harris, and this was just the spark he needed. Their first outing on the stage, *Little Johnny Jones,* about an American boy accused of throwing the English Derby (horse-racing), features two tunes that were destined to become classics: "Give My Regards to Broadway," and "Yankee Doodle Dandy."

Another play that scored was *Forty-five Minutes from Broadway,* which featured the classic "Mary's a Grand Old Name" as well as the title tune. The play *George Washington, Jr.* showcased "You're a Grand Old Flag" for the first time.

Cohan is justly regarded as the father—or one of the fathers—of the modern Broadway musical comedy. His plays were distinguished from the melodramas that preceded him, sophomoric, bathetic, and overly sentimentalized efforts that had none of the drive, slimness, and vigor of the Cohan shows. Between 1901 and 1940 he produced eighty Broadway plays and musical revues for which he wrote the stories, music, and dialogue—and in which he frequently performed.

Cohan was unabashedly American and more than happy to demonstrate that in his shows. They featured flag-waving of various kinds that some critics panned but audiences loved. There is no question that Cohan helped many people feel better about being American, but he did not for a minute imply or state by his work that they should forget their heritage. He was proud of his Irish roots.

Cohan's life, of course, was not all sweetness and light. In 1919 he got involved in a bitter struggle between actors and management, siding with management. By 1920, with vaudeville fading, Cohan's career had similarly paled. Embittered by the fight with the actors, which had spawned Actors Equity, he walked away from show business, vowing never to be part of it again.

But for the true performer the lure of the lights and the boards and audience is always there. Cohan returned to it all in the 1930s, as an actor, appearing in a number of Broadway shows, including those of fellow Irishman Eugene O'Neill.

In 1940 Congress—perhaps, as some cynically suggest, with war on the horizon—awarded Cohan a medal for his tune "You're a Grand Old Flag."

This was a high honor for Cohan, but perhaps his deepest satisfaction came when the brilliant James Cagney—whom Cohan had convinced to play himself—won an Oscar. The film was entitled *Yankee Doodle Dandy,*

Cohan was a complex man. In *Irish America* magazine, a woman who had known him for years described him: "Vain and violent-tempered, childish at times, sulky and temperamental, but a man with a heart and soul, one who was easily hurt and one who could be a great friend. There was a wistfulness always about George and there was never another Irishman born in the world who had his unfailing charm."

In 1959 a statue by sculptor George Lober of Cohan overlooking Broadway was erected. It was a Broadway that, of course, Cohan had helped build. He was also an inspiration to countless other Irish performers, who thought, "If he could do it, so can I." And many of them did.

Walt Disney

Many people are surprised to learn that Walt Disney was Irish American. But he has a line of relatives that go back to County Carlow.

Perhaps equally surprising is that Disney, who presented a huge number of short and full-length cartoons to the public, wasn't a very good artist. Indeed, if he had had to achieve fame on the basis of his artistic ability alone, we probably would never have heard of him.

Disney had a difficult childhood. His father, Elias, a religious fundamentalist, was quick to "chastise" his children with his strap and did not allow such things as toys, games, and sporting equipment in the household.

Elias Disney's undoubtedly turbulent inner life must have been exacerbated by his chaotic job pattern. The family was always moving—from Chicago to Kansas City to Marceline, Missouri, and more—and he worked in such areas as farming, retail railway shops, contracting, and newspaper distributing. He would lose some jobs. On one occasion, following the collapse of a forty-eight-acre farm he owned in Marceline, the family was so poor, they actually had to ride a boxcar to Kansas City.

Disney's happiest time as a child was in Marceline. Theirs was a full-fledged farm, and Walt, who was there from the ages of four to eight, developed a lifelong respect, admiration, and deep love for the creatures there, many of whom would one day find themselves on-screen, delighting children everywhere. The traveling also triggered a lifelong love affair with trains, which would show up in more than one of his cartoons.

In Kansas City, Elias purchased a newspaper delivery route and Walt's education was sacrificed to it. He had to deliver the afternoon papers seven days a week, which often resulted in his being tired and late to school. His father paid him nothing, so at lunchtime he worked in a candy store to earn spending money. School was hardly the happy time for him that many children experience.

Like many imaginative people, Disney was a ham, and in his teen years he earned some money in vaudeville for a while. But he was also developing a burgeoning talent for drawing; he drew a cartoon for a school newspaper and honed his skills at the Chicago Academy of Fine Arts.

Following his freshman year in high school, Disney was smitten by the desire to be in the army, as much attracted by the romance of it all as to impress girls when in uniform. The problem was that at fifteen he was too young. After being rejected by a number of services, his mother conspired with him to create false documents. He was chosen as a driver for the Red Cross Ambulance Corps. He was stationed in France, and his wartime experience was seared into him. It probably contributed to a fierce patriotism, which he would exhibit many years later.

He was eighteen when he was discharged. He settled in Kansas City and there focused on cartooning, developing a great interest in filmed cartooning. His first significant professional creation was *Alice's Wonderland* in 1923, which combined a cartoon figure with a live performer.

At one point he decided to give Hollywood a try. Once there, he succeeded in placing *Alice in Cartoonland* in 1923. This was a very popular series, and he produced fifty-six of the cartoons over a three-year period.

Shortly after this period, Oswald the rabbit, a very popular character, was created, but Disney lost a battle with Hollywood agent and producer Charles Mintz over the rights. Disney knew he would have to create something else, a character that could, he hoped, be just as popular. Somehow his imagination vaulted—to a mouse. He called the mouse Mortimer.

But his wife, Lilian Bounds, whom he had married in 1925, thought the name too "pompous." She suggested something else: Mickey. Mickey Mouse.

Disney liked it. He had his cartoonist partner, Ub Iwerks, whom he had met in Kansas City, draw the mouse—for a simple reason: He was a much better cartoonist than Disney.

The result was a cute little character with an infectious appeal. Disney found appropriate starring vehicles for Mickey. He put him into *Plane Crazy,* based on Charles Lindbergh's achievements, and *Gallopin' Gaucho,* with Mickey doing a Douglas Fairbanks routine. After sound was added, the cartoons were let loose on an unsuspecting public on November 18, 1928.

All that other cartoon figures saw of Mickey from that point on was his rapidly diminishing tail. Disney Studios turned out Mickey Mouse cartoons as fast as it could and also leased the character to manufacturers. It is here that Mickey was a true hero: In the 1930s, Mickey Mouse watches and windup handcars were so successful that they literally saved the Ingersoll Company and Lionel Corporation from bankruptcy.

And it wasn't just ordinary children who had a case of what someone once called "rodent fever"; over the years, Mickey also attracted as die-hard fans such extraordinary "kids" as King George VI of England, Arturo Toscanini, and Cole Porter. Mickey Mouse went on to be the most recognizable figure in the world.

But Disney was not one to rest on his laurels—or on a mouse. His mind was always active, dreaming, looking toward new horizons. And it showed. In the 1930s, he was the first to use Technicolor in a film, in the first feature-length cartoon in history, *Snow White and the Seven Dwarfs,* which was released in 1937.

Disney was riding a tidal wave of success when World War II started in Europe. The diminution of the European market seriously affected his company's fortunes, the losses further increased by *Fantasia* (1940) and *The Reluctant Dragon* (1941), both of which flopped financially.

Disney was also hit with a strike in 1941, and it hit him hard—in his heart. He had thought Disney Studios was one big happy family; now the family members were parading outside the studio with picket signs in their hands. Disney, who had suffered a nervous breakdown in 1931, did not relish the thought of another breakdown. In the midst of the strike, he took off for South America to make U.S. government–authorized films. While he was gone the strike was settled.

Later that year the fiscal hemorrhage was stanched by a big-eared little elephant named Dumbo, who flew right into the hearts of American audiences in the movie named for him.

Then, in 1942, Bambi and all his forest friends came out of the woods in what became Disney's most successful cartoon ever, a movie that had not only irresistibly cute characters but emotional power as well. (Novelist Stephen King said that when as an adult he watched the scene where Bambi's father reveals to Bambi that his mother is dead and says "Mother can't be with you anymore," King ended up "blubbering in my beard.") By the war's end, Disney was on solid fiscal footing again.

Across the forties and fifties, Disney produced both cartoon and live-action short and long films. *Cinderella* (1950) was very successful, as was the live-action *So Dear to My Heart* (1948), one of Disney's favorite films. In the fifties he got into television, producing the *Davy Crockett* series and initiating *The Mickey Mouse Club* and much more.

Disney had a mind that was classically creative. It was said that he could see objects such as chairs and trees change shape and come to life. In essence, he could see something—usually something wonderful—where there was nothing.

All through his creative life he had demonstrated something else: courage. He would need it for what he did next. He had always thought that the amusement parks he and his wife visited with their children were inadequate, and he resolved to create something wonderful. Executives at the Walt Disney Company were dead set against it, but he believed—and he bet a frightful amount of money on that belief.

He built an amusement park in California, and he called it Disneyland. It opened in 1955. It was phenomenally successful and was followed years later, in 1971, by Walt Disney World, built near Orlando, Florida.

In the early 1960s, the buzz around Hollywood was that Disney was getting old and had lost his touch. But he had a touch left, and it was called *Mary Poppins,* a sensationally successful movie that did very well on Oscar night 1965.

Walt Disney was a staunch conservative (unlike his father, who had been a socialist) and anti-Communist. Though born in Chicago, he always seemed to like the rural parts of America best, and his work seemed to reflect small-town values. But as someone once said, Disney never reflected anything except what was in his own heart. It just so happened that his values had been the values of most of America for a long, long time—and still are.

His influence had multiple facets. Within the creative sphere, he influenced untold artists, producers, and creative people. But he also had an impact on ordinary Americans. Indeed, it seems that sometimes the world of Disney didn't stop at the amusement park walls but stretched all across America, Disney values reflecting America's values and instructing in them at the same time.

Always a heavy smoker, Disney died of lung cancer in 1966 at age sixty-four. It seems safe to say that someone like him will not come along again for a long, long time—if ever.

79

Augustus Saint-Gaudens

(1848–1907)

Arguably the greatest sculptor America has pro-
duced and a much imitated sculptural pioneer,
Augustus Saint-Gaudens was of French-Irish stock.
His father, Bernard, was born in France and worked
as a cobbler in his native town of Aspet in the French
Pyrenees. His mother was born in Ireland.

In 1841 Bernard left France, emigrating to Dublin, where he continued his trade of making shoes and selling them to local stores. One
day he walked into a store in Dublin where one Mary McGuinness was
sewing bindings on slippers and was struck by her beauty; he thought
her the most beautiful girl in the world.

They started to see each other and eventually married, settling in
Dublin in a nondescript house on Charlemont Street. Some sixty years
later a statue of the great Irish hero Charles Stewart Parnell, created by
their son, would be standing just two blocks from their home.

From Dublin, Bernard and Mary emigrated first to Boston and then to New York City, with Saint-Gaudens advertising his shoes as "French Ladies' Boots and Shoes."

The couple had two children who died in infancy, but Augustus, born on March 1, 1848, in Dublin, survived. The boy showed artistic ability right from the start. Then one day a patron of the arts, Dr. Cornelius Rea Agnew, confirmed the boy's ability when he came across some pen-and-ink drawings by Augustus in his father's shop. Agnew suggested that the boy had talent and should be encouraged.

Bernard listened, and when Augustus was thirteen, he was apprenticed to Avet, one of America's first stone-cameo cutters. He then continued his artistic education in France, studying at Jouffroy's studio at the École des Beaux-Arts.

When he started sculpting, his genius leaped to the fore. It was evident that this was what he was meant to do. In 1868 he produced his first sculpture, a cast-bronze bust of his father. In his life, he would influence other sculptors to use the same material instead of the standard stone used up until then.

Paris was soon gripped by the Franco-Prussian War, and Saint-Gaudens retreated to Rome. There he met a partially deaf sometime sculptor named Augusta Homer, first cousin of the artist Winslow Homer. Their mutual interest in art turned to romance, and one day they would marry.

When he returned to New York, Saint-Gaudens opened his first studio and waited for work. His first commission was for a statue of Commander David Glasgow Farragut, Civil War a hero. It was the first of many commissions Saint-Gaudens would receive for Civil War sculptures—150 all told.

Saint-Gaudens's genius showed in his sculpture of Farragut, a good example of the nineteenth-century realism that Saint-Gaudens popularized. Instead of using a static, heroic pose, as was de rigueur at the time, Saint-Gaudens depicted Farragut in an action position, his coat lifted by the wind.

Saint-Gaudens married Augusta Homer on June 4, 1877, and moved to New York, where he opened a studio and turned out a variety of sculptures, some of wealthy clients but many of Civil War heroes, including one of the famed general William Tecumseh Sherman. Saint-Gaudens complained he couldn't get a good profile of the general because Sherman kept looking him in the eye.

One of his friends in New York, and someone who was to refer him to many commissions, was Stanford White, the flamboyant architect who designed Madison Square Garden. Out of Saint-Gaudens's relationship with White came one of his most famous pieces, *Diana*, a slim nude resting high on the tower of Madison Square Garden.

In the 1880s Saint-Gaudens took as mistress a woman named Alberta Hultgren. A Swedish-born model, she was the inspiration for much of his work involving the female form; she is quite recognizable in a number of the pieces.

Saint-Gaudens did many great sculptures, but arguably his best was started at the behest of Henry Adams, who wanted a sculpture of his wife, who had committed suicide. He did not give highly detailed instructions, leaving the creation more or less to Saint-Gaudens. The result is the Adams memorial in Washington, D.C. A seated female is swathed in sheets, her face recessed deep inside a sort of hood. Untitled, it is commonly known as "Grief."

Saint-Gaudens lost his New York studio in a fire. He also had a studio, still operative as a museum today, in Cornish, New Hampshire.

He wanted to make his sculpture of Parnell his greatest work. But he was also sick with the cancer that would kill him on August 3, 1907, and the sculpture, while adequate, is not Saint-Gaudens at his zenith.

80

Audie Murphy

(1924–1971)

He was the personification of the "unlikely hero."
When the United States entered World War II in
December 1941, the baby-faced seventeen-year-old
Murphy tried to join the army, but he was rejected
as being too small. He stood only five feet, five inches tall and weighed 112 pounds, a weight-to-height
ratio that more closely reflected the size of the average
woman of the time.

But in July 1942 he succeeded in getting into the army. He went
on to become the most decorated U.S. soldier of all the 18 million men
and women who were inducted into the service. He was awarded an
astonishing thirty-seven medals: eleven for valor, including the Distinguished Service Cross, two Silver Stars, four Purple Hearts, and the
Congressional Medal of Honor, which one commanding officer said he
deserved to get more than once. In combat, he was a pint-sized fearsome

force of nature, single-handedly killing 240 German soldiers and continuously putting himself in harm's way: He once described himself to someone as "a fugitive from the law of averages."

Murphy came from the north central section of Texas, an area straight out of *The Grapes of Wrath*. Both his mother and father were Irish American; his mother came from a family with quite a few soldiers in it. The Murphy family were sharecroppers, meaning they worked cotton fields for someone else for a small—a very small—share of the profits. It was a brutal, soul-sapping life. The Murphys worked endlessly in the dusty fields under the broiling Texas sun, ever in a state of poverty or near poverty, barely able to survive, sometimes living in boxcars provided by the social services organizations of the day. There were twelve children in all, but three died when they were young. Audie's father, Emmet, or Pat, was an alcoholic, and his mother, Josie, though pretty when she was young, lost her looks early. Murphy once remembered her, as reported in Don Graham's excellent biography of Murphy, *No Name on the Bullet,* as a "sad-eyed woman who toiled eternally."

By the age of five, Audie (a name he disliked because it made him seem like a girl) was working the endless lines of cotton plants, hoeing or picking as the season dictated. Years later, Murphy said of his boyhood years, "I never had just 'fun.' It was a full-time job just existing."

School was painful. He was subtly (and sometimes not so subtly) looked down on by some classmates as lower class, and he suffered a grinding sense of shame about his father being an alcoholic and a poor provider.

But he was known as a kid who never backed down no matter what the odds against him. He was daring and a whiz with a gun, particularly when a creature was on the run or in flight. He had an almost spooky ability to detect wildlife—say, a squirrel—hiding motionless in the woods, a sense that would serve him well years later in woods where camouflaged snipers were hiding.

His father, who periodically left the family for short periods, deserted the family for good in 1940, when Audie was sixteen, and a year later his mother died, five months short of her fiftieth birthday.

He joined the infantry and took his basic training at Fort Wolters in Fort Worth, Texas, and Fort Meade, Maryland, where he gained a reputation as an excellent soldier. Following basic, he was assigned to Company B, First Battalion, Fifteenth Infantry Regiment, Third Division.

He did not see any combat until July 1943, when the Third Division invaded Sicily. There, his heroics as a soldier began and became well known, an inspiration to other GIs. On more than one occasion he risked his life to save others or to destroy enemy positions, and he had a reputation as a fearless killer. He said once that he had been afraid all the time, but it was also true that when things got chaotic—as when someone was shooting at you—he did not panic like most people but got calmer. "Things clarified," he said.

He said it never bothered him to kill German soldiers. In combat, he told a friend once, "I had a mean streak."

His derring-do earned him a battlefield commission. After Sicily, the Third Division invaded German-occupied France, and on January

25, 1945, at a place near Strasbourg, on a snow-covered field called the Colmar Pocket, Audie Murphy earned himself the Congressional Medal of Honor.

Hundreds of Germans had poured out of the woods. Murphy, alone, jumped up on a burning tank destroyer, which could explode at any moment, and directed artillery fire while he raked the oncoming Germans with a .50-caliber machine gun. Said one of the eyewitnesses:

> Twice the tank destroyer was hit by direct shell fire, and Lieutenant Murphy was engulfed in clouds of smoke and spurts of flame. His clothing was riddled by flying fragments of shells and bits of rocks. I saw that his trouser leg was soaked with blood.

But he kept firing and during a half-hour period killed fifty Germans, repulsed the assault, and quite likely prevented his company from being trapped.

For Audie the war ended two and a half years after it started. When he returned to the United States, the July 16, 1945, cover of *Life* magazine showed him with the caption "Most Decorated Soldier." He was catapulted to fame.

It wasn't long before Hollywood called, and after a series of false starts, Murphy launched a career in movies that lasted into the 1960s. He had a reputation for being a volatile man (some people were afraid to work with him), a compulsive gambler (he lost hundreds of thousands of dollars), and a womanizer.

Audie Murphy died when he was forty-seven, a passenger on a small plane that crashed on a flight between Atlanta, Georgia, and Martinsburg, Virginia. He was buried far from the cruel place where he had been born and raised, in Arlington National Cemetery. Though many people don't know of him and never will, there are many who do remember and whom he inspired and still inspires. To this day, only John F. Kennedy's grave is visited by more people.

81

Louis Henry Sullivan

(1856–1924)

Louis Henry Sullivan is considered the "father of modern architecture," most particularly the father of the skyscraper. It was Sullivan who coined that most famous of architectural phrases, "Form follows function." And it was Sullivan who nurtured a disciple who was to go on to achieve something of a name himself—Frank Lloyd Wright. Yet, like many great artists—and that's what he was—his greatness was not truly grasped until he was gone. Indeed, his last years were filled with sadness and pain.

Sullivan was America-born, but his father, Patrick, had emigrated to Boston from County Cork in 1847. There he met and married Andrienne List, who had been born in Geneva, Switzerland.

Unlike most of the Irish immigrants, Louis's father, Patrick, was not fleeing from Ireland because of the famine (1847 was known as "Black 47," the worst famine year of all) but simply to start a dancing school, having been an instructor in Ireland.

Louis, born in Boston in 1856, was the younger of two boys Patrick and Andrienne would have. Louis's relationship with his mother was good, but his relationship with his father was stormy. As events would play out, this reflected something in his personality that even he wasn't aware of. Perhaps to annoy his father, he used to describe himself as a "mongrel," part Swiss, part Irish.

Early on, his special abilities became known. He became a draftsman, and his work was clearly superior to that of his fellow students. He also demonstrated a gift for design. At the age of sixteen, he entered the prestigious Massachusetts Institute of Technology (without having attended high school) and then, finding school too constraining, became an apprentice to architects in Philadelphia and Chicago. In 1874 he went to Paris for a year, becoming very familiar with French architecture. He studied at the École des Beaux-Arts in Paris, where he learned one architectural technique—the *esquisse,* or sketch, a quick drawing that becomes the basis for all future work—that he used during his entire career. Indeed, when designing one of his masterpieces, the Wainwright Building in St. Louis, he did an *esquisse* for it in three minutes.

When he returned to the United States, he settled in Chicago and started to practice architecture. It was good timing. The Chicago fire of 1871 had wreaked havoc on the city, and many new buildings were needed.

Sullivan joined the firm of Dankmar Adler, and it was a fruitful collaboration (Sullivan became a full partner in 1881), not only because it melded Sullivan's architectural virtuosity and Adler's engineering skills but also because it allowed Sullivan to stay away from clients and potential clients. Sullivan tended to be quick-tempered, egoistic, and tart-tongued, while Adler was low-key and courteous.

The two men did extremely well. By the time Wright joined the firm, the two partners had, as Robin Langley Sommer writes, in *American Architecture,* "become well known for all buildings of cast iron and steel that were restrained in style and refreshingly original in their ornamentation."

In 1887 Sullivan and Adler were commissioned to design Chicago's Auditorium Building, a behemoth of a building containing four hundred hotel rooms, a seventeen-story office building, and an opera house. Their work was hailed as magnificent. They were feted by all of Chicago—and Sullivan was just thirty-one years old.

In 1895, the year they designed the Guaranty Building in Buffalo, New York, Sullivan and Adler split up, the word being that Sullivan was just too difficult to get along with.

Sullivan was a bachelor, but stories constantly circulated that he was also something of a satyr. One biographer, Robert Twombley, said that word on him at the time in Chicago was that if you lined up all the women he had bedded in Chicago, they would stretch "from one end of the city to the other." Twombley seriously doubted this, but he did not doubt that Sullivan was sexually active.

In fact, the great sensuality of his life seemed to be work—architecture. Then one day, in 1899 while he was walking down a street in Chicago, that changed. He saw a statuesque woman walking down the street with a little dog, and he stopped her, ostensibly to admire the dog but really admiring her. She was only twenty years old and Sullivan forty-two. But they got involved, and the relationship warmed to the point where they were married. They remained married for ten years, but then they split up, in part perhaps because, though he was married, his passions were still directed toward buildings.

His breakup with his wife cost him much of his money and material goods, and business was not good. He was viewed as an architect from the past, and his prickly personality didn't help attract clients. The last twenty years of his life was one long trip downhill.

After he died his work was reevaluated, and his genius as an architect was fully grasped. Frank Lloyd Wright himself acknowledged Sullivan's greatness in his memoir, *An Autobiography,* which was published in 1943. On September 3, 1946, the Boston Society of Architects installed a bronze plaque at 22 Bennet Street, where Sullivan had been born. Recognition came a bit late.

Daniel Patrick Moynihan

(1 9 2 7 –   )

What one biographer said of Senator Daniel Patrick
Moynihan sums him up quite well: "[He has] an
instinctive understanding and compassion for the
plight of the underprivileged." Granted his own
background, it's no small wonder that he does.

He was born in Tulsa, Oklahoma, on March 16,
1927, son of a newspaper reporter, John Henry, and the former Margaret Ann Phipps. But when he was six months old, the family
moved to New York City, and he grew up there.

At first his family did quite well. His father worked as a copywriter
for RKO Pictures but then got into the hard-drinking, nightlife gam-
bling scene, went heavily into debt, and in the mid-1930s deserted the
family. It was all Moynihan's mother could do to keep the family—
Patrick and his brother, Michael, and sister, Ellen—afloat. They moved
from one cold-water flat to another, and on occasion Margaret had to go
on welfare.

But they survived, and Moynihan, a good student, attended Benjamin Franklin High School in Harlem, where he finished first in his class in 1943. He didn't think he could afford college, so he got a job as a longshoreman on the docks. Then, urged by a friend, on a whim, he took the entry test to City College of New York ("To see if I was as smart as I thought I was") and easily passed.

He enrolled, but a year later, in 1944, he joined the navy. He continued his studies, graduating cum laude from Tufts University in Medford, Massachusetts, in 1948 and receiving his Ph.D. from the Fletcher School of Law and Diplomacy. For 1950–1951, he received a Fulbright Fellowship to England.

He liked England and stayed there an additional two years; then he returned to the United States. On the boat back, he had a fortuitous meeting with Paul Riley, a Democratic Party activist, and became involved in politics, first working on the mayoral campaign of Robert F. Wagner Jr., then on the gubernatorial campaign of W. Averell Harriman. As a result, he held a variety of state jobs and worked closely with the governor.

He also lectured at local colleges on political science and citizenship, and started writing articles for the *Reporter*, a liberal, anti-Communist journal.

But his concerns were eclectic. He also got involved in auto safety, and it was said that Ralph Nader used a number of Moynihan's auto safety ideas in his groundbreaking 1991 book *Unsafe at Any Speed*.

In 1960 he was a delegate to the Democratic National Convention and enthusiastically backed the nomination of John F. Kennedy. He then helped write position papers for JFK in urban problems. After he was elected, Kennedy, impressed with Moynihan's expertise—he had garnered a reputation, said one insider, "as a doer and a thinker"—appointed him special assistant to Supreme Court Justice Arthur Goldberg. He was only thirty-six years old. Just a few weeks before he was assassinated, President Kennedy assigned Moynihan the task of writing the government's antipoverty program. This report became the bedrock of what was to be the Economic Opportunity Act of 1964.

Moynihan continued to write, producing a number of very important books, including *Beyond the Melting Pot: The Negroes, Puerto Ricans, Jews, Indians, and Irish in New York City.* His central thesis about blacks—that centuries of discrimination had produced an unstable family structure—was widely misinterpreted as a statement that they were inferior. Moynihan had to do quite a bit of explaining to show those charges as absurd.

The next few years saw Moynihan shuttle between prestigious teaching positions at Harvard and the like and government service, such as being assistant to the president on urban affairs. Indeed, Moynihan was the mainstay of Richard Nixon's welfare reform program.

Moynihan displayed his powerful pen from time to time, and in the March 1975 issue of *Commentary,* he lambasted the United Nations for being too careful in its statements, saying also that America should speak with a clear voice when something is wrong. President Gerald R. Ford liked what he read and appointed Moynihan U.S. ambassador to the United Nations.

Ultimately, Moynihan's outspoken ways resulted in a rupture in his relationship with Ford, and after nine months on the job he quit.

Then, in 1976, he started to run for the Senate. He beat Bella Abzug in the Democratic primary, only narrowly, but by campaigning on issues such as unemployment, inflation, poverty, and economic threats to large urban centers, he rode to easy victory over incumbent James L. Buckley.

From that time, Moynihan never looked back. Over the next twenty years, his legislative record, always informed by his central concern for the underprivileged, old or young, has been impressive. Perhaps his most important work in the late 1990s concerns the future viability of Social Security, a question of crucial concern to millions of Americans.

Moynihan has been married for forty years to the former Elizabeth Brennan, also an author, and they have two boys and a girl.

St. Brendan

(486–578)

J ust what St. Brendan did in his life cannot, at this point, be determined with a great degree of accuracy. A number of biographies have been written, but, like other Irish tales of long ago, they are colored and informed by the individual writer's perceptions and inclinations. In addition, the biographers were writing many years after the events reputedly occurred. More, obvious exaggerations and fantasies have been included.

On the other hand the important point is that St. Brendan's Day (May 16) is celebrated by Catholics worldwide, and his life is revered by many Catholics and has served as an inspiration to many.

The essential facts of his life, detailed in Seamus McManus's *The History of the Irish Race,* are as follows.

When Brendan was born in the latter part of the fifth century, the person who was to become his tutor, Bishop Eire, is said to have been at his birth and to have seen an amazing display: The woods near where

Brendan was born seemed wrapped in an incredible flame, and above them and all across in the brilliantly illuminated sky, there were angels, dressed in bright white, flowing garments.

Brendan was to achieve great fame as a navigator, but before that, he went off to St. Jarlath's school near Tuam to be tutored. Before he left, his mother, St. Ita (she founded the first monastery in Munster and was a miracle worker) warned him to be "not with women nor with virgins lest some should make mock with me." Brendan appeared to take the advice to heart. An event that occurred when he was very young first confirmed the validity of her advice, and he would avoid, if not abhor, female companionship all his life.

Bishop Eire had gone to see the king and queen of the territory where they lived and had left Brendan alone in the chariot. As he waited, a beautiful little princess with curly golden hair approached and got into the chariot—and Brendan summarily ejected her.

Bishop Eire learned of this, and he punished Brendan severely, making him stay alone at night in the cave of Fenit. While there, Brendan in said to have recited psalms all night, loudly enough to be heard at a thousand paces. But this event did not change his attitude toward women, which he would carry all across his long life.

In 556 he started a school and monastery at Clonfert on an island in Lough Deargh in the River Shannon. It was to become one of the most famous schools of Ireland; at one point three thousand people attended. In future generations, the monastery would have as its abbot St. Cummian Fada, one of Ireland's most famous scholars.

Worldly singing was another peeve of Brendan's. He would allow only religious singing, and it was said that one morning after mass at his church in Clonfert, a great bird came to him and sang to him, hiding its bill behind its wing. Brendan was entranced—indeed, he went into a trance—by the sweet beauty of the singing. From that moment on he did not allow any worldly singing to be done in his presence.

But it was not for his attitude toward women and singing that Brendan became famous. It was for his voyage, which was said to last seven years and during which he faced countless challenges. He was even said at one point to have set foot in America—centuries before Columbus. He became famous, being dubbed "St. Brendan the Navigator" or "Voyager."

Brendan went because he thought there was a "Land Promised to Saints" to the west, across the Atlantic Ocean—a land that was probably suited to the life of an ascetic and hermit. He and his monks made the journey, it is said (the history of the journey was written three centuries after it was made), in a wood-and-leather coracle-style boat, and Brendan and the monks with him braved every terror imaginable: Demons hurled fire at them, they sailed past a column of floating crystal (possibly an iceberg), and a sea monster as huge as an island stalked them.

Their journey took them to the Aran Islands, at Iona, then to the "Island of Sheep" and the "Paradise of Birds" (possibly the islands of Strømø and Mykines in the Faeroes), and then to the "Island of the Smiths," where flaming rocks rained down (from a volcano?) and where they dropped anchor for a winter. Then they were off again, through a "thick white cloud" and another "column of crystal."

Just exactly where they landed—in North America—if indeed they landed there—is not known. But in 1976 author Tim Severin plotted a voyage that followed Brendan's route exactly, and he had no problem ending up in "paradise," which happened to be Newfoundland.

84

Maud Gonne MacBride

(1866–1953)

In her 1990 biography of Maud Gonne, writer Margaret Ward says, "At the beginning of this century there was a woman—some claimed a Goddess—with red-gold hair and passionate golden eyes, whose great height towered over those she walked amongst, and whose beauty and charm mesmerized friends and foes alike."

Maud Gonne was one of the dominant women in nineteenth- and twentieth-century Ireland, perhaps in part because she harked back to the myths from early Irish history. Indeed, Irish tales are full of promises that one day a statuesque, beautiful Irishwoman would come to the land and rescue it from tyranny. Maud Gonne (she was beautiful and almost six feet tall) came as close as anyone to fulfilling that ideal.

Like many Irish heroes, she was born in England. Moreover, her parents were not just ordinary citizens but an Anglo-Irish army officer, Thomas, and an Englishwoman, Edith. Her background was privileged. Her great-grandfather, founder of the Cook business dynasty, was a wine importer who when he died in 1869 left two million pounds to his daughters, including Maud's mother, Edith. When Maud was twenty-one, she inherited a portion of that, which allowed her the freedom to pursue her political agenda. That agenda could be boiled down to one thing: freeing Ireland.

It is not clear just why Maud would spend her life in pursuit of this, but at its root her compassion for the downtrodden certainly had something to do with it. She had seen the problems of the Irish firsthand as a young child, when her father was stationed in Dublin, actually as part of a controlling army. Says Ward, "While only a small child riding in the countryside with her father, she [had seen] evicted tenants standing in tears besides their ruined cottages, prevented by the police from returning to their homes."

In her autobiography, the ironically titled *A Servant of the Queen,* Gonne wrote that her realization that the Irish were suffering desperately under British rule coalesced because of a single experience. Writes Ward:

She had gone to stay at a country house, where she was to attend a hunt ball as a guest of a landowner's wife. During dinner her host, a "tall-faced man with an abrupt manner," who appeared to be in very bad temper, suddenly announced, "That damned Land League is ruining our country," and he went on to describe a tenant and his family lying in a ditch, evicted by his agent because of their support for the League. The wife didn't look as if she would live till the morning, and he stopped and told her husband that his political activities were the cause of her condition. When Maud exclaimed in horror, he replied, "Let her die. These people must be taught a lesson." They went on eating but Maud was furious, and sent a telegram to Tommy [her father], asking him to send a carriage as she was leaving the next day. She felt she could not stay any longer in that house.

Her mother died when Maud was only five, but she had a very good relationship with her father. Even years later, when she was an old woman, she used to reminisce fondly about how some people had used to think they were husband and wife. Her father was stationed in Dublin starting in 1882, as part of a garrison to keep the peace. There had been the usual foment, and England was worried that things would get out of hand.

While in Dublin, Maud contracted tuberculosis and went to France to convalesce. There she read the work of a journalist named Lucien Millevoye, whom she ultimately met and fell in love with. Together they forged "an alliance against the British empire," as Ward writes.

They had two children out of wedlock, one in 1893 and another in 1895 (the boy died, but the girl lived), and she also stayed politically active. She raised funds for the Irish cause by lecturing in France, Britain, and the United States. For a brief time, she edited *L'Irlande Libre* in France. She also founded the Daughters of Ireland in 1900.

By that time her love for Millevoye had more than waned. She discovered that he did not share her commitment to Ireland's freedom and, moreover, was morally bankrupt: At one point, to gain a political advantage, he asked Maud to sleep with a couple of politicians.

In 1889 she met W. B. Yeats, who was stupefied by her beauty and charm. They were to begin a thirty-year relationship. He proposed marriage to her on a number of occasions and was always turned down. While her relationship with Yeats was not the way he would have liked it, they said they were "spiritually married." He would write of her as a "glimmering girl," "pilgrim soul," "half lion, half muse."

Gonne was also an actress, and in 1902 she created a sensation when she starred in one of Yeats's plays, *Cathleen ni Houlihan,* at the new Abbey Theatre he had helped found. In the play, Gonne played an old woman, a symbol of Ireland. She hobbled around the stage in a cloak and then, in the climactic scene, shed her cloak and revealed a young, vital, beautiful, new, nationalistic Ireland. That same year, she organized a protest against a visit to Ireland by the king of England and was imprisoned by the British.

Gonne seemed less interested in men than in causes. A close observer once said of her that when she met someone who epitomized the cause, she would be a romantic "goner." Such a man was Captain John MacBride, a soldier in the Boer War who was to become a hero of the Easter Rising of 1916.

She got involved with MacBride and married him. In 1904, she gave birth to a son, Sean, who was to go on to have an illustrious career, achieving high political office and winning the Nobel Peace Prize in

1974. Around the time of Sean's birth, Maud also became a convert to Catholicism.

Unfortunately, the marriage did not work, and they were divorced. Maud returned to Paris. They had been separated a long time when the rising occurred during which MacBride was captured and executed.

Maud Gonne returned to Dublin in 1917. Then, in 1918, she was arrested for her political activities; she spent six months in Holloway jail. Like de Valera and others, she was opposed to the Anglo-Irish Treaty of 1921. She settled in Roebuck House on the outskirts of Dublin, where she organized the Women's Prisoners' Defense League to help Republican prisoners.

Maud doted on her son Sean, and he grew up to be rebellious like her, ultimately becoming head of the IRA. But Sean came to reject the militant and militaristic way of his father and mother and pursued a course of independence by peaceful means. He went on to become prime minister of Ireland.

Maud Gonne died on April 27, 1953, and was buried in Glasnevin Cemetery, Dublin, the final resting place of many other Irish heroes.

85

James Cagney

(1899–1986)

When people think of James Cagney, most probably think of him in his movie roles as a city tough guy—pushing a grapefruit in someone's face, ventilating a trunk by firing into it with a pistol in response to a captive's entreaties for "air," or intimidating someone in some way. This was the kind of role he mostly played in the 1930s.

But the *real* James Cagney was hardly the *reel* one. While he was raised in New York City, he was a farmer at heart—a farmer, painter, and dancer. He loved the land, just plain farming, and when he retired from making movies in 1961, it was to a working farm complete with horses, cows, and other animals.

And though he would show on more than one occasion that he was tough, his was a quiet toughness, more related to his beliefs than to anything else, a far cry from the street-guy toughness in his pictures.

Cagney was raised in the Yorkville section of Manhattan, a polyglot neighborhood of different nationalities and character types, some of which he used quite successfully in his films. "There was this one guy," he once said, "he would stand on the corner of Seventy-eighth Street and First Avenue hitching up his pants and turning his head and spitting. That's all he did all day." Cagney used that mannerism very successfully in his own films.

The Cagney family—his mother, father, brother Bill, and sister—were poor, "but," he said, "we didn't know it." His grandmother on his mother's side was from County Leitrim, but he didn't know much about his father's background. His father, an alcoholic bartender at a local saloon, downed, Cagney once said, an astonishing "sixty shots of rye a day." He died when Cagney was nineteen. The fiscal hard times began in earnest when his father died, but Cagney's mother was a strong woman, and she was able to hold the family together.

Early on Cagney had learned to sing—and dance. He told one biographer that fights in the city had taught him how to move and led him to the dance and also that he loved dancing. Indeed, once, when he was seventeen, he got a free pass to see Anna Pavlova dance: "I wept it was so Goddamned beautiful."

He vowed to use his skills to help support the family. He set off to do just that, getting into vaudeville and taking any job he could. One day he met a dancer named Frances "Winnie" Vernon, who joined him as part of his act. In 1922 they married.

Cagney and Winnie traveled all over the country doing a song-and-dance act, and eventually Jimmy also found work on Broadway, playing Little Red in *Outside Looking In,* a Maxwell Anderson play. He got good reviews and started to be noticed; one of the people who noticed him was Al Jolson. That relationship led to Cagney's starring in a play that Jolson bought and then sold to Hollywood. Cagney and the actress who starred with him, Joan Blondell, did well on the deal.

Sometimes great ones get away. But in the case of James Cagney, Hollywoood spotted the potential greatness immediately, and he was signed up. He would go on to do sixty-two films over a thirty-one-year period, most of them at Warner Bros.

Cagney was cast as a bad guy in a series of movies, some memorable, some forgettable, but all successful at the box office. Over the years he gradually rose to be Warner's biggest star, acting in such classics as *Angels with Dirty Faces* and *The Public Enemy*. By the end of the thirties, he was making a whopping forty-five hundred dollars a week and was one of Hollywood's richest stars.

He refused to make certain pictures, and eventually he got into a to-the-death fight with Jack Warner because of this. Warner suspended him, and he went to his home in Martha's Vineyard while the lawyers in Hollywood fought it out. When it was over, Cagney had won an important victory that was to have a profound effect on legions of actors to come: He had been able to break his contract and sign up with other studios.

In 1940 he got a big scare. A Texas congressman named Martin Dies, who had become aware of Cagney's liberal politics and gifts to migrant farmworkers and other groups, called him in front of a committee he headed to question him about his beliefs. Cagney was able to satisfy the congressman that he was not a Communist, but he wanted also to clear up any residual suspicion the American public had.

He started looking for a project that would do that, and he found *Yankee Doodle Dandy*, the life story of legendary song-and-dance man George M. Cohan. The part was perfect for the way Cagney really thought of himself and portrayed an image that was a lot different from the one the public had of him: As the man he played in the film said, "Once a song-and-dance man, always a song-and-dance man."

Cagney, forty-two at the time, performed like a twenty-year-old, bringing verve, life, and his own special brilliance to the role. And he danced—and sang—his way into the hearts of Americans. The picture went on to become the most successful Warner Bros. picture of all time up to that point—and James Cagney won an Academy Award for best actor.

When he retired to his farm, Cagney also fulfilled a lifelong dream: "I always wanted to be an artist," he said. But his career had gotten in the way. It was on the farm that he spent his days doing what farmers do, as well as painting and drawing and just living the quiet, bucolic life with his wife, Winnie.

There were some unanswered questions about him, things that caused his close friend, the actor Pat O'Brien, to characterize him as the "faraway fella." The main one was hinted at by David Hadju in a review of a Cagney biography in the *New York Times Book Review*: "[His] two adopted children, raised apart from Cagney and his wife in a house built for them behind their parents' home, scarcely knew their father." The obvious question, of course, is why.

James Cagney influenced many in the acting profession with his consummate command of his profession. His fight with and win over Warner Bros. was appreciated by untold actors who followed him. He also affected millions of people over many years in another way: He gave them enjoyment.

He died on Easter Sunday 1986, "a small man," as someone once said of him, "who casts a big shadow."

John Ford

86

(1894–1973)

When Hollywood legend Orson Welles was asked whom he admired as a film director, he answered, "the old masters. . . . By which I mean like John Ford, John Ford, and John Ford."

There was no question that John Ford was an old master. During a career in which he directed dozens of films, he won six Oscars, a feat no director has yet equaled. He also probably created another record by not accepting any of them in person.

The titles of his films read like a list of all-time greats, and include *The Iron Horse,* a brilliant silent film; *The Informer; Stagecoach; The Man Who Shot Liberty Valance; Young Mr. Lincoln; The Grapes of Wrath; My Darling Clementine; Cheyenne Autumn; Fort Apache;* and *Mr. Roberts.*

Nine of his films were made with John Wayne, many of them using Monument Valley, Utah, as a spectacular backdrop. They were films that made Wayne not only a superstar but an icon, a symbol of a certain kind of Americanism with the credo "America: Love it or leave it."

Ford was once described, with some accuracy, as "a crusty son of a bitch." He was not a man who kept his opinions locked in his bosom, and he was also a man who expected—indeed, demanded—absolute loyalty to himself and his films.

Though most of his films do not have specifically Irish themes, Ford's reverence for things Irish and Irish sensibility are apparent. Thomas Flanagan, writing in the book *Out of Ireland,* says that though it doesn't have an Irish theme, *The Grapes of Wrath* may be his most Irish movie, presenting, as it does, the story of a family evicted from their homes, as Irish families were during the Great Famine. It opened America's eyes to a downtrodden part of the American public.

Although Ford was born in America, both his parents were Irish immigrants. They emigrated from Saddal in County Galway, ending up in Portland, Maine, living in the poor section of the city, where Ford became involved in politics and became a ward heeler.

His father wanted him to join the navy, so Ford took the test for Annapolis—but failed. Then, in 1914, Ford, twenty years old, decided to head west, to go to California, where his brother Francis was doing well in the new business known as the movies. Before going, he changed his name. The family name was O'Feeney, his name Sean Aloysius O'Feeney, but he took the lead from his brother and changed it to the simpler John Ford.

In Hollywood, he got a job at a film studio and got involved in everything from editing film to sweeping the floor, learning his trade from the ground up. Then he got into directing, and for ten years he directed two-reelers while he waited for his chance. His chance came in 1924 with *The Iron Horse.*

All his life, Ford was involved with Ireland, and was a supporter, both vocally and fiscally, of the IRA. In fact, on one occasion when he was in Ireland, he lent money to the IRA and was told by the British, who had learned of his activities, to get out of Ireland and stay out; if he returned, he would be arrested.

By the time World War II broke out, Ford was regarded as one of Hollywood's great directors. He proved it once again by taking his cameras to the war zone and shooting a variety of battles, including spectacular footage of the crucial Battle of Midway, for which he won an Oscar for best documentary.

Perhaps the thing Ford rued the most was the charge that he was anti-Indian, that he enjoyed killing Indians in his films. Nothing, he said, could be further from the truth. In fact, he felt a kinship with Indians because their way of life—living in clans—harked back to the way the Irish had lived. And, he said, he had given them what they needed more than anything, an income—not at the puny wages they received when working elsewhere, but at Hollywood union wages.

In 1952 Ford worked with John Wayne to make yet another movie set in Ireland. *The Quiet Man* features a classic fight between Wayne, an ex-boxer, and Victor McLaglen. The movie ran about three hours, very long for its time, but no one really noticed; it was that good.

John Ford died on August 31, 1973.

87

Jack Dempsey

(1 8 9 5 – 1 9 8 3)

Killer instinct: William Harrison "Jack" Dempsey, of Scotch-Irish-Indian ancestry, who reigned as heavyweight champion for eight years, a man nicknamed the "Manassa Mauler," had to have it. In his 1973 autobiography, *Dempsey,* he comes across as sort of reasonable and soft, but not in the ring; there he had that fury, that killer focus that all great fighters have.

Jess Willard, heavyweight champion of the world, experienced it when he fought Dempsey in Toledo, Ohio, on July 4, 1919. Willard was six feet, five inches tall and weighed in at 245 pounds; the glowering Dempsey, who had not shaved in three days, was six feet, one and a half inches tall and weighed 187 pounds, not big for a heavyweight. But thirty seconds after the fight started, Dempsey threw his first punch, a sweeping left hook that dropped a startled Willard on his backside. Willard was almost counted out, and he would go down six more times in the first round.

Somehow Willard came out for a second round, and a third, but at the beginning of the fourth his handlers threw a literally bloody towel into the ring. Willard could not have answered the bell if he had tried. Small wonder: Dempsey had knocked out some of his teeth, broken his jaw in twelve places, and pounded his midsection to veal. The blood-spattered giant looked as if he had been in a traffic accident.

For Jack Dempsey, winning the world championship was the culmination of something he had yearned for for eleven years, since his brother Bernie, also a boxer, had started to train his tough little kid brother in a makeshift gym in the backyard of their home in Manassa, Colorado.

It was an achievement, too, for Dempsey's mother, Celia, because his career had started because of her and a certain incident. One day, a vagabond had come to their house, and Celia had been kind, letting him sleep by their warm stove on a cold night. In return he had given her an old, dusty book by the great bare-fisted heavyweight champion John L. Sullivan recounting his life. Celia had read it and, swept away by the grandeur of Sullivan's life, had used it as a pattern for raising young Jack.

Jack obviously loved his mother very much, but he did not feel the same about his father, Hyrum. (Dempsey got his Irish from his father's side, a long line of relatives coming from County Kildare.) Dempsey viewed him as selfish and self-absorbed. Late in life, after Dempsey's mother had died, his father remarried; Dempsey didn't even go to the wedding.

Dempsey cut his schooling short and left home as a teenager, "riding the rods" (hitching free train rides), living in hobo jungles, doing hard labor working the copper, silver, and cold mines of Colorado and Utah, and periodically fighting—for money.

Early on, he had discovered the power of his fists, and when he came into a new town he would push open the doors of a barroom and announce, in a voice that he loathed for its high pitch, that he could "lick anyone in the house" and was prepared to prove it for money.

More than occasionally, he would fight someone, beat him, then quickly take off with his winnings. For most of that time, he weighed only about 150 pounds. But he was super tough, his hands and facial skin made tougher by soaking them in beef brine.

At one point he started looking for professional fights. One night he substituted in a fight for his brother Jack, also using his name. He won, kept the name, got himself a manager, and fought whenever and wherever he could, in or out of the ring. But it was a tough, hand-to-mouth existence.

Then one day he got a fateful letter from a fight promoter named Jack Kearns. In it was a five-dollar bill for "grub" and a train ticket to San Francisco from Salt Lake City, where Dempsey was living at the time. Kearns said he had heard that Dempsey was a good fighter and wanted to manage him.

Exhilarated and impressed that someone who had never met him would believe in him enough to send him a ticket and money, Dempsey traveled to San Francisco, where he met Kearns. Thus would begin a relationship that would culminate in his fighting Jess Willard and many others and influencing boxing more than any individual that ever lived.

Kearns was hailed by many as the most brilliant manager in the history of boxing. *The Ring* magazine editor Nat Fleischer credited him with having invented the promotional art of ballyhoo. He guided and promoted Dempsey while he cajoled and bullied him into one fight after another across the country, amassing twenty-one first-round knockouts in a row, until sportswriters of the day were writing about the new boxing phenom from the West. Kearns and Dempsey also linked up with George L. "Tex" Rickard, a man who promoted the first million-dollar gate in boxing history.

Following Willard, Dempsey had a series of memorable fights, including one with the great French champion Georges Carpentier. Carpentier was Rickard's idea, and it was cunningly clever. During World War I, Dempsey had been photographed in a work uniform and with a rivet gun in hand, supposedly doing important wartime work. The only problem was that he was wearing patent-leather shoes. Thereafter he was labeled a draft dodger and, though respected as a fighter, was not well regarded as a patriot. Carpentier, on the other hand, was a French war hero. Rickard figured that a big crowd would pay a lot to see Dempsey have the stuffing knocked out of him.

They did. At Boyle's Thirty Acres in Jersey City, New Jersey, Rickard built his usual plain plank stands, which were filled by more than eighty thousand fight fans paying a total of $1,799,238—the first million-dollar-plus boxing gate. Dempsey knocked Carpentier out in the fourth round.

Fights with Jack Sharkey and Luis "The Wild Bull of the Pampas" Firpo, who succeeded in knocking Dempsey out of the ring, followed. The fight with Firpo was the first two-million-dollar boxing gate ever.

Dempsey was making an immense amount of money, hundreds of thousands of dollars, and was the transcendent star of a time (the 1920s) when transcendent stars were not in short supply, what with people such as baseball's Babe Ruth and tennis's Bill Tilden around. Single-handedly, he had made boxing a major spectator sport.

Those who didn't respect Dempsey because of the World War I debacle started to respect him after his fights with ex-marine Gene Tunney. In 1926 Tunney beat him, gaining a ten-round decision in a rain-soaked arena in Philadelphia, where Dempsey lost his championship. Dempsey thought he was over, too old to fight, but he was persuaded to do it one more time—and he did.

The fight, held in Boyle's Thirty Acres, went the way Dempsey thought it would for seven rounds. Tunney, a superb boxer, battered Dempsey until he was near exhaustion. Then, abruptly, Dempsey uncorked a vicious left hook followed by a tattoo of other punches that suddenly had Tunney on his back, looking up at the sky. The referee was counting him out.

But Dempsey made a mistake. Told by the referee to go to a neutral corner, he hesitated. It took him, according to observers, four to seven seconds before he did so and the referee started the count. Gene Tunney got up at the count of nine—after fourteen or seventeen seconds—and to this day there is a debate as to whether Tunney would have been able to get up after nine seconds. He went on to take another decision from Dempsey.

Nevertheless, Dempsey fought some good fights after that one, as well as having some celebrated marital wars with three of his four wives. He also fathered two girls, lost a fortune (three million dollars) in the

Great Depression, and operated a famous Broadway restaurant, Jack Dempsey's, which he ultimately lost in 1950.

Then, in a stirring tribute in New York in 1954, he was elected to the Boxing Hall of Fame, named the greatest boxer of the first fifty years of the twentieth century.

In retrospect, Jack Dempsey may not have been as great a boxer as his reputation suggests. His final record of 69 bouts: He won 47 by knockout, 7 by decision, and 1 by foul; in 5 fights there was no decision, in 4 he drew, and he lost 4 by decision; he was knocked out once. But Dempsey *was* great. He, more than anyone else, with his charisma and his willingness to fight the big fights, brought boxing out of the bars and the two-bit rings, off the mud flats, and into the stadiums of America. A lot of boxers who might otherwise not have gone anywhere in their lives have the Manassa Mauler to thank.

He died on May 31, 1983.

88

John L. Sullivan

(1858–1918)

John L. Sullivan fought in the 1870s and 1880s, a time when pro boxing was closer to the savage "ultimate fighting" of today than to modern boxing. Back then, the fights were bare-knuckled, and the number of rounds was unlimited. A fight ended when one of the men lost consciousness or a trainer threw in a towel—or someone died. Bouts often required a trip to the hospital to have cracked knuckles or ribs, ripped tendons, or the like ministered to. The fights were on a winner-take-all basis, which provided the motivation.

John L. Sullivan was perfectly suited to the trade. He was a rough-and-tumble lad from the Irish ghetto of Roxbury, a part of Boston. Early on, his mother, a large, dominant woman, wanted him to be a priest.

But John, a bruiser with slabs of muscle for arms, wanted to be a fighter and, starting when he was about nineteen, fought local bouts in theaters in the Roxbury area. These bouts were distinguished by being fought according to rules laid down by an English gentleman named the marquis of Queensberry, chief of which were three-minute rounds and the wearing of gloves. A pro Sullivan was at heart, and he liked gloves and the structure of such bouts.

He gradually expanded the number of bouts he fought, and Billy Madden, a great public relations and advertising man as well as a manager, gradually worked the "Boston Strong Boy" into public consciousness.

This led to a bout on February 7, 1882, for the world championship against the champion, Paddy Ryan, whom Sullivan polished off in a little more than ten minutes. He then traveled the country, taking on any and all comers, offering a thousand dollars per bout to anyone who could stay conscious for more than four rounds (they got nothing if they were knocked out). Though some of the men he met were built like trees, Sullivan scoffed, with what was to become his famous line, "The bigger they are, the harder they fall."

And they did fall. To make sure everyone knew he was a world champion, Sullivan traveled to such countries as Australia and England, also taking on all comers, winner take all. How many bouts he had is open to question, but boxing historians suspect it was more than two hundred.

There is no record if he ever fell, this despite the fact that he drank a lot. As Bert Randolph Sugar said in his book *The 100 Greatest Boxers of All Time* (Sugar rated Sullivan number 50), "He never met a saloon he didn't like."

Sullivan became wildly rich. It is estimated that between 1882 and 1892 he made more than a million dollars, a king's ransom in those days. He was also wildly popular, admired not only by boxing aficionados but by people who simply liked sports. His biggest fight of his time was on July 8, 1889, a bare-knuckle bout with Jake Kilrain that was to mark the end of the bare-knuckle era—and almost the end of Kilrain.

The bout took place on a field outside Richburg, Mississippi, because it was the only place where it could be held without too much interference from the authorities, which forbade bare-knuckle bouts. It started shortly after ten in the morning, and it was not yet Mississippi hot—only about a hundred degrees.

The fight took two hours and sixteen minutes and lasted seventy-five rounds. At first Kilrain employed a strategy of evasion, at one point inspiring Sullivan to yell at him to fight. But Kilrain was trying to tire Sullivan out, then move in for the kill. The strategy worked for a while, but Sullivan started to catch up to him, pounding him with powerhouse punches (fighters compared his punch to being hit by a railroad tie fired from a cannon) until Kilrain was a bloody, battered mess.

But he kept coming out for more punishment, until finally a doctor who examined him said that if the bout continued, Kilrain would die. His handlers threw in the towel.

Following this bout, Sullivan went on what was to prove a hiatus, touring the country as an actor at the not insignificant sum of a thousand dollars a week. Still, he went through the money as fast as he made it, and there came a time when he was broke and had to have one more bout with a big payday.

This was with James J. Corbett (played by Errol Flynn in the movie

Gentleman Jim). Sullivan, out of shape and out of time, was knocked out by Corbett in the twenty-first round. Afterward, he announced that he was glad the world champion was an American.

This was his last bout. He was thirty-four but finished as a fighter. Following this defeat, he continued his world-class drinking, ballooning to almost 340 pounds. Then one day in 1905 he woke up and vowed never to have another drink—and he didn't.

Though Sullivan did not live a life that could be characterized as saintly—he was a drinker and lived with a showgirl named Ann Lingston while married—he had qualities that put the lie to the prevailing image of Irishmen as mindless gorillas with savage instincts and appetites. Sullivan was charming, patriotic, and a man's man—a heroic personality who gave people a new image of the Irish and gave the Irish someone to be proud of.

F. Scott Fitzgerald

(1896–1940)

The verdict on the literary merit of F. Scott Fitzgerald's writing is not yet in. Some critics think he is nothing more than a short story writer who also wrote a few novels that were pretty good. Then there is the body of opinion that he is one of the great American writers of the twentieth century and a world-class talent. It is an opinion that is in the majority.

Fitzgerald has been dead for almost sixty years. Yet he is still taught in schools all over America, and, more than occasionally, some writers' group or other is having a symposium on him of one sort or another.

Fitzgerald was born in St. Paul, Minnesota. He was a huge baby—ten pounds six ounces—an ironic fact because all his life he seemed embarrassed by his relatively small physical stature; at seventeen he was five feet, seven inches tall and weighed only 138 pounds.

In *The Far Side of Paradise* biographer Arthur Mizener wrote, in effect, that Scott's childhood was hardly a sitcom. Scott's father, Edward, Mizener wrote, was a slight, ineffectual man who was a salesman for

Procter & Gamble. While Scott loved him, he didn't respect him. His mother, Mollie, whose rich grandfather had emigrated from County Fermanagh, Ireland, was a little dotty, prone to wearing wrinkled clothes with her hair askew. Indeed, she seemed not to care about her appearance at all. On one formal occasion, for example, she wore one black and one brown shoe, her explanation being that it's best to wear shoes in one at a time.

His father, Edward, was also America-born and was a relative of Francis Scott Key, who wrote "The Star-Spangled Banner." Indeed, the novelist's full name was Francis Scott Key Fitzgerald.

Scott was always interested in writing. Though he got rejection after rejection, he kept going and, when he was thirteen, succeeded in selling a short story, "The Mystery of the Raymond Mortgage," to a magazine called *Now and Then*.

He entered St. Paul's Academy in St. Paul, there distinguishing himself as a debater and as a boy whom other boys didn't like. In addition to his debating skills, he had a nasty habit of telling people exactly what he thought of them. And no doubt, other boys were jealous of his looks. He had patrician features, a shock of carefully coifed blonde hair, and mesmerizing green eyes that his friend critic Edmund Wilson was to describe one day. Girls were drawn to him.

At the age of seventeen he entered Princeton and soon thereafter tried—despite his small stature—to get on the football team, fantasizing that one day he would be a starring quarterback. His football career lasted one day, at the end of which the coach told him that football was not "his kind of game." But his desire to complete tasks that were unreachable was typical of Fitzgerald for his entire life. He was always trying to prove his worth in one way or another.

At Princeton Fitzgerald did more partying than schoolwork. By 1917 he was on the verge of flunking out. Then he got what turned out to be a lucky touch of tuberculosis; he was able to quit school for a perfectly acceptable reason before he was expelled or forced to leave.

At the time, World War I was big news, and young men, filled with patriotism, were joining the army. When Fitzgerald's medical problems cleared up, he joined, being commissioned second lieutenant, and performed about as well as he did as a football player because he was not really mentally involved in soldiering: Every chance he got, he worked on writing novels.

He had continued to write, including a novel that he called *The Romantic Egotist*. When it was finished he sent it to Charles Scribner's Sons. No less a genius editor than Maxwell Perkins wanted to publish it, but he was overruled by other editors.

Part of Fitzgerald's sojourn in the service was at Camp Sheridan near Montgomery, Alabama. One Saturday night, he went to a dance in Montgomery and at one point saw a beautiful blond young woman dancing with another soldier. The sight did strange things to his stomach. He wangled an introduction, they danced and talked, and that night, when he was back at the base, Fitzgerald, an almost compulsive note writer, jotted down in his notebook, "Fell in love on 7th."

That beautiful young girl with the vaguely American Indian features was eighteen-year-old Zelda Sayre, daughter of an Alabama judge. She was not only pretty but smart and talented in many ways. As Scott was handsome and talented, too, it seemed like an ideal relationship.

Scott stayed stateside while in the army, a good part of the time at Camp Mills, Long Island. After he was discharged, he set about in earnest the task of trying to make it as a writer—a very successful one. Zelda had told him that before she would marry him, even though they had gotten engaged, he would have to be wildly successful, make a "fortune." Zelda was almost obsessed with money and the security she thought it would bring, and she did not want to marry a writer who might lead her to the poorhouse.

At first Scott gave indications that he might do just that. He settled in New York City and, despite Herculean efforts (at one point he had 122 rejection slips taped up around his room for stories he had written), did not achieve success. Then, in 1919 he sold a story to the magazine *Smart Set,* edited by H. L. Mencken, who paid him thirty dollars.

His relationship with Zelda during this period was chaotic. She seemed to be getting more and more nervous, and he was drinking heavily; they just couldn't seem to get along. She was always dreaming up ways to make Scott jealous, and then she came up with a doozy. She made it seem as if she were having an affair with golfing great Bobby Jones. She and Scott had a terrible argument, and she broke off the engagement.

Fitzgerald tried desperately to get her to change her mind. When she didn't, he retreated to New York and went on a bender that lasted three weeks. But he was always a writer, an observer, and later that bender would result in some memorable passages in his first novel.

When he stopped drinking, he returned to his writing. He revised *The Romantic Egotist,* which became *This Side of Paradise.* Although nominally about the cruel education of a young man returning after World War I, the novel was about much more; it held a mirror up to the time. And it was filled with Fitzgerald's insights and stirring prose, which was notable for its carefully observed detail and well-crafted language. He resubmitted the book to Scribner's and one day shortly thereafter received a letter from Max Perkins, telling Fitzgerald that the book had been accepted for publication.

At twenty-four years of age, Scott was the youngest novelist that Scribner's had ever published. He was euphoric and, he thought, on his way to making his fortune. The book did very well. It was published on March 20, 1920, and before its sales died down in the middle of 1923, fifty thousand hardcover copies had been sold.

Flush with success—and money—Scott became reunited with Zelda. They married, and he became more and more successful.

But their relationship continued to be chaotic. They always lived high. Both drank copiously and argued frequently. Scott, despite doing very well overall as a writer (in good years he averaged close to thirty thousand dollars, not a puny sum at the time), was always fiscally behind, always borrowing from Scribner or his agent, Harold Ober, and churning out numerous magazine articles and short stories to keep the wolf from the door. This was a pattern that he and Zelda created by their lifestyle, a pattern that was to last their entire lives.

In the thirties, mainly to make money, he went to Hollywood and churned out many screenplays, some of them quite good. But despite making very good money there, he never seemed to be able to catch up.

At one point, Zelda started to have mental breakdowns, occasionally to the point of having to be cared for in an institution. There came a time when she had to be permanently committed.

While much of their lives was a blend of endless partying, fiscal woes, and hurt visited on each other and friends, there was love, even after Zelda was committed. She always said that even after their relationship had ended, Scott had been good to her long after another man would have forgotten her.

Fitzgerald has been an inspiration and example to innumerable writers worldwide and will very likely continue to be. His writing holds up. His insights and, particularly in his novels, the characters' longing to capture— or recapture—something indefinable—a sort of lost something a soul seeks—are moving elements that seem to be repeated over and over again.

In *The Great Gatsby,* which many people think is Fitzgerald's finest novel (Fitzgerald himself preferred *Tender Is the Night*), this is one of the major themes. Jay Gatsby, who seems to have everything, is always looking out at a dock at night. At the end of the dock is a small green light that seems to symbolize that which he really wants but can never reach, a world where dreams don't come true.

In the last passage, the narrator, Nick, who has been a witness to terrible things, including Gatsby's murder, thinks to himself:

And as I sat there . . . I thought of Gatsby's wonder when he first picked out the green light at the end of Daisy's dock. He had come a long way to this blue lawn, and his dream must have seemed so close that he could hardly fail to grasp it. He did not know that it was already behind him, somewhere back in that vast obscurity beyond the city, where the dark fields of the republic rolled on under the night.

Gatsby believed in the green light, the orgiastic future that year by year recedes before us. It eluded us then, but that's no matter— tomorrow we will run faster, stretch out our arms farther . . . And one fine morning— So we beat on, boats against the current, borne back ceaselessly into the past.

Knowing his life, one always gets the sense that Fitzgerald was talking about himself. Indeed, the last line of the book is also engraved on his headstone.

Frank McCourt

(1930–)

Five years ago it would have been hard to put Frank McCourt onto a list of the most influential Irish, despite the fact that in the twenty-seven years he taught English at the prestigious Stuyvesant High School in Manhattan, he must have influenced a lot of students who passed his way very positively. At least one senses that.

But the publication of his book *Angela's Ashes* changed all that. Published in 1996 by Scribner's, it had a print run of twenty-seven thousand copies, a respectable number for an unknown author. But as of August 1997, it had been on the *New York Times'* best-seller list for more than a year, sold more than one million copies, and won both the Pulitzer Prize and the National Book Award. The publisher printed 1.8 million copies, and chances are he won't have to burn any.

Why the reason for its success? On the surface, its content—a poor family with an alcoholic father, a stoical mother—seems as though it would reek of clichés. But that's the trick. The book is beautifully written, without clichés, and McCourt has an eye for physical detail, as well as a memory, that is phenomenal. In fact, he told *Newsweek* that something he remembered from when he was three years old had triggered his writing the book: "I'm in a playground on Classon Avenue in Brooklyn with my brother, Malachy. He's two, I'm three. We're on the seesaw . . ."

From that moment on, McCourt could see the story through a child's eyes, speaking in the present tense, and *Angela's Ashes* was born then and there. "It was like a gift," McCourt says. "This was one of those books that had to be written. If I'm happy now, it's because I wrote that book and it's successful. . . . If I hadn't written it, I'd probably be sitting around thinking about going back to teaching. I'd feel unfulfilled, as they say. And I'd die howling."

McCourt says he wrote the book largely to try to put his past to rest, but he found that that was not possible.

Perhaps one central thing the book does is to educate the general population in what it is to be Irish and poor; the book showed what "abject poverty" really is. It's hard to imagine anyone reading this book and not thinking about the Irish poor differently.

The other achievement is that it is an amazing story of survival, showing human beings being put through terrible pressures that, by all logic, should kill them but don't. Not only do they survive; they thrive.

The story starts in New York City, where McCourt's mother and father met and married. Then the action shifts, much to McCourt's regret, to Ireland; the family moved to Limerick in 1934, when Frank was four. He had had three brothers and a sister, but she had died. In Ireland, two more brothers would be born—and would also die.

McCourt's father was a big problem. He was constantly "drinking his paycheck up," leaving the family to more or less fend for itself.

Then, sometime during World War II, his father left, never to return, and the family went from abysmal poverty to superabysmal poverty. Angela, his mother, had to live on welfare, working when she could and scrounging off relatives. At one point, she was in such dire straits that to secure a place for her children to stay she had to sleep with her cousin— only they didn't sleep.

The book ends when McCourt is about twenty. Since the publication of *Angela's Ashes,* there has seemed to be an increased interest in things Irish, and it may well be that this moving book has had something to do with that.

91

Samuel Beckett

The main problem with many of Samuel Beckett's works, one might feel, is that they are difficult to understand; some are even impenetrable. But someone at the Nobel committee must have understood them, because in 1969 he was awarded the Nobel Prize for literature.

Beckett, like his friend James Joyce, was born in Dublin at Foxrock, a suburb of the city, and he was part of a fashionable Protestant family. However, over the years, Beckett would develop even more of a dislike for Dublin than Joyce did. Whenever Beckett visited the city, he would get physically ill. At least one of his biographers said this was because of his relationship to his mother: It was that bad.

He had attended Trinity College, Dublin, then had lived in Paris, and had returned to Trinity to teach French, which was the language he mainly wrote in. But in December 1931, after receiving his M.A., he quit teaching and made a beeline for the Continent.

If he thought he was getting away, he was mistaken. Like a moth to a flame, he was always drawn back by one family crisis or the other, and he suffered the usual ills when he returned. This particular period of disenchantment lasted about twenty years.

Beckett had been writing—determinedly. In 1932 he penned a novel called *Dream of Fair to Middling Women,* which was not published. He then published a collection of short stories, *More Pricks Than Kicks.* He next wrote the novel *Murphy,* which he sent to forty publishers before it was accepted and published in 1938.

During World War II Beckett was not in the garret fine-tuning his prose. He was an active participant in the French Resistance, and following the war, he received the Croix de Guerre for his service.

Critics say his best work was done following the war. *Molloy,* which is considered his best novel, came out in 1951, as did *Malone Dies.*

Beckett was a playwright as well as a poet; late in the decade he wrote what was to be his most famous play, *Waiting for Godot.* It was produced in Paris in 1952, and it caused a deluge of discussion. There was obviously some meaning running beneath the surface of the verbiage—something profound, people sensed—but what exactly did it mean? Waiting for God? The play seemed impenetrable.

Then *Godot* was produced in London and New York, and there were similar reactions. No one ever definitely established what the play meant, but it made Beckett famous. The play had come along when many leading dramatists such as Jean-Paul Sartre, Tennessee Williams, and Arthur Miller were not elusive in their meanings. Beckett was, and audiences loved it.

And so did other writers. Beckett had an enormous influence on such avant-garde stylists as Eugène Ionesco and Harold Pinter. Collectively, along with Beckett, they were characterized as dramatists in the Theater of the Absurd.

Following *Godot,* Beckett did not have much of a literary output, being mostly concerned with translating his work from French into English. In 1957, though, he came out with another play that became famous, *Fin de Partie,* or *Endgame.*

Beckett was influenced by James Joyce, but one thing that is different is his prose. While Joyce's prose, particularly in *Finnegans Wake,* piles "nuance upon nuance," as one critic says, Beckett's prose is clear. Beckett's work is also characterized by an ingenious comic invention, even though the world he writes about is filled with repugnant characters traipsing along in a landscape that seems as if it were bombed.

Beckett died in 1989, at the ripe old age of eighty-three.

92

John Boyle O'Reilly

(1844–1890)

No one could ever accuse John Boyle O'Reilly of not living his life, as Ernest Hemingway once said, "all the way up." Within his relatively brief forty-six years, he was a newspaper publisher, poet, soldier, prisoner, prison escapee, and revolutionary—and an inspiration to his fellow Irishmen and -women. When he died, *Harper's Weekly* called him the most "distinguished Irishman in America."

O'Reilly was born in Drogheda in Ireland, where his father owned and operated a small school. O'Reilly himself was interested in becoming a writer, and, as was the custom, he was apprenticed to a newspaper in Drogheda for four years. He then secured a position on an English paper, the *Preston Guardian*. But after three years he returned to Ireland and joined the Tenth Hussars. He then became a member of the secret Fenian Society, which was dedicated to Irish nationalism, and became very active in its recruitment efforts.

In 1866 he and a number of other Fenians were arrested by the

British for plotting the overthrow of Her Majesty's government, and he was sentenced to death. After two years in solitary confinement, though, his sentence was commuted from execution to a long period in a faraway penal colony. He and a number of other Fenians were put aboard a ship and sent to a prison in Australia. This was virtually a death sentence, as the place was run by taskmasters who would have done well on Devil's Island.

O'Reilly bided his time, always looking for a chance to bolt. But he had to be sure. Then, an opportunity presented itself. An American priest from a whaling boat called the *Gazelle* had come to see the prisoners. He and O'Reilly, a charming man known for his ability to make friends, got along, and it was arranged that O'Reilly would escape and rendezvous with the *Gazelle*.

On February 18, 1869, O'Reilly made his escape from the prison proper, but getting to the ship was another matter. He hid in the bush, avoiding prison patrols, and finally was able to make contact with the ship. He was rowed out—and the ship set sail.

But his ordeal was not over. He had to avoid being captured in England and he finally fled from there to America, where he stepped onto safe ground in Philadelphia on November 23, 1869.

Eventually he got a job as reporter on the *Boston Pilot,* a newspaper that was developing a reputation as the greatest Irish newspaper in America. O'Reilly quickly established a reputation as a highly skilled journalist and was in particular cited for his coverage of the Fenian attack on the Canadians from their base camp in Vermont in 1871. He continued to be successful at the paper, and then, in 1876, he was able to buy it.

He took the paper to new heights, constantly and courageously pressing for Irish Home Rule and social justice, not only for the Irish but for other oppressed minorities such as blacks and Indians. His views were decidedly unpopular with a lot of people.

While O'Reilly was home free, he never forgot his fellow Fenians languishing in the Australian jail. Six years after he himself escaped, he developed a clever plan of escape for six prisoners that was to play out like an action adventure movie.

Chartering a whaling ship, the *Catalpa,* like the one he had escaped on, O'Reilly and coconspirators sailed down to the Indian Ocean, plying the waters off the southeastern coast of Australia. The ship was outfitted like any whaling ship, of which there were many in the area. Moreover, many of its crew were South Seas islanders who did not have a clue as to what was afoot. O'Reilly and his friends counted on the *Catalpa* not attracting attention. At risk, of course, was his own freedom.

Meanwhile, two other Fenians, John Breslin and Thomas Desmiond, sailed from Los Angeles to the Australian city of Fremantle in November 1875 and arranged for the six surviving Fenians and prisoners to slip away from their work parties. They would then be rowed to the *Catalpa,* which would be standing at anchor waiting for them, and sail away.

But it was not that easy. It was not until April of the next year that the prisoners were able to slip away. They made it to the rowboat and started frantically rowing toward the *Catalpa,* which was waiting. But the weather was bad, and they were unable to make it. All night they were tossed around the sea in crashing waves under a lashing rain.

Miraculously, when the weather cleared, the *Catalpa* was still there. The prisoners started rowing toward it, but suddenly they were spotted by a police cutter. The police knew there was an escape in progress and set sail to intercept them before they reached the boat. With a final effort, the escapees made it to the whaler. The police, not knowing what to do, sailed back to Fremantle and notified the governor, who immediately dispatched the steam-powered gunboat *Georgette,* which ran down the much slower, sail-powered *Catalpa* in short order and stopped it.

The captain of the *Georgette* fired a shot across the *Catalpa's* bow and ordered the captain to give up the escaped prisoners. The captain of the *Catalpa* didn't know what to do. His ship was no match for the *Georgette*. They would all die. Then he had an idea. He had the U.S. flag raised on the ship and made something perfectly clear: If the Australian captain fired on the *Catalpa*, he was firing on the United States of America. He then ordered his crew to set sail.

The *Georgette's* captain was unsure; he certainly didn't want to create an international incident. He trailed the *Catalpa* for a while, then turned back toward Fremantle. They had made it. O'Reilly and his comrades kept going, arriving in New York the following year.

The *Pilot* newspaper he bought still lives as the official organ of the Catholic Church in Boston. And it is still edited very well.

93

Alfred E. Smith

(1873–1944)

Irish laborers were always valued by American businessmen for doing certain types of work, such as bridge building. In fact, they were imported to do such jobs. They were strong and fearless (and hungry to survive), quite willing to do high-wire jobs on cables hundreds of feet above a river that, if you hit it from that height, would smash you like concrete.

The problem was that many did fall to their deaths, while others were killed by the bends, a mysterious illness that affected those inside the caissons working deep in the river. (It was ultimately determined that the bends were caused by coming up from the bottom of the river too quickly.).

During the time it took to build the Brooklyn Bridge, ordinary people watched its progress. One of these was Catherine Mulvihill Smith, Al Smith's mother, who, like her husband, Alfred, was an Irish immigrant. Their house was actually under the bridge. As the book *The Irish in America* relates, she had a "vantage point that allowed [her] to witness the bridge's cost in human lives. Dozens of workers died during the decade it took to build the bridge, and many of those left behind large families. There was a safety net for neither worker nor family." Both were left to fate.

His mother frequently communicated her outrage to her son, so it is small wonder that he learned to identify with the have-nots of society—not only his fellow Irish, but his own family, particularly after his father died when he was relatively young.

Smith was not a strong student; books didn't seem to interest him, and he left school at the end of grammar school, when his father's death made it necessary for him to help support the family. This he did in a variety of jobs over the next few years; then, at seventeen, he snagged a job as an assistant bookkeeper in the Fulton Fish Market, the job more that of a laborer than of a white-collar worker.

Early on, Smith looked toward a political horizon. Though he was a moral, ethical person, the only route in politics for an Irish Catholic in New York was through Tammany Hall, which represented the Democratic Party and was usually stained with corruption. Smith plunged into politics full force, using his considerable gifts as a speaker (he had once toyed with the idea of becoming an actor but did not relish the idea of an extended period of poverty) to get ahead.

Despite his affiliation with Tammany Hall, he managed to keep himself clean and his reputation unsullied. It was an achievement. His first party appointment, in fact, was as an investigator of jurors, a job that paid eight hundred dollars a year. For the right person it could have been lucrative, but he didn't make an extra dime. Nevertheless, as the new century dawned, he had bright prospects for some sort of political achievement.

And he was not alone. In 1900 he had married a woman from the Bronx, Catherine Dunn.

In 1903 he was able to wangle the party's endorsement for state senator. He was elected by more than three-quarters of the vote in the overwhelmingly Democratic district he ran from.

His career continued upward, spurred by an ability that served him well: He could see two sides to every story and knew that many things in life are not black and white but gray. This ability allowed him to empathize with both sides and use his personality, which was warm and affable, very effectively. For example, the early 1900s was the time of the reformer in politics, and Smith was able to have one foot in the Tammany camp (with a reasonable surety of getting it back) and the other in the camp of the reformers, such as those led by Franklin Delano Roosevelt, and be trusted by both factions. Indeed, down through the years his effectiveness as a politician was due in great part to his ability to find a consensus among battling parties. His reputation grew, and in 1918 he ran for governor and was elected. He then won an additional three terms, four two-year terms in all.

Another ability Smith had was hiring good assistants; it made his job much easier, and the results were better. Indeed, many of the people Smith hired, such as Frances Perkins, would go on to work in FDR's administration in the 1930s.

In 1924 Smith took the first step toward the ultimate political prize: getting himself nominated to run for president. This was a bold notion because he was an Irish Catholic, something that would play in New York but not in Peoria. He failed, but he tried again in 1928, and this time he succeeded; his opponent was Herbert Hoover.

Smith lost the presidential election for a variety of reasons. First, he was Catholic, and the Protestant majority feared that electing a Catholic was prelude to having the pope move into Blair House as a permanent guest. Second, he was anti-Prohibition, something that foot-stomping, churchgoing, God-fearing—and dry—middle-America still wanted. Plus he was a New Yorker, which automatically conferred on him a patina of fast-talking criminality. He was dead in the water before he started.

But out of the ashes of that defeat came a valuable insight that might well be the reason why FDR was ultimately elected. For the first time, Democrats saw what city voters liked, the very qualities that turned rural voters off. It was a valuable insight, and political strategists used it well.

Smith had been a longtime political ally of Roosevelt's, but in 1932 he committed the equivalent, as someone said, "of striking a king and not succeeding in killing him": He tried to wrest the presidential nomination from FDR. From that time on, his political star descended, and their relationship was further eroded by Roosevelt's not appointing Smith to any post in his administration.

In 1936 Smith became part of the anti-Roosevelt Liberty League, but it was battered in the election. Smith stayed in public life a few more years, but his role as a politician was over.

Still, his influence in his time was great, and he broke the ice, as it were, of the presidency; from then on it was possible to imagine that one day a Catholic could be president. And one day, one was.

94

The Unsinkable Molly Brown (Margaret Tobin)

(1867–1932)

In the dead of the cold night of April 14, 1912, an iceberg beneath the water five hundred miles off the coast of Newfoundland stove in the starboard side of the R.M.S. *Titanic,* the world's premier luxury liner, on its maiden voyage from England to New York. Within hours, the ship, which had been declared unsinkable by the engineers who had designed her, had gone to the bottom, and with her nearly fifteen hundred souls.

One who did not perish, and who was to go on to achieve fame as "The Unsinkable Molly Brown," was Margaret Tobin.

Maggie Brown, born Margaret Tobin, was a wealthy woman who lived in an elegant Queen Anne–style home in Denver with her husband,

James Brown, a prospector who had struck gold in 1893. Maggie, who had been touring Europe, had booked passage on the liner shortly after learning that her grandson in Denver was sick. She was on her way back to see him.

Just exactly what happened that night, or in episodes subsequent to it in Maggie's life, is not totally clear. There is no question that she acted heroically, but this is the kind of event that invites embellishment, and Maggie herself was not averse to gilding the lily.

What is known is that when she learned of the straits the ship was in, she immediately dressed and went topside and into the chaos, where passengers were already being loaded onto lifeboats by crew members, and began organizing people for a more orderly passage into the boats. She said that she did not try to get into one of the boats herself but found herself grabbed by a crew member and unceremoniously deposited in one.

On the lifeboat there was a little crisis. A crew member of the *Titanic* was there, but he seemed unable to take positive action. Brown did. She grabbed hold of the oars and started to row, exhorting other passengers to be of stout heart, that they would make it out alive.

And they did, thanks to the actions of the eagle-eyed Maggie, who, far in the dark distance, spotted the lights of the liner *Carpathia* and was able to intersect with the ship.

Aboard the *Carpathia,* she continued her take-charge style, compiling a list of the survivors—which was easier because many were foreign and she was fluent in a number of languages—and making sure that the list was radioed to New York.

Her courageous coolheadedness during the event made her a national hero, and when she was asked by newspaper reporters why she had survived, her answer was "Typical Brown luck. We're unsinkable."

That was all the papers needed. Someone added "Unsinkable," to her name; someone changed "Maggie" to "Molly"; and the legend was off and running, peaking some fifty years later in a Broadway musical about her life, *The Unsinkable Molly Brown*. The event catapulted her to national fame, and she used the opportunity to speak out on issues that mattered to her. One was the practice of saving women and children first off a sinking ship, which she thought wrong because, as the *Titanic* experience had shown, this had a terrible effect: It left a lot of destitute widows with children to care for—and no means to care for them.

In 1914 she tried to give her voice a more official forum when she ran for the Senate, even though women did not yet have the vote. She lost. Molly also championed the Equal Rights Amendment, even getting an audience with President Calvin Coolidge, though her efforts went for naught.

Part of Maggie's fame was certainly her suggestion that her father had been friendly with Mark Twain. The elder Tobin, John, had first immigrated from Ireland in 1923, settling in Virginia and marrying. But after a few years, he moved on to Hannibal, Missouri, the town that Twain was to make internationally famous through his writing. Her father had married a woman named Johanna Collins from Hannibal, and Maggie was born there. She said that her father had met Twain there. Whether that's true is a matter of debate.

Maggie was rich enough to be a member of the high society there. But she was given the cold shoulder by Denver society folks because she was nouveau riche and her personality was down to earth, her mannerisms more ordinary Irish than anything else.

All was not domestic bliss. Though her husband, James, had suffered a stroke in 1899, he recovered well enough to get involved with another man's wife and have his antics widely publicized in an embarrassing "alienation of affection" suit brought by the cuckolded husband.

James died in 1922. During the last ten years of her life, Molly Brown came upon fiscal hard times herself. For a long time after her death the house she had lived in was in disrepair. But in the seventies it was restored and made into a national monument. Like Molly, it proved unsinkable.

Nellie Bly

Before *Dateline, 20/20,* Geraldo Rivera, and everyone else who does investigative journalism in America, there was Nellie Bly, born Elizabeth Cochran on May 5, 1864, in Cochran Mills, Pennsylvania. As Brooke Kroeger, author of the biography *Nellie Bly: Daredevil Reporter, Feminist* describes her influence: "In the 1880s, she pioneered the development of 'detective' or 'stunt' journalism, the acknowledged forerunner to full-scale investigative reporting." Kroeger adds of her impact on women in journalism, "While she was still in her early twenties, the example of her fearless success helped open the profession to coming generations of women journalists clamoring to write hard news."

Nellie was the daughter of Mary Jane Cummings and Michael Cochran, whose forebears had emigrated from Ireland and settled in the area in the early nineteenth century. Michael Cochran became a person of some importance in the area as well as a judge, and in honor of this the town where Nellie was born, Pitts Mills, was renamed Cochran Mills.

Nellie—or "Pink" as her family nicknamed her because of the pink dresses her mother often dressed her in—had a good relationship with her father, who was considerably older than her mother, his second wife. Unfortunately, he died suddenly when Nellie was six.

There followed a chaotic period for Nellie and her fourteen siblings, because her father had not left a will. Her mother eventually remarried, but her new husband, Jack, turned out to be a drunk and wife beater. It wasn't long before she filed for divorce: Her divorce action was highly unusual, one of only fifteen filed that year (1878) in a county of forty thousand. She was, moreover, one of only five women filing.

At twenty-two, Nellie got her start in the newspaper business with a letter. One column regularly published in the *Pittsburgh Dispatch* was chauvinistic in the extreme, advocating that a woman's place—her only place—was as a homemaker. At one point Bly wrote a savage retort to one of the columns. The editors liked it so much that they contacted her and offered her a job.

About a year later she started freelancing and landed an assignment with Joseph Pulitzer's *New York World,* which created a furor. Posing as a mental patient, she spent ten days in New York's Blackwell Island Institution and wrote of her experiences. The *World* made a big deal of the story, and it was to lead to significant changes in the way mental institutions are run. Nellie Bly—she had adopted the name from a Stephen Foster song, with the spelling of Nelly changed to "Nellie"—was off and running.

Bly was bound to succeed. She was a good writer, but the core of her character was courage and daring. She would go anywhere and do anything. She used investigative techniques to expose sweatshops, slum life, and the world of petty crime.

One of her scariest assignments was a six-month stint in Mexico. She wrote reports from there on life in Mexico, all the time aware that if the authorities didn't like what she wrote, she could easily be arrested and thrown into a Mexican prison. About that, she said later, "I had some regard for my health, and a Mexican jail is the least desirable abode on the face of the earth, so some care was exercised on the selection of topics while we were inside their gates." But after leaving Mexico, she wrote a series of scathing reports on the corruption, abuses, and savagery of life there.

In 1890 she became world-famous when she sought to beat the record of Phileas Fogg in Jules Verne's novel *Around the World in Eighty Days,* traveling by boat, train, and horse. And she did so, making it in seventy-two days, six hours, eleven minutes, and fourteen seconds. When she arrived in San Francisco, her publisher, Joseph Pulitzer, sent a special train to meet her, and when she returned to New York, there was a parade complete with fireworks and gun salutes.

In 1895 Nellie married millionaire Robert Seaman, who was forty years older than she was, and then retired. In 1904 he died, and then she went into business. But she lost most of her inheritance, not the least reason being that she had been bilked by check forgers. Her later years were spent in helping homeless children.

In 1919 she tried to get her newspaper career going again but was unsuccessful. She died three years later, on January 27, 1922. In his obituary, Arthur Brisbane, one of the most prestigious journalists in America, wrote a glowing tribute to her, characterizing her as the best reporter in America—man or woman.

96

Connie Mack

(1862–1956)

Connie Mack influenced the game of baseball—and its lure as a sport—in a number of ways. But perhaps the single most important way was in the dignity he brought to the game, particularly in the latter part of his career, when the team he was managing, the Philadelphia Athletics, lost many games. Another man might have lost his head. Not Mack. He remained a gentlemen during the hardest of times, and by so doing, kept a promise he had made many years earlier to his mother. When Connie was first toying with the idea of going into professional baseball, she was afraid because the people in the game had a reputation for roughness. She felt he might be changed by them. Mack told her not to worry, that he was a gentleman and would always be that way. And he always was.

Mack's father was a product of the potato famine, emigrating to America and settling in East Brookfield, Massachusetts, an industrial town between Springfield and Worcester.

Young Connie loved the game of baseball, though the position he played required extreme courage. He played catcher for the East Brookfield team at a time when there was no protective equipment for that position.

He was tall and very thin, with a storklike neck. He looked as if he might break in half like a matchstick. But he was also wiry and well coordinated, and he was instrumental in his team's winning the central championship of Massachusetts one year.

His father had gotten a job in the local cotton mills, working, as they said, "half days" (twelve hours a day). When Connie came of age, he joined his father. It was grueling, smelly, difficult work, but that did not seem to bother him. Years later, he would speak of his time at the mill with affection and nostalgia.

One day when he was twenty, an event occurred that was to set him off on his baseball odyssey. One of the early baseball greats, Cap Anson, came to East Brookfield to put on an exhibition. Mack was enthralled by it and decided to give professional baseball a try. He found the opportunity in Connecticut, playing for the Meridian team for ninety dollars a month, which was not bad for the time. A year later, in 1883, he found himself playing for the Hartford, Connecticut, team for considerably more—one hundred twenty-five dollars.

"Connie Mack" was actually a nickname he had been called since he was a kid. His birth name was Cornelius McGillicuddy, but for a very practical reason—it was too long to fit on a scorecard—he changed it to Connie Mack for good.

In 1894, at the age of thirty-two, he became the player manager for the Pittsburgh franchise. He compiled a fairly good record, but two years later he was fired. He had no job, but that was not the biggest of his worries. His wife had died, and at the age of only thirty-four, he was a widower with three children to care for.

At just this moment, he got lucky. Another minor-league owner, Ben Johnson, offered Connie the chance to manage his Milwaukee franchise, his pay in part to be a one-quarter interest in the team.

Mack managed the team for four years. As the new century dawned, the Milwaukee team was moved into a new stadium in Philadelphia and given a new name: the Athletics. Mack, of course, stayed on as owner and manager, continuing to manage the team for fifty years. The first thirty years were the best in terms of winning, but overall he managed the Athletics for 7,876 games, 43 of them in the World Series. They won five World Series championships, the first three in 1910, 1911, and 1913. Then Mack went sixteen years without a series but returned to the fray in 1929, 1930, and 1931, when he was blessed with having two baseball immortals in his lineup, Tris Speaker and Ty Cobb. The team won in 1929 and 1930 but was nipped by the St. Louis Cardinals in 1931.

But from 1931 on, the Athletics became the doormat of the league. Mack stayed on until 1950, when, at the age of eighty-eight, he retired. He died at the age of ninety-three, just a year after his sons had sold the team to the flamboyant and irascible Charles O. Finley.

Connie Mack would influence generations of managers with his approach to the game, which was as scientific as he could make it. He kept careful notes on hitters and pitchers and would advise his players on how to hit or pitch to get the best results. Managers are still doing that today.

97

Mathew B. Brady

Civil War photographer Mathew B. Brady did something that no one until then had done in America: Using photographs, he brought war into people's living rooms and hearts; he showed Americans what war was really like. After viewing an exhibit Brady had mounted in his New York City studio, "The Dead at Antietam," in September 1862, the *New York Times* wrote: "If he had not laid bodies and laid them in doorways and streets, he had done something very like it."

The photos from that war are crisp and clear. They show men alive and men dead, men glorious and men horrific and ordinary. (Indeed, he gave many photos to soldiers so they could send them home to loved ones.) Perhaps the most striking thing about the photographs is their ordinariness: We see men cooking, men encamped, men performing the ordinary tasks of soldiers—and then we see them dead.

Brady had been a successful photographer long before he began his black-and-white epic of the Civil War. He had been entranced by the fledgling art and had opened a photographic studio on the corner of Fulton Street in New York City. He was so good at portrait photography that his fame soon spread. Anyone who wanted to be known as someone had to have on his portrait the magic words "Portrait by Brady."

In 1858 Brady moved his studio to Washington, D.C., and there started to photograph many different people, including the high and mighty. When the government, aware of his great skill as a photographer, offered to commission him to travel with the Union army to shoot the war with his camera, he was drawn to the project. "A spirit in my feet said 'Go!' and I went," he said.

Brady's background is murky. It is known that his father came from Ireland and that Brady knew he was Irish but little else. He did not have— or did not dispense—much information about his mother. He didn't even know what his middle initial, "B," stood for. Nor did he reveal why he spelled his first name with one "t." He may even have been illiterate.

His life was plagued with fiscal troubles. When the great fiscal crisis of 1873 occurred, he was driven to the poorhouse. Further problems made him struggle mightily to survive, even after the war and his justifiable fame. So needy was he at one point that he was forced to sell two thousand Civil War photographs to the government, but the money gleaned from the sale mostly went to clear up accumulated debt.

While photographing the war, Brady succeeded in keeping a big secret from everyone, except his assistants. His eyesight was so bad that he had trouble seeing his subjects, and in fact his assistants took many of the photos under his direction. After the war one of the people he photographed was Abraham Lincoln, just days before he was assassinated.

Still, Brady lived his latter years in relative poverty. Then, one day in 1895, he was crossing a street in Washington and, perhaps because he couldn't see very well, was run over. Physically, he was never the same again, and he passed away the next year, on January 15, 1896.

Certainly, however, his photographs did not die with him. Indeed, though it is estimated that three hundred photographers photographed the Civil War, only Brady's work survives. Even now, more than a hundred years after his demise, they show up—literally—in discussions and documentaries about the Civil War. He was the photographer not only of the war but for the ages.

98

Georgia O'Keeffe

(1887–1986)

The marriage of Georgia O'Keeffe to Alfred Stieglitz joined two very special people who certainly saw the world, it can be safely said, differently from most people. O'Keeffe was one of the great artists of the twentieth century, and Stieglitz was a genius with a camera. Indeed, when Stieglitz married O'Keeffe, he was at the apex of his fame and, probably more than anyone else, showed the world what she could do.

Georgia O'Keeffe was born on November 15, 1887, in Sun Prairie, Wisconsin, a town that well described the environment she would do her painting in. She was of Irish, Dutch, and Hungarian extraction; her given name was a female version of that of her Hungarian grandfather, George Totto.

Georgia was one of six children. The family lived on an isolated farm, and her mother, Ida, was lonely. But Georgia would grow to love the farm.

Her father, Francis, had his own demons to contend with: At the time, tuberculosis seemed to run in his family; indeed, it had killed his brother.

Out of fear of tuberculosis, her father moved the family to Williamsburg, Virginia. But Georgia was allowed to stay behind to attend Sacred Heart Academy, which, though it was a Catholic school and Georgia had been raised Presbyterian, was chosen because it was such a good art school. Years later, Georgia would say that she had known when she was eight years old that she would become an artist. She didn't know why—she just sensed it.

Eventually she joined her family in Virginia, also attending good schools. But then she had to quit because her father, who had suffered a series of business losses, could no longer afford it. By 1907 she could afford to attend school again, and she went to New York City to attend the Art Students League.

New York had more than its share of art galleries. One day Georgia visited one named "291"—so-called because of its address—and observed the controversial drawings of Auguste Rodin. The man who ran the gallery, Alfred Stieglitz, was an intimidating figure, so Georgia did not try to speak with him. Little did she know—nor did Stieglitz—that some years later she would end up marrying him.

O'Keeffe supported herself until 1917 by teaching art in various colleges in South Carolina and Amarillo, Texas. But during this period she had arranged for a friend to show Stieglitz some of her drawings, and he was very impressed.

Stieglitz was a great promoter. He put on a show of her paintings. It was a big hit and the first of many shows. Stieglitz managed her work well, releasing only a certain number of paintings at a time to drive up their price.

O'Keeffe's paintings were like nothing anyone had seen, particularly as done by a woman; at the time women were treated just as patronizingly in the art world as everywhere else. The paintings were impressionistic, her subjects mostly drawn from the American Southwest, places such as Texas and New Mexico. They were stunning, and for a while there was much discussion about their explicitly sensual nature. O'Keeffe scoffed at these comments, but Stieglitz, knowing that controversy ultimately translated into dollars, encouraged them. Stieglitz also aided her career by taking a series of arresting photos of her. She was a beautiful woman who always wore her hair pulled straight and tied at the back. A slim woman, she favored black-and-white clothing.

Gradually, her work was noticed more and more by the world. Recognition culminated in 1946 in a show at the Museum of Modern Art in New York.

Her life with Stieglitz was unconventional though successful. By 1929—they had been married in 1924—Stieglitz would regularly live for part of the year in New York because he loved the city so much, while O'Keeffe would stay in the Southwest, in places such as Taos, New Mexico. When she did visit New York, she invariably stored in the trunk of her car withered branches and stones and bones picked up from the desert that she could use as models.

Tragically, O'Keeffe started to lose her eyesight in 1971, developing irreversible eye damage. In 1972 she stopped painting.

O'Keeffe's impact on modern art was substantial. In addition, although she never allowed her name to be publicly linked to the women's movement, she was a role model for other women as to what an independent woman could be.

Seamus Heaney

(1939–)

"Poetry," says the Irish poet Seamus Heaney, "grows like moss inside you and at certain times you start picking it off. You can't sit down and do it just by willing it."

Whatever way he does it, he does it right, because on October 5, 1995, Heaney was awarded the Nobel Prize for literature. As a Nobel winner, Heaney joined other great Irish literary lights such as W. B. Yeats, George Bernard Shaw, and Samuel Beckett. (Other Nobel winners of Irish extraction are American playwright Eugene O'Neill and Australian writer Patrick White.)

Heaney had been picking moss for thirty years, alternately teaching and writing. In fact, he was on vacation in Greece when Harvard University, where he was Boylston Professor of Rhetoric and Oratory, tried to reach him with the news about the Nobel Prize—but couldn't.

Heaney, a low-key person, was born in Mossbawn, County Derry. He went to St. Columb's School, and it was there, he told *Irish America* magazine, that he experienced "his first flicker of genuine poetic pleasure";

he "read the works of Gerard Manley Hopkins. Had he not come into contact with the works of writers and poets, he surmised, he probably would not have written poetry. His was a literate household where books were respected, but not a literary one, he said."

Heaney graduated from Queens University in Belfast and then started to get serious about his poetry. He soon realized that he felt a communion with the farming area where he was raised and started to write poetry related to the land and animals. But it would be a mistake to think that he was simply writing about, say, the life of a frog or the bogs. Heaney said that to have power, everything that he wrote must contain a "universal" truth.

The Nobel committee cited the poem "Lightenings viii" in its announcement:

The annals say: when the monks of Clonmacnoise
Were all at prayer inside the oratory
A ship appeared above them in the air

The anchor dragged along behind so deep
It hooked itself into the altar rails
And then, as the big hull rocked to a standstill,

A crewman shinned and grappled down a rope
And struggled to release it. But in vain.
"This man can't bear our life here and will drown,"

The abbot said, "Unless we help him." So
They did, the freed ship sailed and the man climbed back
Out of the marvelous as he had known it.

Heaney's language is rich, textured, and rhythmic, but his meaning is accessible. In "Churning Day," for example, he writes of buttercream being poured into earthenware pots:

A thick crust, coarse-grained as limestone rough-cast
hardened gradually on top of the four crocks

After the hot brewery of gland, cud and udder
cool porous earthenware fermented the buttermilk.

The 1966 *Death of a Naturalist,* a collection of his rural poems, was his first book, but books that followed were on other subjects. In 1969 *Door into the Dark* was published. In it, Heaney went away from the actual into the realm of the unconscious, myths, and the supernatural. Later he wrote of historical figures. Other books by Heaney include *Wintering Out, North,* and *Bog Poems.*

Besides poetry, Heaney has written a number of volumes of prose. He also wrote a play, *The Cure of Troy,* in the late eighties, based on the story of the Greek warrior Philocretes from an original work by Sophocles.

As with the Irish, the "troubles" have touched Heaney's life. He has been forced to move a couple of times, and he has also written about that.

Besides teaching at Harvard, Heaney also taught in California and has given a number of readings of his poetry in America. In fact, he found this a most positive experience. He first came to the United States in 1969 and found American audiences much more open and receptive to his poetry than Irish and English audiences had been.

Heaney is a shy and humble man and has written not only about the guilt he feels, which he says is a "very Irish feeling," but also about his feeling that he is a fraud. "Poetry summons you," he says. "The real difficulty about being a poet is not in the writing. It's surviving the silence, surviving lack of inspiration and the feelings of fraudulence that are upon you when you go six months and you haven't written anything."

Heaney's impact on poetry is yet to be determined. But by winning the Nobel Prize, he has done wonders for Ireland. Ireland can't help but bask in his reflected glory.

James T. Farrell

(1904-1979)

As so often happens with writers, James T. Farrell was born into the world he was to write about, in his case the working class of Chicago, the "steam-heat Irish" such as painters, butchers, and carpenters, who did not live in poverty like their brethren in Chicago's Bridgeport section but made ends meet and strove for something more.

From 1919 to 1923, Farrell attended Corpus Christi Grammar School. He then went on to St. Anselm's Grammar School and St. Cyril High School, where he earned letters in three sports—basketball, baseball, and football—-and had dreams of becoming a baseball player.

When he graduated from high school, he worked as a telephone clerk, then went to DePaul University, where he studied history, sociology, and English composition. In March 1925, he went to the University of Chicago with plans to study social science and law. Farrell was an intense student, a big reader with a very good memory. At the University of Chicago he decided he wanted to write.

On April 13, 1931, he married Dorothy Patricia Butler, a fellow student at the University of Chicago. They left for Paris, where, encouraged by Ezra Pound, Farrell worked ten hours a day on his fiction, living in poverty.

But Paris was an unlucky place for them. A son born to Dorothy died five days after birth, and Farrell's grandmother, who had nurtured him when he was young, also died. James and Dorothy returned to the United States in 1932 and lived for a while in the artists' colony at Yaddo, in upstate New York. There he finished a trilogy about his most memorable character, Studs Lonigan.

The Washington Square neighborhood in Chicago where Farrell was born is the stomping grounds (sometimes literally) of Studs Lonigan, a young man who is married and has a family but strives for something more. Inside, he suffers from something else, as did others in his neighborhood. As Farrell himself wrote, "Here was a neighborhood several steps removed from the slums and dire economic want, and here was manifested a pervasive spiritual poverty."

Studs appears in three of Farrell's books, *Young Lonigan* (1932), *The Young Manhood of Studs Lonigan* (1934), and *Judgment Day* (1935). The time of the action is from the early twentieth century to the start of the Great Depression. Because it was so hard-hitting and "dirty" for the time, for the first edition of *Young Lonigan,* the publisher put a note on the dustcover that said that the book was intended to be read only "by physicians, surgeons, psychologists, psychiatrists, sociologists and other persons having an interest in the psychology of adolescence."

Farrell's private life was a bit chaotic. He and his wife divorced in 1940. In 1941 he married an actress named Hortense Aldren; they were divorced in 1955. That same year he remarried his first wife, and they were divorced again in 1958.

He was also attacked—in court—for his Studs trilogy on the grounds of obscenity. Indeed, he testified at a 1948 Philadelphia trial to ban his trilogy on those grounds. The trial publicity, wrote Gene Smith in a 1995 article for *American Heritage* magazine, was "what brought teenagers to *Studs:* the dirty parts. . . . Someone told you *Studs* had parts so hot you had to borrow asbestos gloves to turn the pages, and you went out and bought or borrowed a copy."

Farrell was also deeply committed to socialist causes. An atheist, he got involved in workers' organizations as both an apologist and an administrator.

Farrell could probably be fairly characterized as an angry writer when he was young, but as he got older he got more stoical. He wrote other series, too, but never with the success of the *Studs Lonigan* trilogy.

Farrell was a star in a pantheon of writers in the "realistic" school of fiction, writing devoid of the gooey sentimentality of works that preceded it, that tells it as it is—or at least how the author perceives it. Farrell perceived a dangerous world. Studs Lonigan, who tried to become a tough-guy gangster, ends up dead at twenty-nine, and his father loses everything in the Depression. The Studs Lonigan trilogy is not light reading.

Important American writers of this century, such as James Joyce and Norman Mailer, acknowledge a debt to Farrell, perhaps most of all a spiritual debt. And many readers have learned some harsh truths from his books as well.

The latter days of his life were marred by his inability to sell much of anything. He was forever the writer who had written the Studs Lonigan trilogy, and he rarely left his shabby New York City apartment except to watch a Mets or Yankees game.

"Studs," he was quoted in a 1979 obituary as saying, "has been a chain around my neck."

Illustration Credits

℘

St. Patrick, Daniel O'Connell, St. Brigid, Thomas Moore: Tom Philbin III; Michael Collins: Courtesy of the National Library of Ireland; Joseph Kennedy, John F. Kennedy: John F. Kennedy Library; Rachel Carson: Chatham College; William Holmes McGuffey: Miami University Archives, Oxford, Ohio; Catherine McAuley: Sisters of Mercy; Edmund Rice: Congregation of Christian Brothers; William Brennan: Collection, The Supreme Court of the United States, Courtesy The Supreme Court Historical Society, photo by Ken Heinen; Peter McGuire: George Meany Memorial Archives; George Meany: AFL-CIO; Father Edward Flanagan: Boys Town Hall of History; Mother Jones, Sean Lemass, Sean MacBride, Charles Feeney, Bobby Sands, Helen Gurley Flynn, Walt Disney, Georgia O'Keeffe, Thomas Murray:

Bibliography

ುಂ

Books

Abailard, Pierre, and L. S. Berg. *Dictionary of Scientific Biography*. Vol. I. New York: Charles Scribner's Sons, 1970.

Adler, Bill. *Ronnie and Nancy: A Very Special Love Story*. New York: Crown Publishers, 1985.

Boyarsky, Bill. *Ronald Reagan: His Life and Rise to the Presidency*. New York: Random House, 1981.

Boylan, Henry. *A Dictionary of Irish Biography*. New York: St. Martin's Press, 1988.

Buckley, William F., Jr., and L. Brent Bozell. *McCarthy and His Enemies: The Record and Its Meaning*. New York: Arlington House, 1954.

Cagney, James. *Cagney by Cagney*. New York: Doubleday, 1976.

Cahill, Thomas. *How the Irish Saved Civilization*. New York: Doubleday, 1995.

Cameron, Gail. *Rose: A Biography of Rose Fitzgerald Kennedy*. New York: G. P. Putnam's Sons, 1971.

Camp, Helen C. *Iron in Her Soul: Elizabeth Gurley Flynn and the American Left*. Pullman, Wash: Washington State University Press, 1995.

Catton, Bruce. *Grant Moves South*. New York: Little, Brown and Co., 1960.

Chesler, Ellen. *Woman of Valor: Margaret Sanger and the Birth Control Movement in America*. New York: Simon & Schuster, 1992.

Clark, Hunter R. *Justice Brennan: The Great Conciliator*. Secaucus, N.J.: Birch-Lane Press, 1995.

Colum, Padraic. *Ourselves Alone: The Story of Arthur Griffith and the Origin of the Irish Free State*. New York: Crown Publishers, 1959.

Coogan, Tim Pat. *Eamon de Valera: The Man Who Was Ireland*. New York: HarperCollins, 1993.

Crawford, Benjamin F. *William Holmes McGuffey: Schoolmaster of the Nation*. Delaware, Ohio: Carnegie Church Press, 1963.

Davies, Stan Gébler. *James Joyce: A Portrait of the Artist*. New York: Stein and Day, 1933.

Debus, Allen G. *World Who's Who in Science*. Chicago: Marquis-Who's Who, 1968.

Dempsey, Jack, with Barbara Piatelli Dempsey. *Dempsey*. New York: Harper and Row, Publishers, 1977.

Durant, Will, and Ariel Durant. *The Story of Civilization VII: The Age of Louis XIV*. New York: Simon & Schuster, 1975.

————. *The Story of Civilization XI: The Age of Napoleon*. New York: Simon & Schuster, 1975.

Edwards, Dudley R. *Daniel O'Connell and His World*. London: Thames and Hudson, 1975.

Ellmann, Richard. *James Joyce*. New York: Oxford University Press, 1982.

Evory, Ann. *Contemporary Authors*. Vol. 3. Detroit: Gale Research Company, 1981.

Falk, Peter Hastings. *Who Was Who in American Art*. Madison, Conn.: Soundview Press, 1985.

Foster, R. F. *Modern Ireland 1600–1972*. New York: Allen Lane, 1988.

———. *The Oxford Illustrated History of Ireland*. New York: Oxford University Press, 1989.

Gelb, Arthur, A. M. Rosenthal, and Marvin Siegel. *The New York Times: Great Lives of the Twentieth Century*. New York: Times Books, 1988.

Gherman, Beverly. *Georgia O'Keeffe: The Wideness and Wonder of Her World*. New York: Atheneum, 1986.

Golway, Terry. *Irish Rebel: John Devoy and America's Fight for Ireland's Freedom*. New York: St. Martin's Press, 1998.

Graham, Don. *No Name on the Bullet: A Biography of Audie Murphy*. New York: Viking Penguin, 1989.

Graham, Frank, Jr. *Since "Silent Spring"*. Boston: Houghton H. Mifflin Co., 1970.

Grant, Ulysses S. *The Papers of Ulysses S. Grant*. Edited by John Y. Simon. Carbondale: Southern Illinois University Press, 1967–1995.

Greeley, Andrew. *The Irish Americans: The Rise to Money and Power*. New York: Harper and Row, 1981.

Greenfeld, Howard. *F. Scott Fitzgerald*. New York: Crown Publishers Inc., 1974.

Isenberg, Michael T. *John L. Sullivan and His America*. Chicago: University of Illinois Press, 1988.

James, Edward T. *Notable American Women 1607–1950: A Biographical Dictionary*. Cambridge, Massachusetts: The Belknap Press of Harvard University Press, 1971.

James, Marquis. *Andrew Jackson: The Border Captain*. New York: Grosset & Dunlap, 1933.

Jeffares, A. Norman. *W. B. Yeats: A New Biography*. New York: Farrar Straus Giroux, 1988.

Keller, Helen. *The Story of My Life*. New York: Doubleday, 1954.

Kessler, Ronald. *The Sins of the Father: Joseph P. Kennedy and the Dynasty He Founded*. New York: Warner Books, 1996.

Kroeger, Brooke. *Nellie Bly: Daredevil, Reporter, Feminist*. New York: Times Books, 1994.

Kronenberger, Louis. *Oscar Wilde*. Boston: Little, Brown and Company, 1976.

Lacey, Robert. *Ford: The Men and the Machine*. Boston: Little, Brown and Company, 1986.

Lash, Joseph P. *Helen and Teacher: The Story of Helen Keller and Anne Sullivan Macy*. New York: Delacorte Press, 1980.

Lear, Linda. *Rachel Carson: A Witness for Nature*. New York: Henry Holt & Company, 1997.

Le Vot, André. *F. Scott Fitzgerald: A Biography*. New York: Doubleday, 1983.

Lisle, Laurie. *Portrait of an Artist: A Biography of Georgia O'Keeffe*. New York: Seaview Books, 1980.

Mackay, James. *Michael Collins: A Life*. Edinburgh: Mainstream Publishing, 1996.

Mac Liammóir, Micheál, and Eavan Boland. *W. B. Yeats*. New York: Thames and Hudson Inc., 1986.

MacManus, Seumas. *The Story of the Irish Race*. New York: The Devin-Adair Company, 1966.

Magill, Frank N. *Great Lives from History: American Series*. Vol. I. Englewood Cliffs, N.J.: Salem Press, 1982.

Martin, Ralph G. *A Hero for Our Time: An Intimate Story of the Kennedy Years*. New York: Fawcett Crest, 1983.

McCabe, John. *Cagney*. New York: Alfred A. Knopf, 1997.

McFeely, William S. *Grant: A Biography*. New York: W. W. Norton & Company, 1981.

McHugh, Roger. *Dublin 1916*. New York: Hawthorn Books, Inc., 1966.

Meyers, Jeffrey. *F. Scott Fitzgerald: A Biography*. New York: HarperCollins, 1994.

Mizener, Arthur. *The Far Side of Paradise: A Biography of F. Scott Fitzgerald*. Boston: Houghton Mifflin Company, 1965.

Morris, Roy. *Sheridan: The Life and Wars of General Phil Sheridan*. New York: Crown Publishers Inc., 1992.

Mosely, Leonard. *Disney's World*. New York: Stein and Day, 1985.

Nicholls, Mark. *The Importance of Being Oscar: The Wit and Wisdom of Oscar Wilde*. New York: St. Martin's Press, 1980.

O'Brien, Conor Cruise, and Máire O'Brien. *The Story of Ireland*. New York: The Viking Press, 1972.

O'Donnell, Monica M. *Contemporary Theatre, Film and Television*. Vol. I. Detroit: Gale Research Company, 1973.

O'Keeffe, Georgia. *Georgia O'Keeffe*. New York: Viking Press, 1976.

Oursler, Fulton, and Will Oursler. *Father Flanagan of Boys Town*. New York: Doubleday, 1949.

Parry, Melanie. *Larousse Dictionary of Women*. New York: Larousse Kingfisher Chambers Inc., 1996.

Philip, Cynthia Owen. *Robert Fulton*. New York: Franklin Watts, 1985.

Porter, Raymond J. *P. H. Pearse*. New York: Twayne, 1973.

Ranelagh, John. *Ireland: An Illustrated History*. New York: Oxford University Press, 1981.

Reeves, Thomas C. *A Question of Character: A Life of John F. Kennedy*. New York: The Free Press, 1991.

————. *The Life and Times of Joe McCarthy: A Biography*. New York: Stein and Day, 1982.

Remini, Robert V. *Andrew Jackson and the Course of American Democracy, 1833–1845*. Vol. 3. New York: Harper & Row, Publishers, 1984.

Ring, Frances Kroll. *Against the Current: As I Remember F. Scott Fitzgerald*. Berkeley, Calif.: Creative Arts Book Company, 1985.

Robinson, Roxana. *Georgia O'Keeffe: A Life*. New York: Harper and Row Publishers, 1989.

Rovere, Richard H. *Senator Joe McCarthy*. New York: Harcourt Brace and Co., 1959.

Schaeffer, Louis. *O'Neill: Son and Artist*. Boston: Little, Brown and Company, 1973.

Schoenebaum, Ph.D., Eleanora W. *Political Profiles: The Nixon/Ford Years*. New York: Facts on File, 1979.

Schwartzberg, Renée. *Ronald Reagan*. New York: Chelsea House Publishers, 1991.

Shaw, G. B. Edited by Stanley Weintraub. *Shaw: An Autobiography 1898–1950: The Playwright Years*. New York: Weybright and Talley, 1970.

Shickel, Richard. *The Disney Version*. New York: Avon Books, 1969.

Singleton-Gates, Peter, and Maurice Gerodias. *The Black Diaries: An Account of Roger Casement's Life and Times*. New York: Grove Press, 1959.

Stephen, Sir Leslie, and Sir Sidney Lee. *The Dictionary of National Biography*. London: Oxford University Press, 1917.

Swanberg, W. A. *Citizen Hearst*. New York: Charles Scribner's Sons, 1967.

Thurston S. J., Herbert, and Donald Attwater. *Butler's Lives of the Saints: Complete Edition*. Westminster, Maryland: Christian Classics, 1956.

Topalian, Elyse. *Margaret Sanger*. New York: Franklin Watts, 1984.

Twombly, Robert. *Louis Sullivan: His Life and Work*. New York: Viking Press, 1986.

Uglow, Jennifer S. *The International Dictionary of Women's Biography*. New York: Continuum, 1982.

Ward, Margaret. *Maud Gonne: A Life*. San Francisco: Harper, 1993.

Wilson, James Grant, and John Fiske. *Appletons' Cyclopedia of American Biography*. Vol. I. New York: D. Appleton and Company, 1900; republished 1968.

Pamphlets

Helen Marie, Burns, and Sheila Carney. *Sisters of Mercy*. Strasbourg, France: Éditions du Signe, 1996. RSM.
The Congregation of Christian Brothers. *Edmund Rice: Founder of the Christian Brothers*. N.P .n.d.

Internet Web Sites

The Confessio of Saint Patrick. www.mcs.net/~jorn/html/jj/patrick.html
The Diary of Bobby Sands. Irish Northern Aid Committee. http://inac.org
The Irish Hungerstrikes: A Commemorative Project. http://larkspirit.com/hungerstrikes
Information on the Irish State. http://www.irlgov.ie
Old Ireland. http://www.ireland.org
Irish History on the Web. wwwvms.utexas.edu/~jdana/irehist.html#general
The National Archives of Ireland. http://www.kst.dit.ie/nat-arch
Keefe, Thomas E. Keefe Web site. http://www.keefe.org
Sinn Fein. http://www.sinnfein.ie

About the Author

♋

Tom Philbin is the author of a variety of books, both fiction and non-fiction. He has traced his own Irish roots back to 1850 in Ballycastle, County Mayo, Ireland; his grandparents on both his mother's and father's sides were born in Ireland. He first learned about the Irish from his grandmother Honora who cared for him when he was five years old. Tom says "She was a beautiful young woman who lost her own husband when she was just thirty, and pregnant with her fifth child. It didn't beat her. She raised them by scrubbing floors and being a maid and doing what she had to do. As a little boy, watching her and listening to her strange accent introduced me to the idea that the Irish are really something special. She was funny, and she was warm, and she was indomitable-and she had all her own teeth when she died at eighty—four."